Praise for *Until Nir*

"*Until Nirvana's Time* opens wide windows that look out across vivid landscapes of Khmer poetry. Trent Walker's first-ever translations introduce us to the aesthetic and emotional tones of three to four centuries of Southeast Asian Buddhism. Walker translates these songs with tender passion, aiming to make 'the beauty and relevance of Khmer poetry accessible to Buddhists everywhere.' His palpable success makes *Until Nirvana's Time* a major contribution to world poetry and Buddhist humanities. Rarely if ever have the voices of Cambodian or other Southeast Asian Buddhists been so eloquently and evocatively expressed. Accessible, a pleasure to read: this excursion into the spiritual and emotional countryside of premodern Cambodia stands to become a classic voice in the chorus of Asian poetry."

—Peter Skilling, author of *Questioning the Buddha*

"This collection holds a special place for newer generations of Cambodians to gain insight into our ancestors' practices. By centering Buddhist poets from Cambodia, Trent Walker is honoring all the teachers who came before him. It is a work of beauty and utmost gratitude."

—Sokunthary Svay, author of *Apsara in New York*

"A beautifully curated selection of songs, translated with simplicity and eloquence; lucid and touching introductions; and a series of essays, notes, and commentaries graced by impeccable scholarship, artistic sensitivity, and love. Reading and sharing this book will bring great rewards."

—Linda Hess, author of *Bodies of Song: Kabir Oral Traditions and Performative Worlds in North India*

"*Until Nirvana's Time* represents an important contribution to Southeast Asian poetics in translation and shines a groundbreaking light on Cambodian verse and its intersections with Buddhism that was nearly lost during the conflicts of the twentieth century. Trent Walker's efforts at translation are thoughtful and compelling, providing a model for how we might translate and preserve similar bodies of literature across Southeast Asia. A rewarding read that I look forward to returning to many times in the years ahead."

—Bryan Thao Worra, Creative Works Editor, *Journal of Southeast Asian American Education and Advancement*

"Trent Walker's hauntingly beautiful Cambodian Dharma songs bring ancient wisdom to today's troubled world hungering for spiritual truth and guidance. At once disturbing and tender, *Until Nirvana's Time* maps the universal human experience of grief and loss along Buddhist themes of impermanence, gratitude, and transformation. We owe a debt of gratitude to Walker and his teachers for this magnificent collection, which merits a place alongside the *Therigatha* in its contribution to Buddhist and world literature."

—Wendy Garling, author of *The Woman Who Raised the Buddha*

"*Until Nirvana's Time* makes available masterpieces of Cambodian Buddhist poetry filled with piercing renderings of the human condition and wholehearted calls to the path of liberation. With this book, Trent Walker has opened a window to the emotional richness and the depth of human relationships that underlie Cambodian Buddhist culture and life."

—Gil Fronsdal, author of *The Buddha before Buddhism*

"The Dharma song traditions of Southeast Asia are tender and powerful; they still and stir the heart, slowing word and breath, teaching through melody, rhyme, and rhythm. *Until Nirvana's Time* invites those of us unfamiliar with these traditions into new and nourishing ways of engaging the beauty and depth of the Dharma. For years I have taught Trent Walker's work in both dharma centers and academic courses, and I will surely draw on this landmark selection of his translations and commentaries in my future teaching."

—William Edelglass, Director of Studies, Barre Center for Buddhist Studies

"This heartfelt and brilliant series of beautiful translations should become the model of discerning and ethical scholarship. Trent Walker allows the creativity and profundity of premodern Cambodian poets to take center stage. He also provides readers with a detailed explanation of how these poems reveal fundamental qualities of Cambodian Buddhism—offering expert commentary on virtue, merit, and gratitude, as well as beliefs in the power of ghosts, deities, and protective ritual. It is erudite while remaining accessible. It is respectful of local ways of expression, while providing an astute outside perspective. There is simply no other book like this, and it sparkles with insight gained over nearly twenty years of research. With this book, Walker emerges as the leader in a new generation of scholars of Southeast Asian Buddhism and literature."

—Justin Thomas McDaniel, author of *Wayward Distractions*

Until Nirvana's Time

Buddhist Songs from Cambodia

Trent Walker

FOREWORD BY

Kate Crosby

SHAMBHALA

Shambhala Publications, Inc.
2129 13th Street
Boulder, Colorado 80302
www.shambhala.com

Cover art: CamNet / Shutterstock.com

9 8 7 6 5 4 3 2 1

First Edition
Printed in the United States of America

Shambhala Publications makes every effort to print on acid-free, recycled paper. For more information please visit www.shambhala.com. Shambhala Publications is distributed worldwide by Penguin Random House, Inc., and its subsidiaries.

LIBRARY OF CONGRESS CATALOGING-IN-PUBLICATION DATA
Names: Walker, Trent Thomas, translator.
Title: Until nirvana's time: Buddhist songs from Cambodia / Trent Walker.
Description: Boulder: Shambhala, 2022. | Includes bibliographical references and index.
Identifiers: LCCN 2022011534 | ISBN 9781645471349 (trade paperback)
Subjects: LCSH: Buddhist hymns, Khmer—Translations into English. | Buddhist chants—Cambodia. | Buddhism—Prayers and devotions. | Buddhism—Rituals—Texts | Buddhism—Songs and music. | Songs, Khmer—Cambodia. | Buddhism—Cambodia.
Classification: LCC BQ5042.C36 U68 2022 | DDC 294.309596—dc23/eng/20220707
LC record available at https://lccn.loc.gov/2022011534

for my teachers

Contents

Foreword by Kate Crosby xi

Preface xv

Acknowledgments xxi

Note on Transliteration xxiii

Note to the Reader xxv

Part One: The Songs

Narrating Lives 3

1. Chaddanta's Lament 5
2. Subhadra's Lament 7
3. Parika's Lament 9
4. Suvannasama's Lament 11
5. Madri's Lament 13
6. Lullaby of the Gods 19
7. Maya's Guidance for Gotami 21
8. Divine Messengers 23
9. Leaving the Palace 25
10. Maya's Lament 27
11. Indra's Lute 29

12. The Defeat of Mara 31
13. Invitation to Preach the Dharma 39
14. The Buddha's Last Words 43
15. The Buddha's Passing Away 45
16. Mourning the Buddha's Demise 47
17. The Cremation of the Buddha 49
18. The Relics of the Buddha 51

REPAYING DEBTS 57
19. In Praise of the Earth 59
20. The Twenty-Four Vowels 65
21. The Thirty-Three Consonants 67
22. Absolving All Faults 71
23. Filial Debts 81
24. Asking for Mother's Forgiveness 83
25. Orphan's Lament 85
26. Hungry Ghosts' Lament 87
27. Offerings for Monks and Ancestors 93
28. Dedication of Merit 95

BEFRIENDING DEATH 97
29. Funeral March 99
30. This Life Is Short 101

31. The Four Thieves 103

32. The True Fate of Flesh 105

33. This Heap Called a Body 109

34. Song for the Hour of Death 117

35. A Lesson in Meditation 125

36. The Fortunate Eon 133

CHASING PEACE 149

37. Lotus Offering to Reach Nirvana 151

38. A Prayer for the People 153

39. Homage to the Three Jewels 155

40. The Homage Octet 159

41. The Buddha's Eightfold Array 161

42. Homage to All Holy Sites 163

43. Hymn to the Buddha's Feet 165

44. The Dharma of Union 171

45. Lotus Offering to Realize Awakening 181

Part Two: The Essays

THE WORLD OF CAMBODIAN BUDDHISM 189

THE RITUAL LIFE OF DHARMA SONGS 203

ORAL AND WRITTEN TRANSMISSION 209

METER, MELODY, AND RHYME 215

Part Three: Notes on the Songs

UNFOLDING SOURCES, REVEALING MEANINGS 227

Notes 293

Bibliography 309

Index 325

About the Author 337

Foreword

This is the first major literary translation of Cambodian Buddhist literature into English. When asked to provide a foreword, I was struck by the lightness with which Trent Walker conveys to us the enormous sophistication and complexity of these Khmer poems; the lives of the communities who over centuries composed, sang, honed, and handed them down to us; the depths of humanity and the heights of its surpassing that they convey; and the modesty with which he brings to bear his extraordinary ear, skills, patience, and sensitivity. To say that I found myself lost for words would belie the cliché and the fourth precept—words came, but not in accordance with convention. So I ask the forgiveness of the dear reader, author-cum-translator, sources, and publisher, in offering here my unconventional but heartfelt and—to recognize the Cambodian sensibility—liver-moved response:

Do not be daunted by this book's length. It is far longer.
Back to buddhas of foregone ages
more numerous than the oceans' grains of sand,
forty-five poems settle lightly on these pages.

Performances simple capture in a single strand
the eighty-four thousand teachings of the Sage
fathoms deep, as, coaxed out from shade,
Cambodia's poets shine center stage.

Four centuries in the composing, singing,
night-long in the tuning, sounding, ringing,

decades in the neglecting beyond their land
treasures to two crore heirs, far flung, home-bringing,

drawing close to our Khmer temple presence,
quatrains, moon-caught tween full and crescents'
quarters, catch sites, stupas, relics, great events,
cross leagues two hundred eighty thousand.

Two decades of straining, shaping, writing,
capturing the language, meter, mood and lighting,
of melodies to stir us, by karma damned,
treacherous, cruel, and ever-fighting,

our indebtedness to face and understand,
to earth, sun, moon, parents, teachers,
their virtues, so the six-rayed light may reach us
that we may wake to the gems' bright features

and through the maze of lakhs of lives
we billions of beings may recognize
our endless failing inscribed by Yama's hand,
flailing, empty, shifting, agonized;

of tunes, strange tongues' sweet tones
to soothe our loss, still grief, quiet moans,
till in nirvana's citadel we stand,
and bow to buddhas, inward thrones.

For students ahead four essays wait
to tie the poems to the faith and land
to the occasions, powers and rites they fête,
to give the sources form, sound, date.

For scholars each poem is scanned
variants, sources, tunes revealed
with notes to further every field,
Cambodian soundscapes now unsealed.

But readers, the temptation withstand
to pin down, to reach ahead. Stay instead,
ear intimate to lives most distant led,
mortalia of heart, of liver, later head.

Reined-in far-flung realms, infinity in an instant given voice,
the translator's marks unmarked, unseen merits to rejoice,
a free-flowing river carrying us to the further strand,
debts repaid, our vow to their surpassing stronger—
Until Nirvana's Time.

Kate Crosby
Numata Professor of Buddhist Studies,
University of Oxford
Wesak, 2566 B.E.
Flower Moon May, 2022 C.E.

Preface

Buddhist poetry has long informed and inspired Buddhist practice. Think of the ancient verses attributed to the Buddha's earliest disciples, the pithy poems of medieval Zen monastics, or the ecstatic songs of Indian and Tibetan yogis. Buddhists in Sri Lanka and Southeast Asia have likewise expressed their insights and aspirations in verse. Yet very little vernacular Theravada poetry has appeared in English translation. Rarely are the works of Burmese, Sinhala, or Thai Buddhist poets available to Anglophone readers.

Cambodian Buddhist poems are even harder to find; their works are little known outside of Khmer-speaking communities in Southeast Asia and in the global diaspora. This book seeks to change that by centering the voices of Buddhist poets from seventeenth- to twentieth-century Cambodia. Many of the songs translated here were composed or transmitted in and around Oudong, the Khmer capital from 1620 until 1866. The old capital's sacred hill, covered with temples and stupas, graces the cover of this book. For the past seven hundred years, most Cambodians have practiced Theravada Buddhism; their Khmer-language poetry reflects a deep intimacy with the Dharma. The largely anonymous authors translated in this book have produced a rich body of work: frank, devout, and radiant.

For many people around the world, Cambodia is still primarily known for the splendor of its ancient temples and the horrors of its modern history. The wonders of Angkor Wat and hundreds of other largely Hindu stone monuments from the seventh to thirteenth centuries reflect the might and majesty of the Khmer Empire, which once held sway over much of what is now Laos, Thailand, and southern Vietnam. On the other hand, the terror unleashed by the Khmer Rouge from 1975 to 1979, leading to the death of nearly two million Cambodians, speaks to the many traumas the Khmer people have faced in recent times: brutal warfare; colonial subjugation; migration and resettlement; poverty, violence, and erasure. Lost in this bifurcated image are the nation's many contributions to Buddhism, literature, and the arts. Khmer-language poems on Buddhist themes are among Cambodia's most precious gifts to the world. These well-crafted texts offer wisdom and solace for all those seeking a fresh perspective on the Dharma.

The forty-five poems translated in this book are "Dharma songs" (*dharm pad*, pronounced "thoa bot"), verse texts meant to be recited with complex melodies known as *smūtr* ("smot"). I first came to the Cambodian Dharma song tradition as a student in its modern lineage of vocal performance. Studying under the chanting masters Koet Ran, Prum Ut, and Yan Borin in Cambodia in 2005 and 2006, I memorized a significant repertoire of Dharma songs before my literary Khmer was advanced enough to attempt translating them into English. Some of the translations included here I have been refining for the past fifteen years. Others I only discovered in 2016 and 2017, when I spent another two years in Cambodia, this time immersed in the study of traditional manuscripts rather than music. None of the poems have appeared in book form in English. A quarter of them have never been published in Khmer either, transmitted only through oral lineages or on the fragile pages of palm-leaf and bark-paper manuscripts.

This combination of oral and written transmission is common for Cambodian Buddhist poems. Khmer poetry is traditionally chanted aloud in dozens of different melodies, each of which has spawned several variations. Some melodies are fast-paced and use only a few different musical pitches. Others are slow, highly ornamented, and require a wide vocal range to reach all of their many notes. Most of the Dharma songs translated for this book are intended to be recited with such elaborate and elongated styles. Many of the texts are short enough to memorize, with an average of thirty stanzas each. Yet a single stanza can take up to three minutes to recite; a whole poem, several hours. Dharma songs are often recited at night, traditionally in dusk-to-dawn rites of healing, mourning, dedication, and consecration.

The slow pace, complex melodies, and ritual context of these poems are always on my mind as a translator. Each word of the Khmer is designed to linger in the air, carried by breath and music. As readers and listeners, we must be patient, letting the meaning gradually reveal itself to us. Some of the poems are relatively close to modern Khmer, while others have flashes of the archaic, posing a tangle of knots and riddles. But in the long history of Buddhist literature these texts are relative newcomers—and part of a living tradition nourished by Cambodians today. They were written to be accessible, to speak broadly and clearly of the human condition.

My translations aim to bring the clarity and vitality of these texts to life in English. I trust their Cambodian authors; I have not embellished the poems, changed their essential meaning, or elided aspects that run counter to modern sensibilities. On the other hand, the spare, compressed language of the Khmer, bound into tight bundles of rhythm and rhyme, falls flat when rendered literally. Most of my translations maintain the syllable and line structures of the Khmer originals, but only a few preserve their complex rhymes. Translation requires balancing fidelity to letter and spirit; whether I have met this challenge is not for me to judge.

Above all, I hope to have done good by my teachers in Cambodia, who long encouraged me to make these expressions of the Dharma available to the world at large. From their perspective, Cambodian Dharma songs are a universal tradition, one grounded in Khmer culture but whose core messages are intended for all human beings, without exception. We all are subject to death and decay, no matter our background. We all face the challenge of repaying debts to parents, teachers, and the earth. We all must ask ourselves, sooner or later, what human life is really about. I doubted these truths for many years, thinking that Dharma songs were best studied as expressions of Cambodia, and Cambodia alone. I should have heeded my teachers' advice all along. They were wise to recognize that you don't need to be a Khmer speaker to benefit from these poems.

Selected from hundreds of possible works, the poems in this book are intended to represent the highlights of the Cambodian Dharma song tradition. Many of the most popular songs are included, along with others of exceptional interest or literary merit. All of the major themes of the genre are covered: the life of the Buddha, gratitude to parents, the impermanence of the body, and aspiration for nirvana. In deference to Khmer tradition, I have organized the translations into four cycles that follow these themes. Each cycle is preceded by a brief introduction.

These introductions and the translations in part 1, "The Songs," are intended to speak for themselves and so appear without footnotes or other explanatory material. However, for readers eager to explore Cambodian Dharma songs in more depth, this book includes two additional resources. Part 2, "The Essays," is a set of four longer essays that discuss the core teachings of Cambodian Buddhism, the ritual context of Dharma song performance, the dynamics of oral and written transmission, and the metrical and melodic structures of Khmer poetry. These essays are intended to help readers appreciate the doctrinal, performative, historical, and aesthetic dimensions of the texts.

Part 3, "Notes on the Songs," is a series of detailed notes on each of the forty-five poems. Each note tabulates basic information such as the Khmer-language title, meter, melody, date, and author, when known. Most of the translations are based on my comparative editions of old palm-leaf or bark-paper manuscripts in Cambodia. Each note includes citations of these manuscripts, as well as relevant printed books in Khmer. Finally, each note provides a brief commentary on unusual terms, obscure references, and textual parallels, including relevant Pali sources.

Khmer symbols for marking beginnings ៙ and endings ៚ appear throughout the translations, along with one for section breaks ៘. They provide traces of the elegant ways scribes have long carved texts on sandstone and pliant leaves. Portions of the final poem in this book were incised on a pillar at Angkor Wat in 1684. Consonants sit in even rows, packed tight in a floral frame. Vowels loop back in sweeping arcs, a race of lines on rock. As that poem's last line enjoins us: in this fragile world, let's aim for beauty, from now until nirvana's time.

Acknowledgments

Research for this book was supported by Cambodian Living Arts in 2005–2006, 2008, and 2013; the Center for Khmer Studies in 2016, the Robert H.N. Ho Family Foundation in 2016–2017, and Khyentse Foundation in 2018–2020. The writing in 2021 was supported by the Ho Center for Buddhist Studies at Stanford University.

A number of the original Khmer manuscripts translated here were curated and digitized through the collective efforts of the Fonds pour l'Édition des Manuscrits du Cambodge, the École française d'Extrême-Orient, and the Buddhist Digital Resource Center, with the financial support of A Khmer Buddhist Foundation.

Nikko Odiseos planted the seeds that became this book. Anna Wolcott Johnson cared for the project from beginning to end. The rest of the team at Shambhala Publications made a myriad of details come together with patience and precision.

Friends and mentors anchor my practice as a translator. Linda Hess made words real, Peter Skilling gave them new life, and Sharon May put them where they belong. My professors at Berkeley, Stanford, and beyond opened my mind to translation as an ever-receding horizon.

My family made this book possible. Bob and Gail Walker sheltered me as I wrote, grounding these pages in love. Chenxing Han marks my life with meaning, ink on page, star against sky. Her care makes dull words shine.

Vast are my debts to *guṇ grū upajjhāyācāry*; how could I ever repay what I owe? Humbled by the impossible, I bow to my teachers in Cambodia: Koet Ran, Kun Sopheap, Leng Kok-An, Prum Ut, Yan Borin, and Preah Maha Vimaladhamma Pin Sem. May the merits of this work be theirs.

Note on Transliteration

To keep the poems as readable as possible, diacritics have been removed from the translations, with the exception of certain Pali phrases and syllables in small caps. For the essays and notes, diacritics are retained for Khmer, Pali, Sanskrit, and Thai, except for terms in common English usage. For details of the transliteration system, see Walker's "Unfolding Buddhism" (xiii–xvii). Approximate phonetic renderings appear in plain roman type for selected Khmer terms.

For Buddhist terminology, Khmer uses a mix of Pali and Sanskrit spellings. This book generally follows the Sanskrit forms, as these are more familiar in English: for example, Bodhisattva, Dharma, karma, Maitreya, and nirvana.

Note to the Reader

Cambodian Dharma songs may be read silently, but they are intended to be performed aloud. You don't need to know the traditional melodies to appreciate their oral dimensions. Try reading them out loud, and hear how their rhythm shapes their messages. Chant them with a single, steady tone. Or use your own melodies, exploring how your voice can lift the poems into song.

If you would like to study the traditional melodies, I recommend beginning with the thirty-two Khmer and English recordings of Dharma songs freely available at www.stirringandstilling.org. Many Cambodians have learned the art of recitation from imitating audio recordings alone. Though there is no substitute for patient and exacting feedback from a Dharma song master, our own ears provide an essential foundation for study.

Dharma songs are a living tradition, and the best way to learn more is to connect with local Cambodian communities. If you live near a Khmer Buddhist temple, see if there are rituals you might attend; they'll often include the recitation of the original Khmer texts translated in this book. Show appreciation to their traditions with words and actions, and you'll find new friends in the Dharma.

I have translated the present collection with the aim of making the beauty and relevance of Khmer poetry accessible to Buddhists everywhere. Cambodians in diaspora, particularly those who feel more comfortable in English than Khmer: you are always my first audience. These poems are your heritage, letters from your ancestors, invitations for your creative gifts to sing.

May the poems gathered here make way for tenderness, for learning old lessons and weaving new connections. May you find what you seek, and may all beings be well.

PART ONE
THE SONGS

Narrating Lives

The Buddha's journey to awakening was not a solo venture. In his last life as Siddhartha Gautama (Pali: Siddhattha Gotama), and in countless births before that, he traveled through samsara along with a familiar cast of characters: the living beings who eventually became his wife, mother, father, stepmother, cousin, son, attendant, archenemy, and leading monastic disciples, among many others. Cambodian retellings of his numberless lives embed the Buddha in these relationships. Emotional bonds reverberate longer than specific deeds.

The songs in this cycle trace these affective ties over time. Arranged chronologically, they combine into a sweeping narrative arc. The first six poems recount episodes from the Buddha's many past lives: once a mighty elephant, once the son of a blind couple, once a banished prince. The next six narrate his final life as Siddhartha, from birth to the beginning of his teaching career. The final six songs revolve around the Buddha's passing away into nirvana and the veneration of his relics.

Many of the poems gathered here are laments. In some Khmer dialects, the verb "to lament" can also mean "to sing a Dharma song." We hear the cries of the Buddha, his mother, and his wife. We hear the grief of Ānanda, his attendant, and of the Buddha's many other followers. These songs are meant to be felt in our emotional core: our "hearts and livers," as the Khmer phrase puts it. The grief of the Buddha and his intimates can be your grief as well. Let your story be present in the words of these poets.

1. Chaddanta's Lament

Subhadra dear, my old love,
why sow such bitter seeds?
Why send this wicked hunter
to slay me with an arrow?

If you'd just asked for my tusks,
I'd give them up without a fight.
What's the use of having him
butcher me like an animal?

Don't you recall, when you too
were an elephant, how I helped
in your moments of misery?
Perhaps I've been shot by mistake.

Subhadra, I'll talk to the brute
and have him give you my tusks.
May you be happy and well.
Goodbye, my dear; my time has come.

Hunter! Here, take my six tusks.
Walk for seven days to the boat
and tell my love the whole story:
I'm free from pain, fault, and foe.

Pull out my tusks from the root.
I can bear this and much more,
for I have no regrets in death
on the long road to buddhahood.

2. Subhadra's Lament

When Subhadra saw his tusks,
she doubled over, crushed inside,
her heart ablaze, face on fire:
"O Chaddanta, my old love!

"I miss you from my past life!
I didn't know that you'd send
such a message with your tusks.
May I perish together with you!

"This red-white mass of ivory
breaks me down to my bones.
I didn't know that you were
my former mate; forgive me!

"Now I'll die here by your side;
let me suffer the same fate.
I vow to meet you in every life
from now until the very end."

She held her breath till she died,
praying to stay close to him,
to join the future Blessed One
throughout his journey to the goal.

3. Parika's Lament

"My golden love, my dear son,
Suvannasama, come quickly!
The cobra's venom blinds me.
Have pity on your poor mom.

"You're a child, still so young.
My eyes are stung by venom.
Oh, what have I now become?
Curse this loathsome fate of mine!

"My heart trembles for your sake,
for you I quake, child of mine!
My dearest one, love divine,
help me! I pine for you, son.

Crying on the cobra's mound,
she shouted around for her son:
"Suvannasama, come now, run!
I'm blind, undone, all alone.

"Suvannasama, come quickly!
Can you hear me cry and moan?
My eyes are burned to the bone.
I'm on my own. Help me soon!"

4. Suvannasama's Lament

In this wild sanctuary,
who mistook me for a deer
fetching water, fresh and clear?
Feet thunder here, sounds echo.

Why, great king, have you shot me?
My destiny, is it so,
to be pierced by your arrow?
The blood drains slowly from me.

Once I'm gone, who will care
for my parents, who can't see?
Not only one but now three
must die, sadly, as your prey.

Mother, I owe you my whole life.
Why must such strife come our way!
Help me please, save me today,
slipping away . . . before you.

How can I see your sweet face?
Here in this place . . . I leave you.
Mother, come here, help me through,
like drops of dew . . . I vanish . . . .

May all the gods hear my plea:
the king shot me . . . I vanish . . .
tell my parents . . . I anguish . . .
a humble wish . . . please tell them . . . .

5. Madri's Lament

"With the wane of day's red rays,
stirring starts in every heart.
Thunder, lightning, and fierce winds:
Might they cause this deep anguish?

"Until the rooster's hour comes,
flocks of rollers screech and squeal.
Hornbills grunt, like packs of dogs.
The crane cries out piercingly.

"Calling for mates, cicadas chirp.
The duck grieves for a lost love.
The heartsick forest gibbon
pities himself, alone in his tree.

"Why me? Why must I suffer?
Why must I be wrenched apart?
I worry for my two children
and pine for our distant land.

"Having wandered far away,
how this sorrow gnaws at me!
I can't bear these nights and days
with charnel woods for a home."

Madri then said to her kids,
"Krishna and Jali, my two dears,
we live like this forest's our home,
calling the birds our neighbors.

"We came to Mount Vankata
in our hour of grief and gloom.
We have no kin or even friends
to stay with us and ward off harm.

"As for the Lord, your father,
he sits peacefully in a cave,
scolding me with his cold words:
'Madri, let go; don't be attached.

"'For I've become a hermit,
penance now my sacred task.
By night or day, dear Madri,
leave me be inside my hut.'"

Vessantara, the Buddha-to-be,
had given their children to Jujaka.
The old brahman, whose whip was cruel,
dragged his slaves down rocky trails.

"If he hits you, brother Jali,
I will turn to take your place."
"If he hits you, sister Krishna,
I will take the blows for you."

Pity those two, far too young,
walking all day, racked by pain!
Jali felt for his sister's plight
until he could bear it no more.

Their faces both dissolved in tears.
Jali consoled, "Little sister,
we must endure this as our fate
so Father can reach awakening."

Krishna lamented, "But Jujaka
whips and beats us till we bleed.
Look! Our skin is cracked and flayed,
wet with sweat and swollen black."

Jali comforted, "Sister,
do your best to bear this trial.
What can we do? It's our lot
to put up with such agony.

"We once lived in luxury,
free from pain in our palace.
Now we're forlorn and far away,
cut off from our own mother.

"How can we go on without
seeing her face, not even once?
Stuck in these woods far too long,
how much we miss you, Mother!"

Krishna likewise wept and wailed,
"I'm thirsty, Mom. Give me milk.
Come back here! Don't let us die.
You miss us, right? Just a little?"

The evening soon slipped into night.
Deep in the woods only beasts cried,
their tunes haunting, a strange music:
the sounds of grief were all around.

When dusk fell at night's first watch,
pale moonlight spread through the sky.
The poor children whined and moaned
as hunger gnawed them inside out.

Little Krishna asked her brother,
"What can we do to see Mother?
Here there's only the old man
with his filthy hair and beard.

"Look, he's opening his mouth.
He's tied his belt, grabbed his bag!
Jali, come on, let's get going
or he'll catch up and eat us alive."

The cruel brahman Jujaka
tied the children's hands together,
binding them tight to a tree
to sleep upright, back to bark.

Still at the peak of beauty,
Madri went to gather fruit.
When she turned to walk back home,
jungle beasts had blocked her path.

Three gods transformed into fierce
lions and tigers to hold her back,
lest she stop the old brahman
from making off with her kids.

When the sun had finally set,
the gods were moved by mercy.
They let her pass through the woods
so she could get home safely.

But when the princess returned,
seeing neither son nor daughter,
she burst into a flood of tears
and ran back to the forest.

There she heard a cuckoo's cry,
which sounded like little Krishna,
calling for her deep in the woods,
though it was not her daughter.

A breeze blew forth, clearing the clouds,
carrying a jasmine fragrance
from somewhere in the southwest.
Could that be Jali's sweet scent?

"Krishna! Jali! I see the tracks
where you once played with toy carts
and a trail of tiny footprints
on the path in front of our hut.

"I fear a wild, raging beast
or a whole stampeding herd
has snatched you by the maw.
What an awful thought to hold!

"Even as you scream and shout,
you'll be carried far away.
Don't be careless; let me help
free you from those teeth and claws!"

6. Lullaby of the Gods

O wild rooster! Are you crowing, crowing near our hut?
Hey Krishna
        O Krishna
                Hey Krishna, my dearest
Child, don't you cry
Momma's here, Momma's here
        Singing you to sleep.

O cicada! Are you singing, singing near our hut?
Hey Krishna
        O Krishna
                Hey Krishna, my dearest
Child, don't you cry
Momma's here, Momma's here
        Singing you to sleep.

O flute player! Are you playing, playing near our hut?
Hey Krishna
        O Krishna
                Hey Krishna, my dearest
Child, don't you cry
Momma's here, Momma's here
        Singing you to sleep.

Child, don't you cry
Momma's here, Momma's here
        Singing you to sleep.

7. Maya's Guidance for Gotami

Little sister Gotami!
Hold to these words of guidance
I ask you now to receive.
Little sister, forgive me.

Since giving birth to my son,
only seven days have passed.
My life withers to nothing
as I pass on to the next world.

What can I do, when we are
born only to be destroyed?
All humans and animals
die and decay by nature.

Never lasting, never sure,
life is as the Pali phrase:
ANICCAṂ DUKKHAṂ ANATTĀ.
Little darling, you must know.

Now as for me, dear sister,
don't worry, for death is sure;
no more can I hold my son,
the refuge of gods and men.

You who pity your sister,
you, lovely girl, that is why
I ask you to hug and hold
this motherless child of mine.

Nurse him and bathe his body,
attend to him day and night,
care for him like no other—
O my golden girl, don't stop!

8. Divine Messengers

Now I tell of Siddhartha
in the line of the buddhas,
when he, the Lord of the World,
was Kapilavastu's Prince.

He tasted the joy of wealth,
together with the lovely
Princess Bimba, eminent
in her beauty and renown.

From the cradle to the throne,
he lived in strength and splendor;
not a thing could make the Prince
tremble with fear or distress.

When the Prince was twenty-nine,
he rode out to the garden
and saw four men, conjured up
for him by the gods above:

one old, one sick, one a corpse,
and one a wandering mendicant.
He shuddered inside and asked
his charioteer to explain.

The charioteer then bowed low
and told the Lord of the World
the full truth of these four sights,
from the old man to the monk.

When the Lord had heard these words
and perceived their clear-cut truth,
his heart quaked at the cruel fate
shared by him and all beings.

The inspired Lord spoke thus:
"All formations must dissolve.
Living beings are cursed with
the pain of old age and death.

"Only the sight of a monk,
one who plainly sees the pith
and cuts off craving at the root
to reach freedom, brings me peace."

9. Leaving the Palace

At midnight's hour the Lord ached with compassion's throb.
He cried out to young Rahula: "Farewell, my son!
I must go forth.

"Stay with Mother, in peace and joy. May you be safe
and free from harm. May no ordeals, however slight,
cause you distress."

He rode his horse up to the towering palace gates.
Angels opened them for the Lord, who then implored
his lone son thus:

"Dear Rahula! Stay with Mother and be happy.
May you be free from all disease. I take my leave
to wander forth.

"My dear, my son, only just born this very day!
It's wrong for me to leave you here. I should stay back
to care for you.

"Oh, how I wish to hug you close, my newborn child.
If only I could hold you again before I leave
to seek the truth.

"Your mother sets a hand on your chest, her other palm
a pillow for your head to rest. But now you lie
beyond my charge."

10. Maya's Lament

"O my darling, my dear son,
you've become so thin and weak.
As your mother, I'm worn through
by these depths of grief and loss.

"I only lived for seven days
after you came into this world.
Reborn in Tusita heaven,
I now abide among the gods.

"They've told me that you're handsome,
powerfully built, flawless throughout.
What's happened to your figure?
Why have you gone and wasted away?

"Seeing you in such a state,
my grief heats up to a boil,
cooking my own heart away.
How can I go on living?

"O my darling, what went wrong?
Before you had a fine abode.
Maidens met your every need;
not a moment lay empty.

"It's not right for you to die
alone here in the forest;
better it'd be to perish
in your father's grand palace.

"Flesh barely covers your bones,
your eyes clouded, like a corpse.
Can't you see your own mother?
Why aren't you answering me?

"I've come to meet you, face-to-face.
Why don't you call for your mother?
Stand up, my child, my dear son!
Don't just lie there on the ground."

When our Lord, the Bodhisattva,
heard his mother speak these words,
he couldn't move his skeletal frame
but still whispered this response:

"O Mother, my debt to you
is greater than all measure.
I beg you, dearest Mother,
my own master, please don't cry!

"I won't die; that I promise.
I've been like this for a while.
Be relieved of your sorrow
and return to the heavens."

11. Indra's Lute

One day Indra, Lord of the Gods,
descended from Trayastrimsa
with a charming triple-strung lute
to strum and sing for the Great Man.

At first he tuned one string too taut,
and soon that cord snapped in twain.
Another string, too lax, lacked a crisp twang,
so he tightened the slack to retune it again.

The moderate way, not too tight or too loose,
made all fall silent, listening to the strains.
Strung together in songs both long and short,
the melodies rang true in honed harmony.

Once Indra had completely vanished away,
the Prince reflected on his realization:
"To inflict austerities misses the mark,
for I've yet to taste the real Dharma.

"Toils and trials cannot defeat conceit.
The crooked path leads only to diversion.
Just like the lute string Indra overstretched,
exertion without ease cannot be endured."

Once the prince had pondered thus,
he set off to beg for alms in the village.
Having nourished himself with food,
his body soon regained its old shape.

12. The Defeat of Mara

Mara loomed large,
his eyes rolled back,
his face all fierce.
He bared his teeth,
roughened his speech,
and rallied his troops,
their arms raised high.

They aimed their weapons,
blowguns and muskets,
longbows and harpoons,
tips slicked with poison,
javelins and crossbows.
Packed in dense array,
they held their ground.

Clutching their bows,
the frenzied troops
let their shots fly,
rain against earth.
Their darts became
showers of blossoms,
a sprinkled gift.

Then Mara thought,
"This baldy's skilled
in magic might!
We've fought our best,

gasping for breath.
Maybe he'll fall
for one of our tricks?"

So Mara spoke:
"Hey there, hermit,
don't you know that
this throne is mine?
Give up your spot,
your precious seat.
Cede it to me!

"I know what's best;
I've seen all merit
sown in the past.
You're new, smooth-head,
and don't know a thing.
When you're older, squirt,
you'll know what I mean."

The Earth Goddess,
her powers complete,
started to quake:
"Mara, that miser,
that crazy squabbler,
that greedy glutton,
threatened the Lord!

"He's insulted
the Blessed One,
Peak of the Worlds.
Who'll be his witness
and back up his claim?"
She couldn't restrain
herself much longer.

So she dressed up
in her best clothes
and adorned her head:
a shining crown,
gleaming earrings,
diamonds and beryl,
radiant and bright.

Seated at peace
on a golden lotus,
lofty and light,
she burst from the soil
and bowed in homage
to the two holy feet
of the Buddha-to-be.

She told the Lord,
"Stay where you are.
My duty is now
to defeat Mara,
that foolish thief,
who can't even tell
what's merit or sin.

"Poor, wretched Mara
has struggled too long.
He's down on his knees.
If he rallies his troops
to rise from the mire,
he'll only win death
as his grand prize."

So she cried out,
"Hey there, Mara,
you jealous jerk!

The Great Man built up
his merit for eons:
each vow he sealed
with drops of water.

"When an old Buddha
foretold that our Lord
would be a Buddha too,
the water offering
fell right on my head,
four countless ages
and seven eons ago.

"Watch me, Mara,
I'll be his witness."
Squeezing her fingers
down her wet locks,
she wrung out her hair:
a tidal wave crested
and swept all away.

His armies fled
helter-skelter,
total disorder,
scattering wide
in cacophony.
Mara lost his
wits entirely.

He dropped his sword,
let fall his bow.
His yes-men shook
with malarial chills.
Seeing the glory

of the true Sage,
he roared these words:

"Alas, my friend,
you're strong indeed,
best in the world!"
Knowing he'd lost,
he gathered the flowers
scattered on the ground
to make an offering.

Humbled, he said,
"O Blessed One,
Fortunate Lord,
the peak of life,
the spire above!
I recognize you
as our Master.

"Even the deities
in Brahma realms
are no match for you.
For your perfections
exceed all others."
He joined his palms
and bowed in respect.

The Lord then foretold:
"Your wishes, Mara,
won't wither to naught.
For you'll succeed
in your firm goal
to awaken as
a lone buddha."

At that moment,
a mighty throng
of gods gathered
to pay respect,
a swarm of bows
to the Buddha,
showering praise.

They brought garlands
and other gifts
for the Wise One:
flags and sunshades,
fringed with gems,
along with music
for the great Sage.

The sheer merit
of the Bodhi tree
made it grow high,
casting cool shade
on the Lord's throne,
beneath its branches
and verdant boughs.

The Supreme Lord
savored pure bliss.
Bright rays of light
swirled in the sky
across the earth,
the dazzling blaze
of enlightenment.

We offer our praise
to his long journey

of building up merit
until he awakened
as the Wise Teacher—
"The Defeat of Mara"
is now complete.

13. Invitation to Preach the Dharma

At that moment, Sahampati
Brahma, Lord of Our Realm,
knelt before the Teacher,
raised his hands to his head,

and humbly spoke these words:
"Please, have mercy, and be informed
that living beings are soft and weak,
burdened by the weight of their sin.

"They've been waiting for the Dharma,
for their true refuge and reliance.
Now that you are fully awakened,
they'll be filled with joy and zeal.

"Some creatures are laden with lust,
unable to grasp the Three Marks.
Others are ready to comprehend,
thanks to your power, O Blessed One.

"If they could hear you teach the truth,
their wisdom would grow in strength and depth.
Please, O Meritorious Lord,
I humbly invite you to preach.

"Save living beings and slay their sorrow,
their sickness, their passion, their thirst for flesh,
that their darkness might brighten into faith
and deepen with wisdom to reach the truth.

"Worldly realms are fleeting wastes.
Samsara's wheel whirls without end.
Ignorance is the fundamental cause
that sets in motion a chain of effects.

"It leads living beings to suffer,
to drown in cycles of birth and death.
The Five Maras and blind delusion
wrap them tight till they're stuck fast.

"Hence, Lord, please rescue them.
Lift beings aboard your boat
and ferry them across
to nirvana's far shore,

"as if on a water lantern, vast as the sky,
with fractal arrays of dazzling light
to illuminate all living beings
that they might know true peace and joy.

"The true Dharma is the victory drum,
the Vinaya its great shell,
the Sutras its binding strings,
the Abhidhamma its stretched skin.

"The Noble Truths are the mallet
to pound the drum for all to hear.
Beings in the world are sleepy and dazed;
roused by this beat, they might wake up.

"The Four Assemblies of followers
are like lotus buds in the water.
Some will surface, waiting for sunrise,
then bloom at the touch of dawn's rays.

"The Dharma is the sunshine
that rises and gleams, casting its beams,
lighting up the Three Worlds
to make clear the path to bliss."

Sahampati Brahma
bowed down to invite
the Lord, the Blessed One,
with these very verses.

The Buddha consented
and expressed his approval
in silence, befitting
his compassionate state.

He arose from that spot
and walked toward Sarnath,
covering the entire
distance by foot.

He brought beings to the Buddhist fold,
starting with the Group of Five,
by having them drink the ambrosia
that is nirvana's natural taste.

From that moment on,
he preached sermons on the Dharma,
performing a Buddha's duties
for forty-five monsoons in all.

He never stepped back or relented;
the benefits extended across the years.
He achieved acts of merit
for all beings in the Three Worlds.

That is why right in this moment
we are filled with such great joy.
Venerable, O Virtuous One!
We invite you to save us and preach.

Rescue those assemblies
still mired in delusion,
that their wisdom might bloom
right here in this place!

14. The Buddha's Last Words

YO VO Ananda!
Come here now; don't delay.
I'll soon pass away,
leaving you all alone.

O friend, please be well.
Don't suffer needlessly,
for I must leave you.
Don't you grieve, Ananda!

My five aggregates
will break down and dissolve.
Stay, stay, Ananda!
Contemplate your own life.

These days your body
is brittle as fired clay.
It won't last for long,
bound to break in pieces.

Please, dear Ananda,
contemplate this deeply.
When I pass away,
you must bear my teaching.

Truly this Dharma
remains with anyone
whose heart is bright and clear,
who follows what I teach.

Now the Realized One
shall end in nirvana.
Time's curse comes cruelly
to crush and cut off life.

15. The Buddha's Passing Away

I tell of when our Wise Lord
at last entered nirvana
in an old grove of sal trees,
with his students gathered round,

on the fifteenth waxing day
of the month of Visakha,
a snake year, ending in five,
Tuesday morning in bright sun.

Monks both young and old were there,
grieving for the Worthy One.
Some bawled in grief, head in hands,
mourning the Glorious Victor.

Some recalled his sage advice,
others his daily rounds for alms.
Still more remembered his sermons.
None could but feel deep sorrow.

The forest glade resounded
with peals of thunder all around.
Beige-white blossoms fell like rain,
blessing the Lord of the World.

Meanwhile, his attendant
Ananda was out for alms.
Men and women from the town
bowed low before him and asked,

"Venerable Ananda!
The Worthy One, our great Lord,
has not been seen, night or day.
Where has the Lord Buddha gone?

We are used to seeing you
always walking in his steps.
Today we've lost Mara's foe;
our Teacher has disappeared."

Ananda couldn't bear their grief.
Hearing them ask for the Buddha,
the Lord they'd never see again,
he covered his face with his palms.

"The All-Wise One won't arrive
since he's entered nirvana.
We've lost the Lord, our Master;
that's why you see me alone.

"Such is our miserable fate,
bereft of our beloved Prince.
From this day on till forever,
we'll meet only with suffering."

16. Mourning the Buddha's Demise

I bow my head and bend my body,
palms pressed close in reverent prayer,
my heart devoted, straight as time,
to the Chief Sage, the World's Crown.

While the Virtuous One still lived,
he always preached the sweet Dharma
to teach and train living beings,
both those on earth and high above.

But the Buddha, Self-Arisen,
could never stay with us for long
for he was bound for nirvana:
no more sermons to true our minds.

Disciples of the Lord of Lords
gathered around in great numbers,
mourning our Teacher's demise
on that sad day and evermore.

How lonely, Lord, how deep our grief:
we're shocked, we're stirred, we're turned around!
Your true form shines, resplendent still,
our ark, our anchor throughout time.

On the full moon of Visakha,
this very day, our dear Master
emerged from Queen Maya's side,
left the palace to seek out truth,

reached the peak of awakening,
and passed away in nirvana—
these four pivots in our Lord's life
all came to pass on the same date.

After the Buddha's final end,
his students, moved by their teacher,
prepared a raft of offerings
every full moon of Visakha.

This rite lives on to the present.
May all of us gathered here
bow down before the Blessed One,
who best embodies our bright faith.

Having honored the Virtuous One,
I humbly vow to be reborn
in time for Maitreya Buddha,
set to awaken in times to come.

May all my solemn, chanted prayers
never be lost or forgotten!
May I meet the Buddha-to-come
and settle into lasting peace.

17. The Cremation of the Buddha

Today we honor the eighth day
since the full moon of Visakha,
same as when the Malla monarchs
paid their respect to the Buddha,

he who exceeded all the gods,
pinnacle of patience and peace,
his body and mind extinguished,
never to swim in samsara again.

The Malla kings made offerings
of candles and fragrant incense
to the Lord who was freed at last
from the cycle of birth and death.

Once the pyre was all prepared,
a miracle soon came to pass.
The Buddha's body self-ignited:
a final wonder of the Victor.

The Lord's body, replete with marks,
was aflame for thirty-two days,
burning brightly from the power
that blazed within his relics.

Now, at this propitious hour,
good fortune beams, bright as the past,
just as the old sages foretold:
a precious time, imbued with luck.

High above, the stars align,
a perfect constellation forms:
we bow in praise from a distant land
for this auspicious point in time.

We humbly bend our bodies low,
focus our speech, and calm our minds
in fervent homage, full of faith,
to all the relics of the Lord.

18. The Relics of the Buddha

Homage to him! Let me narrate a tale of the past,
when the Buddha entered nirvana in the city
of Kusinara.

His relics were divided up: gods and humans
joined together to distribute them to each country,
eight realms in all.

The crown relics, the four canines, and the Lord's pair
of collarbones: these seven relics were set aside, as they
remained intact.

The remaining relics of the Lord no longer looked
like body parts. As tiny gems, they filled sixteen
tubes of bamboo.

The largest of these mixed-up relics filled five tubes;
the middle-sized ones, six tubes in all; and the smallest,
another five.

His largest relics were each the size of a mung bean,
shining with rays of blinding light, their blazing grace
beyond compare.

The middle-sized relics of the Lord, King of Sages,
shone just as bright in their beauty, each one the size
of a split rice grain.

Their complexion glistened and gleamed like clear crystals,
reflecting light with marvelous rays: such are the relics
of the Buddha.

As for the Lord's smallest relics, each one the size
of a mustard seed, they glowed with lustrous radiance,
like bakul flowers.

A brahman priest, Dona by name, mixed the relics
all together, measured them well, and shared them with
the various kings.

The first portion was for the realm of Rajagriha.
The second was ritually buried in the city
of Vesali.

The third was given to the radiant city of bliss,
Kapilavastu. The fourth was sent to the land
of Allakappa.

The fifth was offered to the realm of Ramagrama,
where the people paraded the Lord's relics
around in circles.

The sixth was sent to the land of Vethadipaka,
while the seventh portion was given to Pava,
a distant realm.

The final portion remained there in Kusinara.
These eight sets of mixed relics remained on earth
to save all beings.

As for the canine from the Buddha's upper right jaw,
Indra had it splendidly enshrined in Trayastrimsa
for gods to worship.

The lower right crystal canine, which blazes red,
was reverently entombed on the island of jewels
known as Lanka.

The upper left one was sent off to Gandhara,
and the lower left, lovely and clear, went down below
to the naga realm.

The right collarbone, blazing bright, was invited
to Lanka by King Sihanatha, rescuing beings
on the island.

The left collarbone was brought to the Brahma realm,
where formless gods built a great stupa in offering,
twelve yojanas tall.

The upper robe of the Buddha was sent to the realm
of Bhaddiya to help its people. His begging bowl
went to Lanka.

As for the Lord's square sitting cloth, it was offered
to the kingdom of Kuva, where gods and humans
praise it to this day.

I bow down low to the highest holy relics
of the all-wise Lord, enshrined in stupas, precious
beyond compare.

I offer my heart, clear in faith, to the Teacher
in place of fine sticks of incense, to burn in praise
    at those stupas.

I offer my words, chanted with care from afar,
in place of gold and silver offerings to the Lord's
    holy relics.

Having made my head and body into a lotus,
I bow and bend in place of flowers, my cupped palms
    raised in reverence.

I worship the Lord's relics with my own two eyes,
offered in place of glowing candles, lit in praise
    to the Blessed One.

The monk Suvannakesar of White Lotus Temple,
resorting to the model of the commentaries,
    penned these verses.

Should a person, male or female, copy, study,
and chant this poem in offering to the holy
    sprouts of buddhas,

they shall achieve the triple bliss: here in this world,
among the gods, and in nirvana, filled with wonder,
    beyond birth and death.

Having faithfully praised the bodily relics of the Buddha,
including his canines, shining like gems, and the objects
    he wore and used,

bowing my body in fervent joy, my palms joined fast,
may I achieve all forms of bliss, dropping delusion,
hatred, and greed.

May I be born in time to meet the next Buddha.
May I listen to his Dharma and reach the fruits
of liberation.

Repaying Debts

We come into this world already in debt: to the parents who birthed us; to those who raised us; to the sun, the earth, and all that sustains us. Who are we without our families? Who are we without our teachers? Who are we without the natural world? Cambodian Buddhists recognize that these debts are fundamental to human life. The Khmer term for such debts is *guṇ*, which means both "debt of gratitude" and "virtue." We owe debts of gratitude to those whose virtues make our lives possible. If we want to be free from suffering, then we must recognize and repay the *guṇ* of our parents, the natural world, and the Three Jewels: the Buddha, his teachings, and his community.

The poems in this cycle remind us that Buddhist values are grounded in human relationships. Our connection to parents, teachers, friends, and all beings is what makes spiritual progress possible. Like the Buddha, our journeys to freedom are not undertaken alone. We rely on the patience of the earth. We learn by forming karmic bonds with our teachers. We breathe thanks to this body, given to us by our parents. And when we hurt others, committing sins or karmic faults, it is our responsibility to seek forgiveness and make amends.

Some of the songs gathered here express *guṇ* in the form of "heart syllables" in Pali. These poems draw on the esoteric dimensions of Cambodian Buddhism, in which select Pali syllables contain the essence of particular Buddhist teachings, meritorious entities, or even parts of the body. By intoning, inscribing, or visualizing these syllables, we learn the Dharma, praise virtuous beings, and repay our debts. Other songs in this cycle refer to specific rituals: the funeral of a loved one, the mid-April Khmer New

Year, or the autumn festival for honoring ancestors, Pchum Ben. Whether expressed in one letter or a multiday rite, the invitation is the same: to reflect on our lives, thank those around us, and honor debts with love.

19. In Praise of the Earth

I now shall chant in praise of the Earth, majestic goddess,
who supports the worlds' creatures, the birds, the beasts,
    and all the trees.

Her thick soil shows her merit, her vast extent
some two hundred and eighty thousand yojanas wide,
    her mass unknown.

Mother to all, she supports whole realms and all our homes,
never angry or prone to move, despite what we
    have done to her.

We dig deep holes, build villages, carve paths and roads,
plant fields of rice, and plow the mud; we shit and piss
    but she doesn't mind.

Those who repay their debts to her shall be reborn
on lofty thrones in Indra's heaven and soon attain
    awakening.

As for the cruel and the careless, their sins are grave.
They're sure to lose all their riches and take rebirth
    deep in the hells.

The Buddha preached: "A roasting pot, filled with water
and brought to a boil, retains its heat for long after
    the water's gone."

In this simile, our sins are fire; our belongings, the water;
our body, the pot. Even after our own home boils away,
we'll keep burning.

If you seek merit, then repay your massive debts
to your parents, your relatives, your preceptor,
and your master,

as well as your debts to the gods, the Moon and stars,
the Wind, the Sun, the Rain above, the Fire below,
and Vaisravana.

Vaisravana, the god of rice, helps all succeed
as our guardian, a mother to all, a father too,
blessed with virtues.

As for the Buddha, Dharma, and Sangha, their vast virtues
exceed measure. The Lord leads countless beings
to liberation.

Whoever joins their palms together to chant praises
and repay debts to those endowed with vast virtues
follows the Lord.

Seeing their debt to the Buddha, they chant, in praise
of his virtues, his epithets, beginning with
"The Blessed One."

All people should hear the Dharma and chant in praise
of its virtues, in keeping with the Pali texts
of the scriptures,

and thus repay their weighty debts to the Dharma
by intoning all its virtues, beginning with
"Well-expounded."

All people should give rise to joy within their hearts
and chant praises of the Sangha, in accord with
the Pali texts,

to thus repay their priceless debts to the Sangha
and its virtues, beginning with "Well-practiced is
the Lord's Sangha."

All people should hear the scriptures and chant praises
of the Buddha's great perfections, amassed from birth
till nirvana.

Listen, wise ones! Chant in the morning, chant in the evening,
and chant at noon. Hone your practice so that you reach
heavenly bliss.

Buddhas of old repaid their mothers through great sermons
on Abhidhamma, the deep teachings that help repay
maternal debts.

To repay their debts to the virtues of their fathers,
they preached the tale of Vessantara, the final life
of Lord Buddha.

For your teachers, who guide the path, you should intone
the Akaravatta to repay debts and wipe away
all trace of sin.

For kith and kin, you should recite one of the tales
of the Pannasajataka, fifty past lives
of the Buddha.

We must also repay our debts to the Earth herself,
to Fire, Wind, Rain, and Vaisravana, our mothers true,
who care for us.

The fourth lunar month, or Phalguna, is rare indeed,
a crucial opportunity to pay back debts,
so take good care.

On the full moon of Phalguna, build a stupa
of sand to make the central mound, paying your debts
to the vast Earth.

Make a small mound in the Southeast to pay back Fire,
who blazes bright as the full moon, endowed with light
and brilliant rays.

Make another in the Southwest to pay back Wind;
show thanks to Rain in the Northwest and Vaisravana
in the Northeast.

In the next month, known as Caitra, make more stupas
for the three days of the New Year, as the Buddha
has guided us.

Drop all your work; pray to let go of bad karma;
make your heart calm. Finish the mounds and do good deeds
to seal your merit.

Bathe all buddhas and pay respect to monastics.
Bow down to all your ancestors and elder kin,
so they live long.

If you're beset with fear and dread of ghosts and ghouls,
you must recite the Mahametri to release you
from those spirits.

Go meditate to soothe your heart, and then intone
the friendly prayers of this sutta. All gods will come
and listen close.

As for the Sun, to pay it back you should recite
the Sun Sutta on those days when Rahu obscures
the solar orb.

As for the Moon and all its stars, you should recite
the Moon Sutta on those days when the lunar disc
becomes eclipsed.

Listen, my friends! Follow the path of the Buddha.
Don't be heedless, for such people, laden with sin,
drop to the hells.

A reckless man forfeits his own ordained life span.
He'll die alone, his wealth used up and merit gone,
so thick his sin.

Merit and sin take after us, a long shadow
through samsara. There's no way out if you can't lick
your lack of care.

Think things through. Stop and reflect. See with wisdom.
Spare no effort to make merit. Don't be careless
with pain or sorrow.

Any person who gives their all to the Dharma
shall not be born on earth again; they'll reach the goal
of nirvana.

Here ends this chant expressed in words for all beings
that they might know the ancient law on all the debts
they must repay.

20. The Twenty-Four Vowels

With NA and MO I pay homage
to the virtues of my parents.
BU stands in for the pure Dharma,
DDHĀ the virtues of my dear kin,

and YA those of my wise teachers.
The All-Knowing Buddha devised
these syllables for us to chant
as acts of worship, day by day.

SI stands for the Abhidhamma,
DDHAṂ recalls the Vinaya rule.
The next vowels, A, Ā, I, and Ī,
comprise the corpus of the Suttas.

The letters U, Ū, and UV reveal
what's soon to come in future lives.
UV is the Lord, preaching to us;
U and Ū, the Dharma's fathers.

Ṛ and Ṝ, the Victor's perfections,
dazzle with light, blue and white,
leading the mass of living beings
to the far shore, nirvana's isle.

Ḷ and Ḹ capture the moment
when the Buddha was enlightened.
E and AI embody the Lord's
awakened mind when he preached.

O and AU are hard to fathom
within the Dharma and its spells.
Rare indeed is someone fit
to solve the riddle of O and AU.

AṂ and ĀṂ are rules for monks,
established once and for all time.
AḤ was laid down as the pathway
for all beings to come and go.

This teaching was expounded
by the Buddha, Supreme Lord,
so that the people of the future
know how to bow and venerate

the virtues of the Dharma
every day throughout their lives,
so as to reach perfect peace
and cease this round of rebirth.

21. The Thirty-Three Consonants

I rouse my mind awake and bow my head down low
to my exalted mother, whose virtues are supreme.
I honor my dear father and kneel before my preceptor.
The legacies of these three are precious beyond compare.

Poor as I am, what can I do but sit by their side at death?
I haven't got enough to repay my debts with alms.
I've only got my heart and a mind to see clearly
the legacies of the three who gave birth to my life.

My preceptor translated the pith of Pali words;
everything he taught me holds fast within my body.
As for my own parents, even lofty Mount Meru
can't measure but a third of their soaring grace.

They fed me, cradled me, and nursed me through the night.
They guarded me from foes and saved me from all harm.
I bring these legacies to mind each day without a lapse.
Sitting upright, I honor them through their undying signs.

The virtues in the consonants are thirty-three in all—
I've learned them as the letters that gave birth to my being.
The Pali phrase IMASMIṂ KĀYE means "within our very selves."
And hence inside my body, I find these thirty-three:

> KA gives birth to the hairs on the head;
> KHA to those covering the body.
> Our heads sport some nine million,
> the rest of the body ten times more.

GA is the nails, twenty in all;
GHA gives rise to the teeth.
Our Teacher, Lord Buddha,
had forty teeth in total.

People these days aren't so complete,
with thirty-two or maybe thirty-three.
Some poor folks have only twenty teeth,
and hence there's no fixed number.

ṄA is the skin, wrapped around
our bodies like a jujube fruit.
Conjure this image, clear as day,
and hold it within your mind.

CA is the flesh, thirty muscle groups;
CHA the sinews, pulled to and fro.
JA is the bones, three hundred in all;
JHA the marrow; ÑA the kidneys; ṬA the heart.

ṬHA gives birth to the liver.
In the bodies of the ignorant,
those whose wisdom is blocked,
this organ is bulbous as a pika fruit.

But the livers of the wise,
those endowed with courage,
are sharp as lemongrass,
barbed like spiked betel.

ḌA is the diaphragm,
holding in digested food.
ḌHA, the stomach's bag, is foul;
contemplate its transience.

ṆA is the lungs, pressed to the chest;
TA the intestines; THA the mesentery—
study them, remember them well
to perfect your magical power.

DA is undigested food,
the daily source of life.
DHA is digested mush:
odious, rank, and vile.

NA becomes the gallbladder.
PA gives rise to phlegm;
PHA to pus; BA to blood;
BHA to sweat, flooding our pores.

MA is fat, whorled in endless little rings;
YA our tears, seeping from our eyes.
RA is grease, our flesh soaked through;
LA becomes saliva, knower of tastes.

VA is mucus, oozing daily
and constantly changing;
SA is the fluid of passion,
obscuring right and wrong.

HA is urine, a stinky dribble,
staining the earth below;
ḶA is known as the skull;
and A, the brain within.

Thus the letters are expounded; study and see them in your mind.
Divide them as appropriate; memorize them beyond doubt.
Twenty-one consonants are gifts of my father:
KA to DHA is his share, along with the lonely ḶA.

My mother gave me twelve, from NA to HA, plus A.
The wise know these thirty-three and honor their true legacies.
What great rewards redound to the pious men and women
who learn and prize these words! For ancient scriptures say:

> One who daily chants these letters
> shall take rebirth for hundreds of lives
> as a blissful, righteous monarch,
> blessed with beauty and speech divine.

22. Absolving All Faults

BHANTE BHAGAVĀ! I place my head beneath your feet,
my ten fingers raised high above in veneration
of the Three Jewels.

May I take leave of my own faults, from conception
up to the present. While pregnant with me, my mother's
sinews went slack,

her body racked with stabs and pangs. Fearing spirits
would torment her, she bore a long, heavy burden
in constant pain.

After one month, a blood-drop became a solid mass.
After another month or two, five limbs formed above
the placenta.

Nursed and fed by the umbilical cord, my body curled
into a crouch, my front turned back to face her spine
behind the womb.

Like a monkey, abused and whipped, I turned and kicked.
When my mother ate sweet desserts, joy and pleasure
surged within me.

But if her food had too much salt or excess spice,
I'd writhe in pain, burning inside, my coiled-up limbs
shaking in the womb.

She took good care and honed her mind so I'd be ready
in ten lunar months. When my time came, a fierce wind blew:
    the force of fate.

It turned me around so that my head could safely emerge
from the birth canal. At that moment, I was careless,
    not yet conscious,

as if first hurled to the final wall that rings the world,
and only then leaving my mother. As consciousness
    arose, I screamed.

As for my mother, I had caused her searing pain.
She laid above a blazing fire for nine full days
    to heal her body.

Absolve this fault: my mother raised and nurtured me.
Whatever the cost, she made no mistakes. She always bore
    that weighty task.

Absolve this fault: my mother faced countless trials,
sleeping in my urine and feces when I was young—
    I leave this sin behind.

Absolve this fault: my mother cared for me with love,
hugging me close as I suckled her breast, even as I bit
    and beat her chest.

I take leave of this fault, lest any vengeance remain:
while my mother was deep in sleep, I cried and cried
    till she woke up.

Karmic traces, wanting revenge, surely follow me.
When I was young, I screamed and hit and kicked her:
    I leave this sin behind.

Farewell, the sin of fighting my mother; may feuding cease.
Goodbye, the sin of ignoring my father. I leave such sins;
    may faults be cleared.

I take leave of this fault, lest any vengeance remain:
I competed and quarreled with my relatives, hurling
    words of abuse.

I was heedless when I fished, taking creatures' lives.
I now take leave of those cruel sins. May all hostile
    remnants be appeased.

I lacked ideas, skills, and knowledge, so my relatives
taught me all I know. Yet I was careless with their trust,
    and spit back lies.

For all the times I mocked the Sun, the Moon, or the stars;
the Lords of the Wind, Rain, Fire, or Water, or other gods:
    I take leave of those sins.

I seek to absolve the fault of deriding the king,
lord of the realm, earthly ruler. I take my leave
    of all such sins.

Another fault: I mocked mandarins and generals.
For all the times I uttered curses and crude insults,
    I take my leave.

Absolve this sin: when I was a young, foolish novice,
my master taught me well, yet I was naughty and rude,
shrugging him off.

I take leave of any malice and faults that remain:
I was churlish with my teacher. I cursed with anger
behind his back.

Farewell, my faults! I leave you now, thoughts of vengeance.
Master, help me, block all those sins. Stop them, bar them,
leave them behind.

Absolve this fault: I lied and tarnished your good name.
May none of this return to me, O master please,
let these faults go.

Absolve this fault: when I was still a novice monk,
I swore at others and fought with them, even cursing
at their mothers.

When I was twenty-one, ordained as a full-fledged monk,
I chided and scolded my novice charges, telling them lies
to help them learn.

In my anger, I snapped at them, my face all red.
I glared down at my students, hoping they'd beat
their ignorance.

I didn't hold back, even with my slow-witted kids.
I shouted and swore, desperate for them to learn
to read the texts.

Absolve this sin: I beat and whipped my animals.
Some beasts I rode, some I trampled, some I pummeled
    without pity.

When I came down with a fever, an astrologer checked
for evil forces and found the source: I needed to free
    the ones I hurt.

He told me to tell a healer that I was haunted
by those I abused, and needed to have a smoke
    and down a drink.

After I die, I'll have to swallow molten bronze;
for such intoxicants betray the Buddha's pure
    monastic law.

I now take leave of that grave sin: drinking alcohol.
O Lord Buddha, I rely on your incalculable merit:
    have mercy on me.

Goodbye, my sins, lest traces of wrong deeds remain!
Cats and dogs, ducks and chickens: I made them yelp,
    I made them yowl.

Deafness, ignorance, orphanhood:
may I never face them again, no matter where
    or when I'm born.

Leprosy, ringworm, ulcers, arthritis, uneven limbs,
broken bones, amputation, blindness, hermaphroditism,
    a hunched back,

throbbing aches, muteness, timidity, frizzy hair, matted locks,
a blocked nose, an irritable disposition, and simmering pain:
    may I be free of these.

Misshapen face, stocky limbs, swollen feet,
leprous lesions, crossed eyes, blurred vision,
    bad cataracts,

broken teeth, sunken face, double chin, hooked nose,
and a permanent grimace, like a monkey eating betel:
    so long to these!

I take leave of facial scars, blisters, whitened hands,
whitened feet, a darkened face, and crooked limbs:
    may they be gone.

Farewell, all types of baldness: hair only in the back,
just in the front, or alone on top, so the head seems
    to float in space!

Bowlegs. An awkward gait. Short, squat, or stupidly tall.
Eyes that gaze up or out to the sides, like wild people—
    I take my leave.

Goodbye, pustules, goodbye leprosy, goodbye, thrush!
Impetigo, sores and lesions, rashes and rings: may I
    never have them.

I take leave of disfigurement and wasting away,
sickness, calamity, misfortune, and disturbance.
    May I be done.

Farewell, splayed fingers, farewell choked veins!
Farewell, open sores and wrinkled, scarred lips!
    May I be free.

I leave duplicity, falsehoods, all lies and tricks.
Goodbye to my dim, foolish acts, dishonesty
with my own kin.

The right. The wrong. The laws of kings and of the Lord.
Farewell to not knowing these truths. An end to lies:
I take my leave.

As for taking random strangers as my own kin,
may I never make this mistake again, for each
and every life to come.

Absolve these sins! I leave behind thoughts of revenge,
retribution, deprivation, pain and hardship,
all states of woe.

I take leave of violating the five precepts.
Absolve these sins; may they never come back to me,
not even once.

Farewell, the sins of killing creatures great and small!
I abandon the faults of stealing, smuggling, and swindling;
absolve them all.

Absolve the faults of adultery and dishonesty,
my careless words, untimely jokes, and hurtful speech.
I leave these sins behind.

Breaking the fifth precept by drinking is worst of all:
I lost my wealth, town and temple, my own good name.
May this fault end.

Absolve this fault: on holy days I failed to keep
the eight precepts, during New Year, Pchum Ben,
and the rains retreat.

During these times, I boxed, wrestled, wore ogre masks,
held whips and shovels, drank in the temple, and defied
the Buddha's words.

Cart races and elephant rides. Hair in a turban, shoes on my feet.
A parasol above my head. A boast about my shuttlecock game.
My hands clutching a sharp chisel:

I did such sins and more at the temple in every life.
I made offerings while slouching against the wall,
without a care.

I spit and acted thoughtlessly within the Buddha's own abode.
Forgive me, Lord! Save me, Master—I now take leave
of all such sins.

When monks chanted sacred texts and preached the Dharma,
I didn't listen. Chin in my palm, I chatted with my neighbors,
thinking of other places.

I take leave of this sin: I built a shrine for a tutelary spirit.
Such sheds are worthless and wasteful; they open the gates
to lower realms.

Absolve this sin: I defamed those who guard the precepts
and the Buddha's virtues. Like a traitor, I called them flat
as the earth's plane.

I vow to succeed to the pure lineage of the Buddha.
Forgive my faults, Merciful One! Guide me, O Lord,
and all beings.

May I retain the five precepts within my mind.
The eight precepts: may I guard them with my being,
without a lapse,

just like buddhas who made the Dharma sweet to hear,
who kept pure rules and noble vows, who led beings
to nirvana.

May I rely on their merit and perfections.
May I be born in a palace in the heaven
of Tusita,

where gentle songs will soothe my ears, where a retinue
will serve my needs, equal to gods and goddesses
in realms divine.

May the Buddha, with his wisdom, bring Mara down.
May he be crushed, so I can quell all greed, craving,
and defilement.

To help others, may I forsake a monarch's crown,
even my spouse, even our children, that I might end
endless rebirth.

My absolutions and aspirations: may both come true.
May I achieve the paths and fruits until I win
the final prize.

23. Filial Debts

Noble mother and father!
I burn in longing for you.
Ever since I took this birth,
you've toiled so hard to rear me.

O my masters, how precious!
You've borne so much suffering,
cradling and caring for me—
words can't record all you've done.

So I humbly join my palms,
raising them and bowing low
to your feet, my peaceful lords;
forgive my faults and failings!

While you ate, I cried and screamed.
You rushed over and held me,
gently singing lullabies
with affection till I slept.

Spit and piss and even shit,
any nasty thing I'd ooze,
you'd pick up with your own hands
and wipe me clean without disgust.

Mother, Father: my debt's huge,
my tally's long in arrears.
I honor all I owe to you.
May you be well, lords of peace!

May I share the merit I make,
settling my vow to practice
giving, ethics, and meditation:
may all that's good flow to you.

May you receive with full joy
what my sincere heart offers
in these words of truth,
this dedication to you.

24. Asking for Mother's Forgiveness

I now ask your forgiveness
for all I have done to you
and for all my careless words:
O mother, please forgive me!

My debt to you is immense.
I offer my body and speech
and bow in respect to you:
O mother, please forgive me!

I prostrate myself to you,
hands raised in prayer, head lowered
to touch your feet, O mother:
Please release me from my faults!

When I was inside your womb
I put you through constant pain,
whether you walked, stood, or sat,
and made you eat simple food.

Salty, spicy, hot, or cold:
these you eschewed for my sake.
You suppressed your desires
to protect me in the womb.

For nearly ten months you toiled,
the pain spreading through your body,
without a moment's relief
to bring you joy, ease, or peace.

I offer you the merit
that may arise from this gift
of the Teaching, so lucid.
Receive it, mother, and rejoice!

I dedicate this merit
to my mother and father.
May the three treasures be theirs
and may they be free from pain.

25. Orphan's Lament

Woe, woe! I'm now an orphan;
I'm broken without Mother.
All alone will I suffer,
this grief never to leave me.

Nursing me by your own breast,
O Mother blessed, you raised me.
But then Death came so cruelly;
suddenly I'm without you.

Because of my old karma
I am torn apart from you.
O dear mother! Death comes to
turn me into an orphan.

On the pyre the fire burns bright,
setting alight this searing pain.
Only my karma is to blame
for the fierce flame that brands me.

I've been broken, through and through.
I long for you in agony.
My dear mother, you've left me;
now there's only bones and ash.

Mother, you're gone! You've left me
in misery and anguish.
Even my pain and joy vanish,
leaving me wordless and empty.

In this life I'm all alone,
with no one to care for me.
Endless is my misery,
solitary is my plight.

O night, how long and how deep!
Before I'd sleep, you'd hold me tight.
Mother, you'd sing through the night,
lest I, in fright, wake and cry.

Mother, I wail for your grace.
Never again your face will I see.
Alone, I burn in agony.
What misery, day after day.

26. Hungry Ghosts' Lament

All you people of virtue,
young and old, men and women:
The month of Pchum Ben has come;
time to go to the temple.

Don't stay shut up at home
or go out heedlessly, thinking
"Making merit can't beat wine"
and cursing loudly in the streets.

Enough already! Quit it.
Stop and reflect carefully.
Go! Offer alms with the rest.
Don't be idle or useless.

Parents live for their children.
When death comes and this life ends,
no one knows where they'll be born:
among gods, men, or hungry ghosts.

If born on earth or in the heavens,
such rare goodness has a cause.
But how fearsome to become a shade,
belly swollen from lack of food!

Only eating pus, blood, and shit,
walking alone, with a hideous face:
what a torrent of misery,
a fate without certain end.

This is what comes to parents
who harm others to feed their kids,
sowing seeds of bitter fruit.
Learn this lesson carefully.

Now in this month of Pchum Ben,
the ghosts cry out for their kin.
Lord Death lets them go to find
their children, wife, or husband.

Woe, woe—how pitiable!
The suffering ghosts shed fresh tears
as they wander to each new temple,
still not seeing spouse or child.

They only find strangers' homes,
where families join to prepare
rice and sweets for their forebears;
lonely shades won't get one bite.

But even more miserable still
are ghosts with no kin at all.
They pummel themselves in agony
outside the walls in searing pain.

Pounding their chests, they lament
"Woe, woe, this body of mine!
Before this, I bore heavy loads
day and night for my kids' sake.

"Now I've fallen to the ghost realm,
while those above eat their fill.
Woe is me, bereft of kin,
bitter, lonely, miserable."

Thus we should reflect and quake.
Pity all those starving shades,
facedown in the muck and mire,
wailing out their tales of woe:

"My golden child, my dear love!
I bore this pain all for you.
But now you're gone, good as dead.
I can't find you at the temple.

"Don't you know that your father
suffered so much for your sake?
I gave up my entire life
so that you might be happy.

"Now this karma bears its fruit,
for your dad is never at peace.
My mind knows pain, never joy.
I suffer alone without reprieve.

"My child, please know right from wrong.
Remember me, your father,
starving as a hungry ghost,
never knowing my next meal.

"Pchum Ben is almost over;
Lord Death is summoning me.
My dearest, my precious child!
Where have you gone? Where are you now?

"Before I return, may we meet?
So I can taste a bite of food?
Until my death, my child, my life,
I'll never say no to you again!

"I've gone to all the temples,
but you've never come at all.
I've lost hope of finding food.
Farewell, my child. I leave you!"

The ghosts wail until hope ends,
from dawn until day fades to night,
their cries choked back in their chests,
wondering when their kin will come.

I'll cut this story short a bit
for all you people to reflect.
Don't you see who this tale's for?
For you as sons and daughters.

Your parents killed and harmed creatures
to find you food and nourish your life.
Because of their deep love for you,
they suffer now, after their deaths.

If we're truly grateful children,
we must remember this vast debt.
Don't make offerings at the bar!
You'll be haunted if you dare.

For Pchum Ben, come offer alms.
Prepare rice balls with great care.
Make merit for your ancestors,
friends and kin who've passed away.

Let them enjoy some sweets and snacks,
prepared with skill by your own hands.
Once they've eaten, they'll bless you
with peace and true prosperity.

If anyone who's wise and kind
can make good on these offerings,
the fruit will be returned to you:
a joyful boon till nirvana.

27. Offerings for Monks and Ancestors

Permit me, monks, to speak to you!
In keeping with the Order's rules,
we now offer these gifts of food
to fill your bowls up to the brim.

We dedicate these to our kin:
curries prepared with art and skill,
along with candles, incense sticks,
banners, lamps, and parasols,

betel nuts and areca leaves,
scents and perfumes, buds and blossoms,
garlands of flowers and strings of jewels,
all crafted with beauty and care,

sunshades fringed with long festoons,
lanterns hung from strings and poles,
casting light across the temple,
all prepared in pious prayer,

food to round off your alms bowls,
measured well and tightly packed,
with many kinds of fruits and cakes—
all these we give to the Sangha.

Without stealing a cent from others,
we've prepared these gifts with zeal
for the community of monks,
releasing a flood of great merit.

We fix our minds with pure intent
on this secure resolution:
to make this surge of benefits
flow to departed ancestors.

May all the spirits and the sprites
who live in quarters near and far,
along with gods in heavens high,
rejoice in our dedication.

May this deluge of merit pure
cascade to all our ancestors
by means of our sincere efforts
in making these fine offerings.

Now please, O venerable monks,
may the swift stream of our merit
bring nourishment to those we love,
our ancestors throughout all time.

We humbly chant this solemn prayer
that it come true, just as we wish,
and one day reach that crystal isle,
the yonder shores of nirvana.

28. Dedication of Merit

May all I've done with care and craft, both words and acts,
help me find bliss, shake off distress and cross to reach
nirvana's shore.

In every life may I give alms and hold precepts.
May all my vows be soon realized, my boons, my bridge
to realms supreme.

I share the fruits of my merit with my parents,
my preceptors, my wise teachers, and all my kin,
gone and to come.

May my forebears, no matter where they now reside,
share in the joy of my blessings. May they find peace,
free from all pain.

Befriending Death

Anicca. Dukkha. Anattā. Fleeting, painful, not yours. These are the Three Marks, the facts that haunt our lives. Born in a human body, all of us must, sooner or later, grapple with three stark realities: this body is limited, destined to suffer, and doesn't belong to us in the end. The Dharma songs in this cycle find dozens of ways to bring this message home.

When we're healthy, happy, and content with our lot, it's hard to see how fragile everything really is. But illness or accidents can shatter our complacency. The poems in this cycle are intended to be recited for the dying, the dead, and the bereaved, for only when death is near do the Three Marks become easier to recognize. In the depth of our grief and fear, we are shaken to the core. The songs gathered here emphasize this experience of spiritual urgency, or *saṃvega*, as the end of life draws near. They also provide a path of practice: training the mind to swim beyond the waves of birth and death.

Some of the verses translated here are hard to swallow. The poems are direct, filled with do's and don'ts. Horror and gore abound. Some are cryptic, sketching a map without naming the roads. The poems in this cycle aren't mean to be comprehensive manuals. They are pithy guides, wise as old friends, reminding us of truths we already know.

29. Funeral March

A drum-and-oboe dirge resounds:
"The lives of all living beings
never last long; they soon must end.
Birth leads to death, all forms decay."

A drum-and-oboe dirge resounds:
"All you people must understand:
gods and humans, even children,
none can escape impermanence."

A drum-and-oboe dirge resounds:
"O good people, follow what's right.
Seek out the truth and fix your mind
on ceasing wrong and foolish deeds."

A drum-and-oboe dirge resounds:
"Youth slips away, death's never far.
Old age stalks close and can't be shaken;
it must answer to karma alone."

A drum-and-oboe dirge resounds:
"Go beyond death: know the Four Truths
and take their pillow to the far shore.
Rest free from pain in peace and bliss."

30. This Life Is Short

This life is short: you are born
with bodily form that can't last.
You'll never be free or get past
the shadow cast by distress.

Nothing is yours: all is void,
all is devoid of essence.
No fame, no rank, no parents,
no one precious, nobody,

not even those born before,
not even your family.
Your own body is empty.
Listen to me: make this known.

Discarded deep in the forest,
with none to trust as your own,
save wild beasts who grunt and groan,
you'll be alone, through and through.

Your wealth, the worst poverty:
you can't take anything with you.
You'll lie there, nothing to do,
your body truly worthless.

All merit gone in your wake,
your kin will take your carcass
to woodlands cloaked in darkness.
They'll leave, tearless; there you'll stay.

The dead must be abandoned,
their bones and flesh thrown away.
Your body's bound to decay;
your name, they say, soon unsaid.

Reflect on this and be stirred.
Don't be deterred but instead
take refuge in what's well said.
Hear this and tread the right course.

Give gifts, keep rules, train your heart:
three ways to start from the source.
To wipe your brow of remorse,
don't do what's coarse. Thus I preach:

Build your merit. Guard your mind.
Always be kind. Strive to reach
all those in need. Make your speech
match those who teach the true path.

31. The Four Thieves

The Buddha's words save beings
by making the Dharma their anchor.
Give up your cruel and violent thoughts.
Cast them away, don't cling to them.

The places to seek true refuge
are reached through meditation;
engage in preparatory rites
to ward off ill and ignorance.

Calm your body, make it steady.
Focus your awareness, still the mind.
Breathe in and out with perfect ease
so that you might soon reach the goal.

Your situation is as dire as this:
You're like a man, fearing for his life,
frantically chased by four thieves,
who seek to catch him at every turn.

Shaking with fright, he sprints away
and finally reaches the water's edge.
Breakers crash and whirlpools spin,
too swift for him to cross the foam.

Right then he spots a drifting corpse,
carried by the churning tides.
He leaps to hold it in his arms,
floating his way across the sea.

Once he alights at the far shore,
he cleans himself of filth and rot
to enter the deathless country
known to all as nirvana.

This parable, drawn from old texts
in the scriptures, is thus untangled:
The four thieves who chased the man
are birth, old age, sickness, and death.

The ocean is the great abyss
that sinks creatures in samsara.
The violent maelstrom is craving,
dragging beings down to the deep.

The floating corpse is our body,
bound to be broken apart,
lacking any stable essence,
not able to endure for long.

Don't drown! Swim on, strive hard.
Study the path of the Buddha
and his Sangha, our true masters,
real saints beyond all scales or tests.

To be a saint means that your mind,
reborn across infinite lives
in the swirl of heavens and hells,
exceeding all our dreams of time,

has finally made manifest
the crystal realm of the deathless,
with grief and sickness gone for good
and no return to birth and death.

32. The True Fate of Flesh

All you people
with hearts of faith!
Learn the Dharma:
your body's old,
ready to break.
Let the true fate
of flesh stir you.

All bodies share
one destiny.
Lord Time knows when
the young turn old
against their will,
yet who but Time
bears this in mind?

Be your refuge.
Count your merit,
pray drop by drop.
Ask Time to help
record your deeds.
These earnest prayers
will be your raft.

Your human life?
Short and painful.
Remember this
while you're still here.

When you must go,
hop on your raft
to the far shore.

Carnality
makes waves as tall
as snowcapped peaks;
few stay afloat.
The sea's the same:
most drown instead.
What misery!

Reflect on your
fragile body—
this Dharma's true.
Those who practice
and make pure vows
with radiant faith
can cross the sea.

Care for your body
to learn the Dharma,
even just one page.
Don't be thoughtless
and call the Lord's
Teachings useless;
you'll fall to hell.

Lift the Three Jewels
above your head,
raise them up high.
They will save you
from fires below
to reach real bliss,
merit's own fruit.

The true Dharma
beats all wonders
and bests all scales.
Cradle it close;
contemplate deep.
Treasure its boons
more than your life.

The great Dharma
is most precious.
Hold it within.
Guard it, keep it,
and hug it tight.
Study daily
and meditate.

For flesh and bones
rot and scatter:
they can't go on.
Pity this body!
It will leave you,
while your spirits
will join the Dharma.

You'll get nothing:
your kids, your heirs,
will stay behind.
Your poor spirits,
the Dharma's wards!
Time grabs their throats,
all disappears.

O Lord Buddha
of vast virtue,
incomparable!

Please ferry us
upon your raft,
lead all beings
to nirvana.

33. This Heap Called a Body

You're no different.
You've got one too:
this heap called a body,
liquids, solids, a source of heat,
two ears, two eyes, and a tongue.

But heaps don't last.
You'll die in pain,
pummeled senseless
and bound in chains
by Death's little men.

Your breath goes first,
down the body, through the palms,
out the soles. Winded,
you plead with your captors
for one last talk with your kids.

But Death's minions,
full of rage, won't let you go.
They curse you: Damn thief!
You think you can cheat death
without seeking the path of saints?

When your time's up,
make a pledge and we'll assent.
But don't you dare

talk back to us—
no last words for now.

Death, waiting in the wings,
swoops in to seal your doors.
Closed off, you cry inside,
Mom! Dad! Save me!
Show some love for your child!

"Soon this body
shall be cast away," or so the scriptures say.
Your fever spikes, your breath quickens,
letting out more than you take in.

You try to turn back,
and shout with muffled tones,
calling out for your family.
You might recover enough
to give your final will.

Yet karma soon resumes its course.
You gasp for air. Your body goes slack
as you lay weak, helpless on your bed.
Others may feel for your pain,
but what can they really do?

Loved ones gather, kids and kindred souls,
their hoarse throats lined with prayer.
They slot a coin through your lips,
a gift for worlds to come, yet nothing
they do can halt this march of death.

In, out, held—
so goes the breath.
Winds leave but no longer come.
Veins and vessels twist and twirl
as life sighs into death.

Your body is orphaned,
lonely, unguarded.
The souls within wander,
bereft of a body.
A ghost takes shape and leaves.

Unconscious, unmoored,
this specter laughs without a care.
Men shoulder your corpse
deep into the woods,
and score a cross in the soil.

Your ghost frolics, heedless, headless,
but soon pines for its old abode.
Floating off to the forest
it finds the cross, and at the crossroads,
byways blocked by thorns.

Your ghost pauses, then wonders aloud,
Who dared to call me dead?
Look! They've laid out brambles
and carved an X in the earth,
blocking my escape.

And look at my fingers!
Before I had five on each hand,
but now I'm down to four.
In fear, it cries, Mom! Dad!
Why have you thrown me away?

You hate me, don't you?
Why not keep me at home
or bury me in your yard?
You didn't say you'd dump me
out here in the wilderness.

Help me, Mom! Save me
from this den of savage beasts.
Here, far from human life,
the fleshy eyes of owls
track my every move.

The woods lie still and hush,
prowled by tigers and wolves,
elephants and dholes,
monkeys and packs of dogs.
My carcass lies there, alone.

Thus it wails and stomps its feet,
stamping its mark in the earth
from daybreak to noon
in the fearful forest,
forlorn and flooded with tears.

Your ghost sits by your grave,
bemoaning its former host.
This swelling flesh,
those bulging eyes!
The neck sinks down,

the limbs splay wide,
the trunk splits open.
Blood flows from all nine holes,

staining the body,
soaking the soil.

After seven days,
sinews break apart,
leaving only bones.
All falls away,
no body remains.

Soon, for your ghost,
only pain endures,
days and months
of hunger and lack,
a wake of misery.

Your kin cover the corpse
with a thin cotton shroud.
And so your ghost wanders
to beg from strangers
until your bones bleach white.

Reflect on this cycle of birth and death,
a tale of hundreds of thousands of lives.
Hear this, dear friend, and be stirred.
Study the virtues within your body
that lead to freedom from pain.

Don't get caught in suffering;
move on, let go, find peace.
While you're still alive,
change your own fate,
for karma cuts through all.

Hold to what's good,
cultivate yourself,
keep wise words on your lips.
Forsake your wealth; give it away.
Don't be greedy or grieve past gifts.

Keep your eye on the highest truth,
keep your patience, keep your vows.
Help others and live with thanks.
Adore the seeds you sow,
a basis for future boons.

Death himself will grant you favor,
the gods will rejoice and lift you high.
You'll rise to the heavens above,
dodging the hells below
and other stations of woe.

Good friend, pure in deed,
listen close to this advice.
These teachings aren't easy,
but they are the bud
that blooms in bliss.

Rare are these words,
and rarer those who take heed.
For death is sure for all who are born.
You'll lose everything, carts and chests,
priceless bracelets and wish-granting gems.

You'll be parted from all that,
save for a mouthful of betel
and a silver round, pushed between your lips.

You'll even lose that single coin,
for once you're gone, they'll snatch it back.

Strive hard while this body remains.
Perfect your conduct, give with abandon,
bridge the ocean of birth and death.
Etch your prayers deep in your chest
and point the mind to lasting peace.

34. Song for the Hour of Death

Pain binds your body, intensifying,
subtle to serious, throbbing, flaring;
you face it alone, right till the end.
Pain seizes, squeezes, and makes you sick
with fevers that wreck you from within,
from life to death, from death to the void.
Your body knows but constant change:
unchecked, short-lived, bound to decay,
once light, now dark, once rising, now falling.

Your voice sang clear, but now it's hoarse.
Your eyes once ranged both far and near,
but now they've changed, and all grows dim.
Your hair once gleamed, black and oiled,
but now it's dull and gray as ash,
white to the tips, like river-grass buds.
Your teeth once snugly meshed together,
mashing your food without a hitch.
Now your gums swell and your teeth shake.
They slip from their roots and fall from your mouth.
Whatever you eat, you can't bite it through.
You chomp down and swallow, fearing hunger.
Your ears grow deaf. Your supple skin,
once tightly wrapped around your flesh,
goes slack and droops; what beauty remains?

Your body's parts aren't really you.
You can't even call them your own.

To love them's useless—what refuge are they?
You coax your hair, "Stay as you are.
Don't go gray." But your hair won't listen.
You woo your teeth, "Stay as you are.
Don't fall out." But your teeth won't listen.
You plead with your ears, "Be kind to me!
Don't go deaf!" But your ears won't listen.
You beg your eyes, weeping and wailing,
entreating the gods to offer their blessings,
"Dear eyes, have mercy! Stay as you are.
Don't go dark." But your eyes won't listen.

Death, our foe, rallies his troops
to storm in swiftly and seize your body.
They grasp your head, hands, and feet,
pin down your waist, and never let go.
They grip your chest and squeeze your heart,
pinching the thirty-two vessels within.
They knock you down and tie you up,
pulling you forward, pushing from behind,
tugging and tossing you left and right.
Crumpled and pummeled, you wither in pain,
by agony crushed, by anguish beat,
tormented, tortured relentlessly.
Your chest contracts and blazes red hot.
Thick phlegm creeps up, crowding your throat.
The body's four elements slink away,
but your mouth sticks open, gasping for air,
your nose all clogged, your last tears dry.
What a struggle to breathe! The wind element
slips away, twisting your vessels in knots.
Your eyes roll back, as you shiver and shake
and quake inside, pursued to death by Death.

Your snot, once yellow, turns black and sticky;
your body soon grows noxious and foul.
Strangers haul your corpse to the woods,
throwing you out like trash, without regret.
In the charnel grounds, your body's forlorn,
beneath gibbons, civets, and flying squirrels;
hounded by wolves, dholes, and wild dogs;
eyed by owls, osprey, and circling hawks,
whose hoots and shrieks resound in the woods,
hemmed in by crows and circled by vultures,
who summon a flock to join their feast of gore.
Soon all these beasts rush in to peck and hack,
gnawing and tearing your corpse to shreds.
They mob en masse as your last entourage.

Dead for a few days, your limbs swell up.
Your body bloats, your eyes bulge out,
your tongue slops down over your chin.
Your arms buckle, broken and contorted.
Your hair sticks up, shameless and indignant.
Your belly balloons like a water jug.
Your legs splay out, miming an ogre,
as blood and pus and putrid fluids
seep out from your nine orifices.
Worms burble within, pockmarking your skin,
while swarms of flies feast on your foul corpse.
Soon your lungs and flesh are gone, and all
that remains are bones, sinking in the mud
and sliding down deep to oblivion.

You can't control this body, for it's not yours.
Reflect on this carefully, ponder it well.
See the path before you—don't be careless.
You bathe yourself, put on a lace-hemmed skirt,

an embroidered silk blouse, a blended scarf,
smiling and thinking you're not too bad.
You trim your hair, massage it with oil,
and shave the sides so you can show off.
Adorned with gold and gleaming with jewels,
you walk with grace, swinging your arms.
You never stop preening, but this body
is loathsome; its fate, disgusting, certain
to decay. Take a moment to think it over.

Reflect in detail on your fragile body,
strive to tame and train your wild heart.
Don't be too bold, don't lose awareness,
don't get aroused. Contemplate your own
physical form. Don't think of the pleasures
of men and women, gold and silver,
horses and elephants, buffalo and cattle,
or rising in rank—these thoughts are futile.
Such attachments bind your neck, waist, and ankles,
your whole body shackled like a thrice-bound corpse.

Rare are those who can loosen these cords.
To succeed and reach complete freedom,
you must study the forty-five subjects
the masters selected for meditation.
Clear your mind and concentrate well
on the lucid guidance of your teachers.
Filled with pity, they admonish you
to vanquish the evil trapped within
and abandon all five of the obstacles.
Quick, cast them off; don't let them get near
or you might get stuck and fail to progress.
Having gained the hard-won jewels of virtue,
hold them tight; keep them safe and secure.
Don't be a fool and forsake the manual

that guided you this far. Don't let your mind
wander, don't hold grudges, don't be sly.

The sages of old learned, upheld, and vowed
to realize the truth of the Buddha's teachings.
Completely detached, they accrued good deeds
and strove to cast off numberless evils.
They rooted the Dharma in their bodies,
aiming to one day reach its highest fruits.
All doubts they severed, all sins they ceased.
Fletchers of the mind, they trued their resolve.
Their aim was sure: to complete their practice
and find real bliss before life's window shuts.

Should you succeed in meditation,
you're certain to win a divine prize.
Once you've mastered the true practice,
keep it fixed and firm within your being.
Suppose you had a hoard of gold and gems,
all squirreled away in a secret cache.
If you were able to protect it well,
your treasure would keep you secure for life.
But if you were to relax your guard,
and spend a little here, a little there,
soon your vast riches would be scattered
and you'd be ruined, worse than before.

This is just like one who wins the Dharma
and gains freedom yet can't live up to it.
Resting on success, he loses his zeal.
Unstirred by urgency, he fails to strive
and keep up all the progress he's made.
He assumes that now he's a master,
with vengeful karma all melted away,
he can just be careless with his body

and not bother to think things through.
But one can never cheat the price of sin.
Don't doubt this, for evil fast accumulates
when you fail to hold yourself upright.
When you take up the Dharma, be careful:
study the mind, keep it pure, stick to truth.
Deepen your tolerance and compassion;
find the path of kindness from within.
Take care of yourself, be steady and settled,
follow your teachers, don't mess around.

Learn to speak softly; keep your voice reined in.
Learn to walk modestly; don't swing your arms.
Learn to wear your sarong in the proper style.
Learn not to boast; don't praise the forest sprites.
Learn to eat with grace and courtesy;
only consume what's free of fault and fear.
Learn not to cause strife; don't neglect your lords.
Learn not to ruffle feathers; don't be too nosy.
Learn not to harm creatures, not even with words.
Learn not to fight or quarrel; don't scheme or sue.
Learn to listen to sermons. Take the Dharma
as your object; find the path and its fruits.
Learn the precepts; don't be lazy or idle.
Learn to be grateful and know your debts
to teachers, to parents, and to neighbors.
Learn to be patient, to be poor and hungry;
don't swindle strangers or abuse your friends.
Learn to see your own faults; keep them in mind.
Learn the scriptures; engrave them in your heart.

In times to come, you'll have nothing to fear,
for if you study these teachings with care
and a pure intention, you need not doubt.
Should you aspire to reach the heavens,

soaring above in distant Brahma realms,
or even return back here in human form,
your hopes and prayers shall be fulfilled.
At last, this exposition's complete.
The facts that haunt our lives are plain:
constant change, ceaseless pain,
and nothing to call our own—
now these wise words must end.

35. A Lesson in Meditation

I pay homage, bowing my head in veneration,
and make a vow, born out of faith, to explicate
the signs with care,

as written in the text known as "On the Body,"
which bears the Lord's teachings on the four foundations
of awareness.

The contemplation of the body was taught by means
of syllables that trace a path within ourselves
for seeing the signs

and their counterpart images. This path conforms
with what the Lord called ultimate truth: study it well
to reach the goal.

The contemplation of sensations is the second
foundation of awareness, complete with signs
to learn in stages.

The contemplation of the mind is the third,
expounded within our physical bodies:
know it clearly.

The fourth is based on various mental factors:
remember its signs and images to reach the goal
of nirvana.

May I commence with a firm vow to cultivate
wisdom and faith within this life, to grasp the objects
of meditation.

I vow to make my bodily realm a sphere of joy,
to be aware of the sign of contact, the base for all
stages of bliss.

I contemplate the syllables NA MA BA DA
to know each kind of sign, mental factor,
consciousness, and awareness.

The concentrated meditator knows these letters
in secret ways but establishes just three of them
as instructed.

In fact, within us there are four awarenesses,
known as "bodily contemplation"—study them
within your being.

These four are embodied in the four syllables:
aware and awake to hot and cold, consciously
knowing all scents.

Inhalation opens the gate to states of trance,
accompanied by water and wind that guide our minds
at every door.

The body stands like a tall tree, verdant and lush,
rooted in the earth. This is the abode of Prince
and Princess Mind,

the city of Ayudhya. It glows with rays of many hues.
standing on nirvana's path, guiding the prince
and the princess.

On top are two round bushes, lovely and fresh,
adorned with leaves, growing beneath the path
to nirvana.

Beneath them lie two gates, the means for the conscious
knowledge of trance, which open and close as our breath
flows in and out.

Below them is the gate made for the lord of the realm,
the monarch of the glorious city of Ayudhya,
our own body.

Two bushes sprout on the sides, a pair of supple wings.
These are our two ears, the means of wisdom that lead
to nirvana.

Above and all around grows the forest of Himavant,
laden with fruits, both black and white, ninety-nine
million in all.

The first foundation of awareness centers the body,
unfolding through four main stages. Remember them
to see clearly.

Once you grasp the sign, its fixed counterpart can arise:
bright as the day, beaming with rays that sparkle and shine
upon the waves.

The beams glisten and gleam in the gates of our eyes,
glaring and blinding, as if the sun had arisen
inside your mind.

The contemplation of the body: maintain it well,
stable and clear, within your being—don't split your mind
from your body.

Establish it as your firm base, a stone platform,
steady and fixed, within your mind, inside the city
of your body.

Perfect your vision, full like the tide coming to shore,
each wave crashing directly against your body,
making all clear.

The second foundation centers all sensations
within the city of your body, a clear method
to rise in stages.

The fixed image features a burst of purple beams
in ornate arrays, like fields of flowers, their braided stems
twisted and coiled,

circling like wheels, perfectly round, splitting in pairs,
like flying snakes playing tag in the sky, their mouths clutching
flower stems and diamonds.

The third foundation centers the mind within
our own bodies. Its marks include a violent storm,
spiraling into the sky.

The fixed image has moon-soft beams of yellow hue,
which float down close to our bodies, filling our minds
with faith and joy.

A spectrum of rays, five colors in all, shines like a jewel.
Brilliant bolts of lightning flash bright in distant skies,
then circle the body.

Heavenly realms appear, with palaces filled with deities,
their bodies peaceful and light with joy, beyond all fear:
how fortunate!

The fourth foundation centers the factors of the mind.
Its fixed image looks like a blaze of blood-red fire,
extending far.

It's like the sun—when it rises, it shines yellow
and blue with solar resplendence: dazzling, luminous,
incandescent.

It's like the Moon—when it rises, many facets appear,
a realm of bliss. The body changes: light to heavy;
still, then moving.

It's like a naga—it flies, clutching a radiant jewel,
moving, then still; it takes its gem atop the city
of Ayudhya.

NA MA ARAHAṂ: short syllables fixed as letters
for the virtues of the bright jewel inherited
from our mother.

They're like the ocean, vast and profound, beyond compare.
Even the earth and all its seas can't top the virtues
of our mother.

Among the four jewels inside our body, this is the first.
Named *manijoti*, with clear-hued rays, this jewel was given
by our mother.

The Lord established this ultimate jewel as a pure realm
of subtle bliss. Unmixed, unalloyed, our mother bestowed
this jewel on us.

The virtues of this precious jewel lead to nirvana.
Like twinkling stars, it scintillates; like flower stems,
it rises at dawn.

The second jewel, named *maniratna*, shines luminous,
its blue-yellow rays as bright as the sun, its many beams
awash in color.

This jewel's the pure method bestowed by our father.
The many virtues of this jewel are fixed as syllables
for meditation:

U Ū ARAHAṂ, for the earth disc in all four realms.
This jewel's virtues sit in the body as a method
for meditation

within the mind, for all of us to venerate,
to strive to know its marks clearly, within the city
of the body.

The third jewel, named *manipaduma*, gathers together
fiery red rays, with smoky tails of many colors,
up to seven.

The Patthana, precious book of the Abhidhamma,
gave it to us, a jewel that hides within our bodies,
filled with wisdom.

A Buddha's sprout, this jewel's for us to worship.
It's like a cart, a divine chariot, swiftly carrying
us back and forth.

This jewel's a method, a means to reach the city
of nirvana, a vehicle for all, a bridge
to the heavens.

The fourth jewel, named *vaidurya*, shines with clear rays,
like the jewel of the sky itself, its beams colored
with countless hues.

This is the jewel of the King, the Buddha himself,
the Thrice-Omniscient Lord, who gave it to us
to venerate.

It illuminates living creatures, blessed with bright beams
of matchless splendor, with rays of yellow, white, and green,
seven hues in all.

The virtues of this precious jewel always ferry
sentient beings across the waves of samsara
to nirvana.

36. The Fortunate Eon

RŪPAṂ DUKKHAṂ—such agony, endless, untold!
For young and old, pain boils within without relief,
till death ends all.

ANICCAṂ—not fixed, not firm, not prone to last for long.
Once dead, only your corpse remains. All turns to soil:
flesh, bone, sinew.

ANATTĀ—nothing, no form, no name, no accolades,
no fame, no rank, no high, no low, no friends, no love,
no wealth: all gone.

So reflect well; care for your heart. Calm your anger,
soften your heart, like mother and child. Calm your anger,
let it all go.

In the Three Worlds, turmoil arose, since billions of beings
lacked the merit to pay their debts. The empty eon
thus came to be.

After some time, there was a Lord, his Sangha pure,
the first Buddha who saved beings in our own time,
the Fortunate Eon.

Then came a second, and soon a third, who each awakened
to bright wisdom, always shining to liberate
living creatures.

Their eras glowed without a fault, reigning supreme.
A fourth Buddha then awakened, saving beings
with the Teaching.

Our eon is blessed with five buddhas, Omniscient Ones,
who each awoke to the Dharma and preached to help
all living things.

Kakusandha: the acacia was his bodhi tree,
six-colored rays were his luster, forty thousand
his life in years.

Konagamana: the fig his tree of awakening,
six colors ablaze as his splendor, thirty thousand
his life in years.

Lord Kassapa: the great banyan was his bodhi tree,
six-colored beams were his radiance, twenty thousand
his life in years.

Lord Gautama: our own Teacher became awakened
on the dazzling diamond throne where Mara lost
to our bold Lord.

Our Perfect One, with six-hued rays, sat on this throne
as Mother Earth flooded Mara and his armies
till they bowed down.

His teaching will last five thousand years, but his life was short:
eighty monsoons. His Dharma remained to save beings,
both men and gods.

Lord Maitreya, Buddha-to-be, blessed with bright rays,
will awaken as predicted: eighty thousand
        his life in years.

He'll reach omniscience beneath a laurel, with fruits and flowers
the size of wheels, so large his tree, pollen falling
        like sheets of rain.

The sweet fragrance will waft and float to fill the air
in all quarters, reaching the four great continents
        and heavenly realms.

Our lucky eon birthed five great ships, blazing with jewels
on their four sails, ready to cross to the far shore,
        braving harsh winds.

With grace and ease, they glide across the vast ocean,
breaking through fog and schools of fish, flanked by serpents
        and briny beasts.

Buddhas are bound to help countless throngs of beings.
Their great ships sail to reach the shore, where sunstone lines
        the jewel-paved path.

There all the buddhas, in vast numbers, uncountable,
resort together in the crystal city, the realm of peace,
        incomparable.

The crystal city resounds in song, with tender tones:
bliss beyond bliss, suffering long gone. The buddhas lead
        all beings there.

Jeweled wheels revolve in seven rings around the city,

each a wing of awakening, a blaze of rays
 of brilliant light.

The peerless city shimmers and shines in endless joy,
untouched by time, forever fine, a glimmering jewel,
 a priceless gem.

Lord Death praises and Lord Time blesses all who follow
the path to release, far from this world, for our planet
 shall end in fire.

Realms of pure form, blissful heavens, and all beings
will burn to ash, their merit gone. Once their karma
 is exhausted,

they'll be reborn in human form once more in samsara,
the endless stream of birth and death, drowned by desire,
 like brutes, like beasts.

Four buddhas awoke, but you're still trapped, far from their light.
Regret your fall; ponder things deeply. You're fortunate
 to meet the Dharma,

so praise all buddhas, wells of merit, springs of virtue.
Lift their feet high, above your head, each night and day
 without a lapse.

Make your mind bright as the sun's orb, suffused with light.
When your life ends, your mind will soar, reaching the highest
 heavenly spheres.

Study your mind. Learn to reflect on every state:
the good, the bad, the calm, the clear, the sore, the sad,
 the final goal.

One thought shatters into a thousand five hundred
unwholesome states. Marred by greed, you shun the good,
    the path of merit.

The wise know their mind, and there abide, a lotus in mud.
Single in thought, their minds don't leak out the nine doors;
    they stay focused.

Keep your heart bright as the Moon. Know your own breath.
When inner winds are clear and at ease, the centered mind
    attains the goal.

Billions of beings boil with pride and seethe with anger.
Most wait till death to seek the goal, but Death's guards
    bind them with five cords.

In life they failed to take the Teaching as their refuge.
They lost awareness on the deathbed, as monks' chants led
    to worlds beyond.

Their bodies died here, their minds went there: reborn below
in fiery hells, they roast alive, their skin scorched black
    in agony.

Countless past sins will burn their bodies through the ages.
Singed by flames, screaming in pain, they're stuck in torment
    for eons to come.

Think this over and be afraid. Find someone wise
to guide you to the true Dharma, the most profound,
    to reach the goal.

It's too late for a thousand good deeds; your sin's too strong.
Death's loyal men will seize your mind and bind it tight
without a care.

Hear this warning and be shaken. Find someone wise.
Heed your own mind, not fame or wealth. Learn this for good;
don't wait too long.

If you've built up a mound of merit, you might awake
with a cleansed heart, your vision clear, your mind eager,
no need for sleep.

In the still night, sit upright in meditation.
Recall the Dharma, sublime and pure. Be diligent
as long as you can.

Think how Indra and all deities, lovely in form,
reside in radiant palaces, with angels waiting
by the thousands.

Ponder how universal monarchs excel all ranks,
replete with seven treasures, divine companions,
and jewel-like consorts.

Seek joy in trance; make your heart soft and expansive.
Torpor will wane and bliss will blossom as you meditate
on the Three Jewels.

Once you achieve the Teaching's goal, drop all your fear,
for the treasures of Indra, Brahma, and wheel-turning kings
are already yours.

Take the Sangha as your family; keep your mind close.
Guard the Three Baskets, inner and outer. Let monks guide you
in the Dharma.

Nothing beats the Dharma, for it's the force, driven by wisdom,
that carries you high up to the heavens until the day
Maitreya comes.

Lord Death's four men, who always lurk inside your body,
will lack the means to seize your mind. They'll soon rejoice
and bless your progress.

When your karma's run its course, Lord Death speaks out,
telling your Prince or Princess Mind to flee the suffering
of the hells below:

"Quiet your thoughts. Study to achieve the Three Baskets
within your heart, and free yourself of sins and fetters
to reach true bliss."

If you're ready, you'll find delight in his stern words,
and seek rebirth in Maitreya Buddha's future time.
Lord Death exhorts us

to make merit. Hold to these words. Recall all virtues.
Don't let your mind slip from the good; this way in death
you win the heavens.

Life ends, but your merit endures, the font of faith.
You won't regret your wretched life if you achieve
the true Dharma.

If you are born for many lives, stuck in samsara
for far too long, then it is said that you still fear
Lord Time himself.

With his great power and countless scores of mighty troops,
he records the date of your coming doom and takes you away.
None can fight back.

Even great kings, Indra, Brahma, ogres, and nagas
only borrow their bodies. They might keep them
for a billion years,

but then Lord Time hastens their end, making them know
their hour has come. Death is certain for living creatures;
all die in the end.

Your material body, marked by nine holes, is guarded by wind,
water, earth, and fire. These four elements maintain the life
of flesh and bones.

The mind abandons this heap of a body, like a charred log.
Pity your body! Your mind splits apart. Time, in his fury,
prepares your rebirth:

"Vile and virtueless, you'll be reborn as a stupid beast.
You only borrowed this human body. You can't keep it
for endless lives.

"You stubborn brute! I'll menace you and bind your body,
your mind in knots. You'll suffer as I squeeze your vessels,
all thirty-two.

"I'll make you cry. I'll tire you out and make you starve.
Your inner flame will burn you up. My men will bind you;
you won't say a word."

Brave are those who give their bodies to reach omniscience.
Only one in a hundred thousand become buddhas, saving
beings in all worlds.

The wise know this, casting off the worries of samsara.
They respect Time, knowing he can ask for their body
any year, any day.

One hundred and twenty years after the Buddha passed,
there was a ruler, filled with earthly and spiritual power,
named King Ashoka,

who enshrined the relics. An array of saints, five hundred strong,
flew through the air to ask Ashoka's son to join them on
the isle of Lanka.

Prince Mahinda taught the island's king, Devanam Raja,
along with his queen and his harem. He ordained monks,
tens of thousands.

After five hundred years, a handsome king named Milinda
came to the throne. He blazed with radiant wisdom, as bright
as a golden swan.

He sought debate with thousands of saints, but all of them
fled to the woods, fearing his sharp mind. Not a single monk
dared face his questions.

So Indra raised his concerns in the realm of Tusita,
and there invited a god to take rebirth as the sage Nagasena
to best Milinda

and praise the path of all the saints. Indra then returned
to his own realm, and Milinda learned to raise up high
the Lord's teachings.

Eight hundred years after the Buddha's nirvana,
a mighty king named Dutthagamini vanquished
all the heathens.

After a thousand years, the Dharma's letters were nearly gone,
the seven limbs scarce, the eighty-four thousand scriptures
only in Lanka.

Indra asked a god named Ghosaka to take human birth
and translate the texts from the Lankan tongue of Sinhala
back to Pali.

Ghosaka accepted this charge and left behind
the heavenly maidens to take rebirth in a line
of brahman priests.

After ten months, he exited from his mother's womb.
His parents were overjoyed to see their handsome son,
Buddhaghosa.

From a young age, he studied hard. Once in orange robes,
he memorized all the scriptures, the whole Three Baskets,
inner and outer.

A saint served as his preceptor. He wisely taught
Buddhaghosa. But once his teachings had run out,
he grew quiet.

The pupil thought, "Is this the end of his knowledge?
Or are there depths to his insight still left unsaid?
Why won't he talk?"

The saint spoke up: "Buddhaghosa, don't defame me.
To end your sin, I must punish you. Set out and translate
the texts of Lanka.

"Find Mahinda and translate all the commentaries
on the Three Baskets from Sinhala to free yourself
from this grave fault."

He accepted this task without delay: "Since I transgressed
the Vinaya rules, I will translate the entire holy scriptures.
Please forgive me!"

Buddhaghosa boarded a merchant ship to cross the strait.
Indra descended to open the sails, along with nagas
and other gods,

to help the boat swiftly across the ocean swells.
The journey took seven full days, with banks of mist
at each sunset.

An elder monk, Bodhidatta, returning home from Lanka,
met Buddhaghosa there on the waves, giving him Indra's
sharp lead stylus.

Once near Lanka, he saw thousands of ships arrayed
in the harbor, below the ramparts of the great city,
a maze of roads and fields,

rising with spires, crowded with palatial towers,
and peaked by a mound for the Buddha's footprint
on the highest hill.

The jewel canine relic was there too, blazing bright
with six-hued rays; people with eyes to see this wonder
bowed down to its light.

He stayed there three months to translate and inscribe
the Three Baskets, eighty-four thousand sections in all,
on fresh palm leaves.

Then he preached to the magnificent king of Lanka.
Tens of thousands, both humans and gods, came to hear
the precious Dharma.

They offered gold, silver, jewelry, linen, silk, and fine rugs
in vast amounts. The sea merchants shared these treasures
to bless Buddhaghosa.

He then boarded his ship to return back to the mainland.
The gods pushed him to arrive in the city of Phnom Penh,
where four rivers meet.

There the pious king, Ketumala, built Wat Lanka,
a lovely temple, created to grant joy, space, and ease
to Buddhaghosa.

Grateful, he then translated Sinhala texts into Khmer,
making all eighty-four thousand parts of the Dharma
speak in our language.

The Buddha's teaching prospered then: four thousand
years remained. Four men of merit, wise in their words,
made the religion shine:

Ashoka, the emperor; Nagasena, the sagely monk;
Dutthagamini, the fearless king; and Buddhaghosa,
the translator.

Two thousand five hundred years after the Buddha's death,
—year of the rooster, first of the decade—a person of merit
will boost the Lord's way.

But first, in a pig year, ending in one, violence shall reign.
Calamity will ensue; no refuge will remain until the day
a true king comes.

We still must wait one hundred and twenty-four years,
for now it's two thousand three hundred seventy-five,
a dragon year.

O good people! Listen well and don't be careless.
Strive hard: in the year of the pig, ending in one,
a wonder will arise.

After thirteen years of the dragon, during a dog year
the people will return from the woods to pay respect
to the true king.

Soon, at two thousand three hundred and eighty years,
you must be careful; take refuge in the path of the Lord
to reach nirvana.

The power of Time is measured by the billion and trillions.
It gnaws at all of us each day and will come without fail
in thirteen years.

Seek the four fruits. Be very careful in the year of the dragon,
ending in four, through the monkey, rooster, dog, and pig,
till your merit is ripe.

Listen close to the passing of the Buddha's era.
Be afraid, good men and women, as you reflect
on our eon.

Contemplate and bring it to mind each day, thinking:
"Alas! Time chides and reprimands me each morning
and evening."

Don't yield to greed. Don't fall for hate. Don't let delusion in.
Don't steal someone's child or spouse. Uphold the precepts
and you need not fret.

For you'll receive boons and blessings from all quarters:
gold and silver, precious gems, gleaming jewels, linen,
silk, rice, and wheat.

Maitreya Buddha will awaken in accordance
with the predictions of the previous Buddhas
of our own time.

I raise all five buddhas of the Fortunate Eon
above my head: they kindly preach to save us,
humans and gods.

Here in Jambudvipa, all will swell with joy; men and women
will shine in beauty. Those of pure faith, made wise in mind,
who give without pause,

who keep the precepts, shall never lack for the three treasures.
Their joy will never fade. All of them will know the Dharma
and win the first fruit.

They'll gleam, in want of nothing, with the three kinds of bliss
by the sheer force of their perfected merit, until at last they win
nirvana's prize.

Chasing Peace

What brought us to this moment? What do we make of this rare human birth? How should we orient our lives in the midst of decay, disease, and violence? Cambodians have long been gripped by these questions. The Buddhist poems gathered here converge on a unified response: in our short, uncertain lives, the best we can do is seek peace, for ourselves and others. A peaceful heart in this life is the basis for greater ease in lives to come. And when our time in samsara comes to an end, no joy can match the peace of nirvana.

The poems in this cycle are focused on the image of the Buddha. Some of the texts are recited for the consecration of a new Buddha image, bringing stone to life. Others are daily prayers of homage to the Three Jewels. All of them center the figure of the Buddha as a model for our aspirations. If we wish to reach nirvana, the historical Buddha, Siddhartha Gautama, is our guide. If we hope for rebirth in the time of the future Buddha, Maitreya, then meeting him becomes our goal. If we seek buddhahood ourselves, then the path taken by countless past buddhas is ours to tread.

Cambodian Dharma songs often speak of the "three treasures": the felicities of human life, heavenly rebirth, and nirvana. Each captures a different dimension of peace: safety and well-being, ease and pleasure, silence and release. Such felicities are grounded in devotion to the holy sites and symbols that embody the Buddha, the Dharma, and the Sangha, including Bodhi trees, sacred scriptures, powerful diagrams, and even the marks on the Buddha's feet. The Khmer poems in this cycle pay homage to these sources of stillness and renewal. If we are to chase peace, we need a road, a set of landmarks, and a vision of the goal. This final cycle provides us with such a map.

37. Lotus Offering to Reach Nirvana

Our hearts brim with joy,
clear faith overflowing.
We've come to offer
flowers to the Teacher.

May we earn the boons
that lead us from rebirth
and the heat of strife
to the Lord's cool refuge.

We take these blossoms,
weave them into garlands,
fragrant rings and wreaths,
and give them to the Lord,

to his true Teachings
and his Community,
to the Triple Gem,
crown of the Three Worlds.

Here we're all bereaved,
worn out, beat up, broken,
whirled by worldly life,
sundered from our spouses.

We're bound to suffer
in rounds of birth and death.
No one can help us,
ours alone the anguish.

We offer these flowers
to you, Lord, so that we
might from fault be freed
and break the grip of age,

flee the pit of pain,
leave death in the dust,
and one day delight
in nirvana's repose.

May our prayers fly straight,
made true by honesty.
Real bliss: may it come
for us all, step by step.

38. A Prayer for the People

I bow down to the Buddha,
unparalleled in the world,
teacher of gods and humans,
his students in the Dharma.

He showed us the Middle Way,
the path to pass beyond pain,
peril, danger, and distress,
saving us from birth and death.

Even today, all those blessed
with karmic roots from the past
for the study and practice
of the Dharma can be free.

No joy equals that of peace;
nothing else can end suffering.
Here in this world and beyond,
peace is the cause of true joy.

I bow down to the Dharma
and to the great Disciples.
Joined together, these Three Jewels
cast cooling shade on the world,

while relics and images
remind us of the Teacher.
May their boons guide our people
to happiness for all time.

39. Homage to the Three Jewels

The Lord, the final
refuge of all beings,
vowed to earn merit
over the span of ages,

myriads of eons
beyond count or concept,
to reach omniscience
as our only Teacher,

his deeds exceeding
what humans can number
braving many trials
for the sake of all life.

I give my body,
speech, and mind to the Lord,
the Merciful One,
our refuge forever.

We're born, then we die,
as we're tied to karma,
caught in a vortex
of rebirth in all realms,

blind to the Dharma,
sublime, perfect, and pure,
practiced by buddhas.
With my mind I bow down

to that most special
and outstanding Dharma
that cuts through darkness
and dispels defilement.

The Lord's disciples,
blameless and without flaw,
perfect in conduct,
concentration, wisdom,

freedom, and knowledge,
devoid of pollution:
the field of merit
in which pure seeds may sprout.

I lower my head
to the Noble Sangha,
heirs of the Buddha,
blessings for all beings.

I humbly bow down,
palms raised up, my head low,
to the Three Worthies,
higher than the Three Worlds.

May this great merit
now be present for us,
full as the wide earth
and vast like the ocean.

May it bring an end
to all strife and danger.
May woe stay away
and may we find safety.

By the mighty force
of this rising merit,
may joy and blessings
surge toward us without end.

Through my pure homage
to the lofty Three Jewels,
may the benefits
lead us to nirvana.

40. The Homage Octet

Homage! I bow down in worship
to the Supreme and Worthy One,
the Rightly Self-Awakened Buddha,
endowed with numberless virtues.

Homage! I bend and bow with joy
to the Dharma, peerless teaching,
preached by our Lord, King of Sages,
in tender tones upon the earth.

Homage! I bow to the Sangha,
equipped with pure precepts and views,
clean and faultless, beyond all doubt,
the true order of Noble Ones.

Homage! I bring my head beneath
the sacred feet of the Three Jewels,
expressed as the sublime union
of three letters: A, U, and M.

Homage! I humbly bow in praise
to the resplendent Triple Gem,
unsullied by mud, dirt, or grime,
freed from all things base and low.

Calamities shall be destroyed
by means of the power produced
through chanting these eight stanzas
of homage to the Three Worthies.

May there be power and glory,
and may there be prosperity
for all days and nights to come
by means of this act of homage.

I fervently wish to achieve
spiritual strength and magic might
within this rite by the sheer force
of my homage to the Three Jewels.

41. The Buddha's Eightfold Array

I make my mind alert
and bend my head in prayer
to the supreme Lord,
who sits in the center.

Around him are eight saints
in circular array,
preaching the Dharma
with joy and constancy.

On the Teacher's right
sits wise Sariputta.
Ananda's in the west,
behind the Blessed One.

To the left, in the north,
sits firm Moggallana.
Kondanna's in the east,
in front of the Buddha.

In the northwest corner
sits noble Kaccayana.
Upali, rule master,
defends the southwest.

Over in the southeast
sits Mahakassapa.
Rahula, the Lord's son,
holds down the northeast.

All those who maintain
the Buddha's array in mind,
who guard it within
and honor it with care,

who bow down in worship
to this mandala each day,
holy scriptures assure
that they'll be free from pain.

No sadness, illness,
or bad omens will arise.
Fear, distress, or strife
will never torment them.

They'll thrive in success,
their bodies made secure,
free from pain and woe
till they reach nirvana.

42. Homage to All Holy Sites

I humbly bow down
to all sacred stupas,
to the crystalline
relics of the Buddha,

to all Bodhi trees,
held in highest respect,
with my mind kept pure,
my two palms joined as one,

and to images
of our Lord, the true Sage,
found in every place
on this vast and wide earth.

By means of the Lord's
transcendental virtues,
which always free us
from pain, fear, and danger,

may I find true peace
and be freed from suffering.
My foes, far and near:
may they fast become friends.

May I meet the Lord
Maitreya, most precious,
and see the Dharma.
May my wishes come true!

43. Hymn to the Buddha's Feet

UKĀSA PĀDAYUGALAṂ NAMĀMI'HAṂ. I humbly bend
down to the earth beneath his feet, shining as bright
as radiant jewels.

Here's my own head, instead of flowers, here's ten fingers
for gold candles, here's my two eyes to take the place
of glowing lamps.

My words express and pay homage to the Marked Lord
in place of whiffs of fine incense, my mind in place
of fragrant tastes,

my whole body presented as a golden jar,
bedecked with gems: all these offerings I humbly gift
to his two feet.

The Marked Lord's soles have wheels with wrought-iron axles
and a thousand spokes; auspicious signs; fine parasols
from all quarters;

golden bullhooks; towered temples, spires soaring high,
replete with jewels; gem-studded thrones; white umbrellas
and royal swords;

palm-leaf and peacock-feather fans; whisks made of gold;
diamond-tipped pikes; maidens clutching candleholders;
exquisite crowns;

ribbons fringed with mottled gems; wish-granting stones;
bowls of radiant gold and silver; bowls forged from jewels;
    lotus flowers;

water lilies; gorgeous gold trays; silver pitchers;
jugs made of jewels; the lush woods of the Himavant;
    the world's sheer edge;

Mount Sumeru and its foothills, the Seven Bands;
the Seven Seas, the Sidantara, successive rings
    of oceans deep;

the Sun; the Moon, rising lustrous, sky-chief among
the host of stars, of radiant rays; four continents;
    two thousand isles;

conch shells; the king who conquers all, his ministers
in tow with flags and parasols; Indra; Brahma;
    Shiva; Vishnu;

the mountains and Seven Rivers; delightful ponds
in seven rows; the salty sea, its limits vast
    and most profound;

fish of silver and fish of gold; golden turtles,
sharks, and serpents in deep waters; junks and frigates,
    gold and silver;

nagas, garudas, lions, tigers; the elephant king
Uposatha; Balahaka, king of horses;
    the snowy peak

called Mount Kailash; gold swans and geese; the elephant king
Eravana; starlings, parrots, kinnara; the sea
    goddess Mekhala;

karavika birds; peahens; peacocks with tails displayed;
the violent king of the vultures; waterfowl with
    blazing red hues;

lions who stand and those who walk; white bulls and cows,
with suckling calves; the six-tiered heavens high above,
    where senses reign,

pure Brahma realms, sixteen in all, with gold mansions—
all these appear on the Lord's feet, his marks totaling
    one hundred and eight.

The Three-World's Lord strode on his feet to cross the earth,
saving beings in all kingdoms, with lotuses
    sprouting up

from the earth to meet the Sage's soles at every step,
with no footprints left in his wake; only when seated
    did the blooms cease.

From time to time, flowers might fail to greet his feet,
as when he walked on paths where winds cleared away
    all motes of dust

beneath his heels, carrying them up and far away
then blowing them back to earth as crystalline sands
    that soon dissolved.

No matter where the Lord would walk no prints remained,
lest anyone should tread upon his holy feet
    and incur sin.

Our mighty Lord, nirvana-bound, had goodwill for
all deities, gandharvas, gods, titans, nagas,
humans, and beasts.

And so to save them he made five shrines for his footprints:
one pair on the summit of Mount Suvannamali,
a pure abode;

one pair on the summit of Mount Suvannapabbata;
one pair on the isle of Lanka, on the fine Mount
Sumanakuta;

one pair on the mountain known as Saccabandha,
where people may gather all kinds of offerings
to worship them;

one pair on the Nammada's banks, where the Lord stepped
into the mud so that the fish might bow down low
in reverence.

Before he went to nirvana, the Ten-Powered Lord
saved beings through these five footprints, made to last for
five thousand years.

Alas, we are born too late to meet the Lord;
only his true Teachings remain. We can't even reach
those distant shrines.

And so we bow from far away, chanting in praise
of all five pairs. May there be joy, fortune, power,
and victory.

May greed be beat, so too hatred, folly, danger,
suffering, sorrow, illness, and fear. May there be joy
till nirvana!

Whoever aims to know the marks on the Lord's feet,
who learns them well, free from all flaws, who always strives
to chant them aloud,

they're like someone who's born in time for the Buddha,
leaving behind the four base realms, those filled with woe
and vile karma;

for one hundred thousand eons, they'll know no pain,
never falling into the hells, tasting the joy
of their merit;

their whole body will be complete, without a fault,
besting all men, flawless and fit, most lovely and
most loved by all;

they'll know merit, sin, and virtue; work and duty;
the meaning of texts; reputation, determination,
and firm ethics,

they'll be born in a lofty line of warrior caste;
rulers with full sovereignty, lords of all lands,
mighty and strong;

their enemies from all quarters shall crouch down low
out of sheer fright, cowering in humble submission
to such majesty;

and they'll be wise, skilled in all arts, their doubts removed
till nirvana—such boons arise from chanting the praise
of the Lord's feet.

44. The Dharma of Union

We bow down in homage
to the footprints
of the supreme Victor,

adored by throngs of gods,
humans, ogres,
and poets each day.

We worship his Dharma,
whose nine stages
are like a precious ship.

We bow to all his Sons
and his Daughters,
who teach and tame beings.

By means of our pure praise,
may we be free
from danger and distress.

We vow to make merit,
give alms, keep rules,
and fill our minds with love.

We invite the relics
of the Buddha
in realms both high and low:

come here, come here quickly!
May you fly swift
and never be delayed.

Merge with our new icon.
Bring your bright rays,
ablaze with prismatic light.

The relics of the Victor:
in all cites,
on the isle of Lanka,

here in Jambudvipa,
in high heavens,
and down in naga realms—

come, O relics, come quick!
Enter into
this new Buddha image.

The Lord's top-right canine,
bright as a gem,
high in Trayastrimsa;

his bottom right canine,
enshrined for all
to worship on Lanka;

the Lord's top-left canine
in Gandhara,
brought there in ancient times;

his bottom left canine,
clear as crystal,
deep in the naga realm—

come now, come here quickly!
We call on you
to enter this icon.

The Lord's right clavicle,
a rare relic,
resides on Lankan shores.

The relic on the left side
shines high above
in the Brahma heavens.

His hair and mid-brow tuft,
whose rays shine far,
are in Pataliputra.

The Lord's thirty-two marks,
his two eyebrows,
his forty perfect teeth,

and his fine fingernails:
we call them all
to merge with this image!

The Victor's round halo,
in full radiance,
bright beams beyond compare;

his brilliant aureole,
aglow with rays
of white, blue, yellow, red,

green, and all these combined,
a six-hue light,
an effulgent spectrum,

blazing throughout the sky,
illumining
the ten cardinal points,

like the sun on the snow
of the Himalayas,
or an iridescent rainbow—

come here, rays of the Lord!
Gather as one
and enter this image.

The Ten-Powered Buddha:
ten perfections,
each one with three levels.

The Teachings of the Lord:
nine supreme states,
eighty-four thousand paths there.

The Buddha's profound wisdom,
deeper than all
the seas around Meru.

His focus, his knowledge,
his clear insight,
revealing all meanings.

His vast, fathomless mind,
comprehending
the layers of all realms.

The Lord taught the Dharma,
saving beings
throughout the Triple World.

We call on the Teaching
to penetrate
this statue of the Lord

and merge with its fine robes,
lower, upper,
outer, inner, and the belt,

well-sewn with saffron threads,
as bright as gems
imbued with flecks of gold,

their orange color as rich
as fresh blossoms
of frangipani and pomegranate.

Our icon is flanked with fans
and wrapped in robes,
all carefully prepared.

We invite this image to sit
upon its throne,
gilded and resplendent.

We consecrate this Buddha
that it may last
as the Three Worlds' true king.

O buddhas of the past,
whose ranks exceed
the ocean's grains of sand;

O Maitreya Buddha,
next to wake up
in our fortunate eon;

O uncountable saints,
vast in number,
beyond all known figures;

all you blessed with merit,
who save beings
and attain all three treasures—

may the supreme powers
of all you saints
and perfected buddhas

enter into the image!
Raise up its glory;
increase its might and charm.

We have gathered here today
to faithfully
make offerings with zeal:

puffed rice, candles, incense,
and floral blooms,
for reverence day by day.

All these gifts, made with care,
marked with beauty,
we offer to the image.

Flywhisks and fans crowd below
tiered parasols.
Oil lamps exude warm light.

Above, silk banners fly,
casting cool shade,
as candles blaze below.

Leafy towers, left and right,
handmade with care,
help sacralize the space.

In the center, a bowl
of sweet milk-rice
is perched, perfectly cooked.

We offer all perfumes,
fine and fragrant,
scents wafting in the air.

Tasty, refined desserts
are placed in rows,
along with savory foods

of every known cuisine,
delectable,
alive with flavor and spice.

Powdered scents and sandalwood
pervade the air,
along with balms and creams.

Coconuts adorned with leaves
and cigarettes
join lanterns and festoons.

Bottles of fragrances
hold waters fit
to come from naga realms.

Some are even fine enough
to be taken
for heavenly ambrosia.

The dishes laid out here
are as tasty
as those served to the gods.

We raise all these offerings
to the icon,
the holy Buddha image:

may the Lord's perfections
enter inside
and dwell in this statue.

We ask for praise, power,
and victory
to crush Mara's armies

and destroy all danger,
illness, and pain;
may they never harm us.

May we secure success
from the image,
to see great boons in this life

and in the heavens after death.
May our wishes
come true in every way.

We hope to be born in time
for Maitreya,
the Blessed One to come,

and under his guidance
win the treasures
that last throughout all time.

The Dharma of Union,
kept most succinct,
is finally complete.

45. Lotus Offering to Realize Awakening

I cup my palms in humble prayer,
my ten fingers and their ten nails
joined like the petals of a lotus
made from airy sheets of gold.

With joy in my heart, I offer
this lotus bud, ready to bloom,
mud-born blossom, stalk and stamen.
Hands to my brow, I bend down low.

By grace of this fine offering
of a single, perfect flower,
my decade of digits raised high
in reverent prayer above my head,

I pay respect to the Buddha,
placing myself beneath his feet.
Hail the first of the Three Jewels,
the glorious Lord of our realm!

How bright his adamantine throne,
how artful its inscribed designs,
how skillful its ornate carvings,
soaring fourteen cubits in height!

The Blessed One, our Lord Buddha,
sits in repose upon this throne,
witness to each creature's birth,
the beasts below and gods above.

How dazzling his radiant light,
six-colored rays arrayed in rings,
rings whose circles ever expand,
expanding out, encircling all!

How vibrant the brilliant hue
of the Buddha's bodhi tree,
how vigorous its lush verdure,
how leafy all its golden boughs!

The Lord's feet bear special marks
arranged in rows and ringed by wheels,
with symbols of supreme fortune
unmatched by all in the Three Worlds.

I place my head beneath the dust
under the feet of the Lord of Men,
my mouth filled with chanted praises
of the all-wise Omniscient One.

May I, in all future eons,
in every life that's yet to come,
be born when each Buddha appears,
to serve them with my whole being.

May I be rich, flush with vast wealth,
gold, gems, and wish-fulfilling jewels,
like the merchant Jotikasetthi,
whose riches were beyond compare.

May I be kind toward all creatures,
giving them gifts with firm resolve,
without any hesitation,
like the great Prince Vessantara.

May I be like Prince Temiya,
my heart always patient and pure.
May my mind glow with goodness,
pleasing to both men and women.

Should some commit capital crimes
or be condemned to endless pain,
may I free them from such rulings,
so that they may regain their lives.

May I exchange my life for theirs,
just like all buddhas have resolved.
May I serve as the guarantor
for all creatures, their last refuge.

May I be skilled in every way,
impressing all in every place.
May I be skilled in every art,
like the craft of Vishvakarman.

May I recall the Three Vedas
and all their spells to perfection,
with total ease and efficacy,
like Lord Shiva, best of the gods.

May I be blessed with a brilliant mind,
my answers to riddles roundly praised,
my resolutions of doubts so marvelous
they raise the hair of all around.

May I awaken to the vastness
of the Dharma while still young,
memorizing the Three Baskets
of the canon in seven years.

May my voice be resonant,
resounding with sonorous tones,
charming the ears of all who hear,
just like the voice of Lord Brahma,

so when I chant the true Dharma,
my voice astounds the gods on high,
hailing them down from the heavens
to rejoice in the Buddha's teachings.

May I be like Sariputta,
my wisdom sharp, my thinking clear.
May I rival Moggallana,
with magic powers and stores of merit.

May I equal Mahakassapa,
my mind sharpened by awareness,
my discipline unstoppable,
my senses tempered and at peace.

May I be filled with awesome might
to defeat those racked by anger.
May all my foes, however strong,
be crushed without even a fight.

May I be packed with fearsome strength
to vanquish hordes of violent brutes.
However wicked they might be,
may they grovel in submission.

May I be free from pain and danger,
from illness, fever, and despair.
May I be blessed with great beauty,
just like Mahakaccayana.

May I be built with heft and brawn,
with vigor bursting from my bones.
May my staggering power be matched
only by the mighty Vishnu.

May I shine with a retinue
of hundreds of millions
of adoring angels, more than
the sand grains in the Ganges;

with a colossal entourage
of kind and skilled assistants;
and a host of well-versed sages
to perform the ancient rites.

May I be wedded to a consort
who is gentle, faithful, and true,
filled with joy, endowed with charm,
their whole being without a fault,

who never gets angry at all
or quarrels with their spouse.
May I always be surrounded
by a throng of friends and fans.

May I be freed from poverty,
cruel hardships, and bereavement.
May I not once endure the pain
of being orphaned and alone.

May my merit increase forever,
my rank rise, my followers grow.
May my attainments be complete,
just like Lord Indra, Thousand-Eyed.

May I be close to all the sages,
my heart released from jealousy.
May I decipher all the scriptures
and meet with love in every life.

May I encounter Lord Maitreya
and respond to his disciples' doubts.
May he predict my buddhahood
in the future just as I vow.

By the grace of this lotus flower,
mud-born blossom, stalk and stamen,
a bud ready to burst in bloom,
its petals gleaming bright as gold,

that is, these ten fingers and nails,
cleansed and cupped in devotion,
raised up high, above my head,
as I bow low, down to the ground,

please, O Lord, may all the boons
for which I so fervently pray
come true at once and come to be
from now until nirvana's time!

PART TWO

THE ESSAYS

The World of Cambodian Buddhism

Dramatic changes rocked the Theravada world between 1850 and 1950: The rise and fall of colonial powers. The adoption of print and the decline of manuscripts. The promotion of the Pali Tipiṭaka and the decline of vernacular texts. The valorization of Western science and the denigration of indigenous medicine. The spread of Burmese-style vipassana meditation and the collapse of local meditation lineages. Modernization changed many aspects of Buddhist doctrine, cosmology, and practice in South and Southeast Asia.[1] To understand the world of Dharma songs, we have to return to an earlier age.

Most of the poems in this book were composed in the seventeenth, eighteenth, and nineteenth centuries, and reflect the viewpoints of that era. We can provisionally use the term "traditional" to describe this period, though we should be aware that traditionalism and modernism are co-constitutive; we cannot have one without the other. As such, many of the ideological frameworks adopted by pre-twentieth-century Cambodians are still current for some Khmer Buddhists today.[2] What is this traditional worldview, and how is it present in the Dharma songs in this book? This essay surveys the doctrinal and cosmological universe of traditional Cambodian Buddhism as a response to these questions.

Virtue and Debt

As expressed most clearly in the second cycle, Repaying Debts, the central doctrinal notion of Cambodian Buddhism is *guṇ*, the Khmer form of the Pali/Sanskrit word *guṇa*. In most Indic contexts, *guṇa* means "constituent part" or "quality," and by extension "good quality" or "virtue." The term is rare in the Pali canon, though it is used extensively in the commentarial literature, particularly in the sense of "virtue." Thus the commentaries frequently invoke the term *buddhaguṇa* to refer to the perfected qualities of the Buddha. This sense of *guṇ* is primary in Khmer as well but is accompanied by the secondary sense of "debt of gratitude."[3] The *guṇ* of our parents refers to their virtues and to the debt that we as children owe to them, as seen in "Filial Debts" (poem #23 in this collection) and "Asking for Mother's Forgiveness" (#24). The same is true of the *guṇ* of the Buddha, the Dharma, and the Sangha, and of teachers, relatives, and various deities, including the Earth herself, as made clear in "In Praise of the Earth" (#19).

The *guṇ* of these worthy entities may be enumerated in the form of lists; each quality enumerated is also a debt to repay. In spoken Khmer, the phrase *ar guṇ*—literally "I rejoice in your virtue/my debt to you"—simply means "Thank you." The notion of gratitude is expressed in Pali as *kataññutā*, "knowing what [others] have done [for you]."[4] This is rendered into Khmer as *ṭiṅ guṇ*, or "knowing *guṇ*." To be a grateful devotee of the Buddha or a grateful student of a teacher, we must know their virtues and the ways we are indebted to them.

Traditional Khmer texts on meditative practice draw on esoteric systems practiced widely by Theravada Buddhists prior to the twentieth century.[5] According to these systems, the *guṇ* of various entities can be expressed as "heart" syllables (Khmer: *paṇṭūl*, "pith"; cf. Thai *hvă caï*). These syllables, drawn from the vowels and consonants of Khmer script, have the ability to encapsulate a range of specific *guṇ*. Intoned as mantras, inscribed in magic diagrams (*yantra*), or tattooed on the body, these heart letters take on the power of the *guṇ* they represent.[6] Indeed, to hold these syllables in mind is one of the key methods Cambodian texts recommend for repaying debts to *guṇ*-filled entities (Pali: *guṇavant*, "endowed with *guṇa*"; Khmer: *ṭá mān guṇ*, "replete with *guṇ*"). Moreover, these *paṇṭūl* and the *guṇ* they contain may be mapped onto a range of other qualities, including the four elements of earth, wind, fire, and water; the organs of the human body; names of past and future buddhas; and doctrinal lists drawn from scripture. "The Twenty-Four Vowels" (#20) is one of several poems that link *paṇṭūl* with specific *guṇ*.

Perhaps the most important nexus of *guṇ* and heart syllables in traditional Khmer Buddhism concerns the thirty-three parts of the body. According to this anatomical list in Cambodian sources, inspired by the canonical Buddhist meditation practice, twelve parts of our bodies are considered liquid elements and connected to the *guṇ* of our mothers.[7] Each of these twelve parts are likewise associated with a different letter of the thirty-three consonants in the Khmer alphabet.[8] The remaining consonants are each paired with the twenty-one solid parts of the body, understood as the *guṇ* or legacy of our fathers. To repay our debts to our parents, we must first know the body they have bequeathed to us, and the way its parts can be encapsulated in thirty-three heart syllables that embody specific *guṇ*, as articulated in "The Thirty-Three Consonants" (#21).

A wide array of other Buddhist lists connect *guṇ* with letters of the Khmer alphabet. Esoteric meditation practices use these letters as substitutions for key qualities on the path to enlightenment. These letters are visualized as "crystal spheres" (Khmer: *ṭuoṅ kèv*), glowing balls of light that are brought into the body, manipulated through key doors (Sanskrit: *dvāra*) and inner channels (*nāḍī*), and eventually brought into the abdomen to nourish the development of a Buddha within.[9] Colorful, vivid signs of progress (Pali: *nimitta*) allows teachers to verify their students' practice. Such signs figure prominently in "A Lesson in Meditation" (#35).

At their core, these meditation techniques are based on normative Theravada sources, including the Abhidhamma and the *Visuddhimagga*. At the same time, they bear a superficial resemblance to Vajrayana practice: dazzling visualizations, intoned and inscribed seed syllables, and private master-disciple lineages. While Tantric forms of Buddhism were popular across Southeast Asia in the first millennium, concrete historic links to esoteric Theravada practices remain elusive.[10] Khmer forms of meditation are best appreciated as an extension of classical Pali forms of meditation, reshaped through local developments, including the central notion of *guṇ*.

Arhats and Buddhas

The esoteric process of gestating a Buddha within one's own body is also connected to a broader trend in Cambodian Buddhism, namely the valorization of buddhahood, rather than arhatship, as the ultimate goal of religious life. Some Khmer texts articulate arhatship (Pali: *arahattaphala*) as the aim of practice; indeed the Khmer concept may simply be translated as "the goal" (*arahaṃ*, an inflected Pali form of *arahant*). "Lotus Offering to Reach Nirvana" (#37) is one of many such texts. Others celebrate buddhahood as a higher goal, one requiring the arduous path of a Buddha-to-be or bodhisattva (Pali: *bodhisatta*). "Lotus Offering to Realize Awakening" (#45) presents an aspiration to this lofty ideal. Between the sixteenth and nineteenth centuries, many Cambodian Buddhists left records of their "truthful aspirations" (Khmer: *satyapraṇidhān*) to awaken as buddhas in the future.[11] This does not mean they were Mahayana Buddhists, but rather that they were inspired by the path of the bodhisattva in Pali Buddhist contexts.[12]

In keeping with this goal of future buddhahood, traditional Cambodian Buddhist texts are deeply invested in the worship of infinite numbers of past and future buddhas.[13] Khmer Buddhist inscriptions of the sixteenth to eighteenth centuries frequently invoke a multitude of buddhas, "as numerous as the grains of sand [in the Ganges]" (Khmer: *braḥ buddh aṃpāl khsāc'*).[14] Of these uncountable buddhas, the most important are the five of the present "Fortunate Eon" (Pali: *bhaddakappa*), namely the three most recent past buddhas—Kakusandha, Koṇāgamana, and Kassapa—plus the historical Buddha Gautama (Pali: *gotama*; Khmer: *samaṇagotam*) and the first buddha of the future, Maitreya (Pali:

metteyya; Khmer: *si-āry metriy*, from Sanskrit *śrī ārya maitreya*).[15] "The Fortunate Eon" (#36) describes these five buddhas in brief.

Many Cambodians put special emphasis on Maitreya when making an aspiration for awakening as a worthy saint (Pali: *arahant*; Sanskrit: *arhat*) or a Buddha. This is because they hope to be reborn again in human form when Maitreya Buddha begins to teach so as to be his direct disciple, as described in "Homage to All Holy Sites" (#42). Those who wish to become buddhas likewise aspire to meet Maitreya, but rather than seeking to become his disciple they hope to receive a personal prediction from him about their own future buddhahood, an aspiration made clear in "Lotus Offering to Realize Awakening" (#45).

No matter their specific aim, Cambodian Buddhists often envision the journey to nirvana (Pali: *nibbāna*; Khmer: *nibbān*) as a long process. While the esoteric meditation tradition advocates the achievement of nirvana in this very life through the creation of a Buddha inside our own bodies, many Khmer texts frame the Buddhist journey as one that unfolds over many lives. Cambodian Buddhists regularly speak of the three treasures or attainments (Khmer: *sampatti*), namely those of humans, those of the gods, and those of nirvana.[16] To be reborn as a human being or as a denizen of the heavenly realms is considered extremely fortunate. While nirvana itself remains the only escape from samsara, there is no shame in cultivating merit in the hopes of being reborn as a human or a god on the long path to nirvana.

Merit and Sin

The making and sharing of merit (Sanskrit: *puṇya*; Khmer: *puṇy*, pronounced "bon") are cornerstones of Cambodian Buddhist life. Merit accrued through Buddhist practices can and should be shared with others, including those owed a debt of gratitude, such as one's parents and teachers, and indeed with all beings. Meritorious acts include the foundational practices of giving (Pali: *dāna*), to monks as well as the poor; ethical conduct (*sīla*), especially keeping the five precepts throughout one's life and the eight precepts on holy days; and mental cultivation (*bhāvanā*), such as prayer, chanting, and silent meditation. The moral economy brought to life through the exchange of merit makes karmic connections and good fortune possible within the vicissitudes of samsara.

That said, Cambodian Buddhist texts also emphasize the horrors of being trapped in the round of birth and death. Khmer poets have long viewed samsara as a treacherous jungle, filled with snares and dangerous beasts.[17] To cross through this forest and reach nirvana requires mastery of the powerful forces of greed, hatred, and delusion within ourselves. Another common metaphor for samsara is as an ocean that divides living beings from the far shore of nirvana, as seen in "The Four Thieves" (#31). In "The Fortunate Eon" (#36) and other texts, buddhas are described as magnificent ships, powered by the Dharma's sails, for ferrying beings across this gulf. In esoteric texts, nirvana is described not in abstract terms like "the deathless" or "extinction" but rather more concretely as a crystal city (Khmer: *nagar kèv*) or sometimes a jeweled island (*koḥ kèv*).[18] "A Lesson in Meditation" (#35) and other practice manuals make clear that this city of nirvana is in fact the city of our body, and the journey to nirvana takes place within the human person.[19] Other Khmer Buddhist texts simply describe nirvana as the realm of ultimate happiness or perfect peace, the final antidote to the suffering of samsara.

Spiritual progress in samsara is limited by our own failings. The human tendency to stray from the path to nirvana is personified through the figure of Māra, a lofty deity whom early Buddhist scriptures depict as the embodiment of evil, tempting the Buddha-to-be to abandon his quest for enlightenment. Khmer texts sometimes speak of Māras in the plural, as the array of passionate attachments that keep us bound to samsara. These attachments push us away from merit and toward *pāpa* (Khmer: *pāp*), a term often translated as "demerit" or "fault." But these terms fail to capture the gravity of *pāp* in the Khmer Buddhist imagination, which is closer to "sin"—a transgression against the ethical principles laid down by the Buddha.

In Buddhist thought, sins are not preordained but produced by individuals through intentional action. From some Cambodian perspectives, however, sins are a natural and sometimes unavoidable dimension of human life.[20] The *pāpa* of killing animals to feed one's family, for instance, might not be preventable in some contexts. Nevertheless, the karmic consequences are grave if we fail to confess and seek atonement for our transgressions. Although Buddhist repentance practices originated in monastic law, Khmer Buddhist texts extend these rites to laypeople as well. Just as achieving nirvana requires a firm aspiration, so too does confessing and seeking absolution from our sins. According to texts such as "Absolving All Faults" (#22), we must regularly recount and then aspire to abandon (Khmer: *lā*, literally "to depart from") both our transgressions and the negative karma they generate. Only then may we make progress on the road to liberation.

Death itself proves a formidable obstacle on the path, for our life spans are limited by forces far beyond our conscious control. In Khmer conception, all beings in samsara live under the sway of Yama (Khmer: *yamarāj*), the god of the dead in both Hindu and Buddhist scriptures. Some Khmer poems present him as one and the same with *braḥ kāl*, meaning "Lord Time" or "Lord Death" (Sanskrit: *kāla*); others make a distinction between the two deities. As witnessed in "The Fortunate Eon" (#36), the process of death and rebirth is overseen by Yama and his henchmen (*yamapāl*).[21] As death approaches, Yama's lackeys cruelly tie our bodies into submission, though the chains that bind us are merely our own worldly attachments, a point made in "Song for the Hour of Death" (#34).[22] We are then dragged before Yama himself, who reviews our tally of merit and sin in this life before determining the circumstances of our next birth. Yama thus represents an anthropomorphic take on the impersonal process of karma. Khmer Buddhist texts take his existence quite seriously, on both the literal and metaphorical level.[23] As such, our journeys through samsara require reckoning with this personification of time, death, and karmic retribution.

The Buddha, the Dharma, and the Sangha

Escaping the clutches of Yama and his henchmen requires relying on the Three Jewels: the Buddha; his Teachings or Dharma (Khmer: *dhaŕm*); and his fourfold community of monks, nuns, laymen, and laywomen, collectively known as the Sangha. The jewel of the Buddha includes not only the historical Buddha, but also all past and future buddhas throughout space and time. For Cambodian Buddhists, the Buddha is not an abstract notion or a long-dead teacher. He is a living entity, made real through his images (Pali: *rūpa*), relics (*dhātu*), perfected qualities (*pāramī*), and sixfold rays of light (*chabaṇṇaraṅsī*).[24] All of these are objects of devotion in their own right, along with the sacred Bodhi tree under which the Buddha was enlightened. The Buddha's feet are likewise a special locus of reverence, as "Hymn to the Buddha's Feet" (#43) makes clear. In the Cambodian tradition, as in Laos and Thailand, the soles of the Buddha's feet are depicted with an array of sacred marks and symbols, usually numbering one hundred and eight.[25] The precious *guṇ* of the Blessed One are not only his internal qualities of wisdom and compassion but also the way his perfections are embodied in specific physical features.

The second jewel, the Dharma, is likewise understood as replete with *guṇ* and worthy of our veneration. The Dharma is enumerated in various ways: the nine Dharmas or stages of sainthood, culminating in nirvana (Pali: *lokottaradhamma*);[26] the thirty-eight virtues or *guṇ* of the Dharma (*dhammaguṇa*);[27] and the 84,000 divisions of the Buddha's teachings (*dhammakkhandha*). In more material terms, the Dharma is understood as the words of the Buddha in Pali, particularly as inscribed on palm-leaf manuscripts or recited as sermons and chants by monastics. The notion of the Three Baskets (Pali: *tipiṭaka*) of scriptures is frequently referenced in Khmer texts, though usually only to refer to Pali writings as a whole, rather than specific texts deemed canonical or noncanonical. Some poems, such as "The Fortunate Eon" (#36), refer to an "inner Tipiṭaka," found within our bodies, in contrast to the "outer Tipiṭaka" of written scripture. The outer Tipiṭaka in traditional Cambodian conception contains many protective texts (Pali: *paritta*) and past-life narratives (*jātaka*) that are not found in modern printed editions of the Pali Canon.[28] The inner Tipiṭaka is a way of connecting particular *guṇ* of the Dharma with the interior, body-centered practice of meditation.[29] From this standpoint, the various visual signs, or *nimitta*, that arise during meditation are aspects of the Dharma to be worshipped and propitiated in their own right.

The third jewel, the Sangha, concerns both the Buddhist community writ large as well as specific individuals singled out for veneration, typically monastics and other teachers. These include the chief male and female disciples of the Buddha as well as one's own preceptor or master. Disciples of the Buddha invoked in "The Buddha's Eightfold Array" (#41) and other poems include Ānanda, Koṇḍañña, [Mahā]kaccāyana, [Mahā]kassapa, Moggallāna, Rāhula, Sāriputta, and Upāli.[30] In former times, nearly all boys and men in Cambodia spent at least a brief portion of their lives as monks. As such, almost all males had a personal monastic preceptor (Pali: *upajjhāya*) who was responsible for their ordination. Likewise, many men—and also some women who studied meditation and other Buddhist practices—can point to a master (Pali: *ācariya*) under whom they studied. The emphasis on masters extended beyond the monastic realm, as lay priests (Khmer: *ācāry*, from Sanskrit *ācārya*) and teachers (*grū*, from Pali *garu* or Sanskrit *guru*) were often responsible for training in letters, chanting, meditation, music, magic, astrology, and medicine. Cambodian Buddhist traditions retain a deep reverence for teachers up to the present, and the *guṇ* of teachers, both monastic and lay, is frequently invoked, as witnessed in "Dedication of Merit" (#28) and other texts. To be a grateful student means to know and respect the *guṇ* of one's teacher, to approach them with ritual offerings and appropriate deference, and to study and live their teachings with care.

Gods and Ghosts

Khmer texts extend the notion of *guṇ* beyond one's parents, relatives, teachers, and the Three Jewels to encompass the natural world and the nonhuman beings who inhabit earthly and heavenly planes. Cambodian Buddhists divide samsara into six realms: that of hell beings (Pali: *naraka*), hungry ghosts (*peta*), titans (*asura*), animals (*tiracchāna*), humans (*manussa*), and gods (*deva*). The gods, in their status as protectors of the human world below, are thought to be replete with *guṇ*, even if they can't compete with the glory of the Three Jewels. The six lower heavenly realms, those of the world of desire (*kāmadhātu*), are frequently mentioned in Khmer texts, including the heavens of Tavatiṃsa (Sanskrit: Trāyastriṃśa), presided over by Indra (Pali: Inda or Sakka); Tusita, the abode of Maitreya, Buddha-to-be; and Paranimmitavasavatti, home of Māra. Above them lie the heavens of pure form (*rūpadhātu*), the abode of the Brahma deities, including Sahampati Brahma, lord of our world system and the principal character in "Invitation to Preach the Dharma" (#13). Though their exact location in Buddhist cosmology is not specified, Khmer texts also refer to gods more commonly associated with Hinduism, including Śiva and Viṣṇu. They too are honored as deities with rank, power, merit, and *guṇ* above that of ordinary beings.

The natural world itself, including the Sun, the Moon, and the stars, are likewise recalled as repositories of *guṇ*. The traditional Khmer calendar follows an Indian lunar system of months and a solar calculation of the year, and Cambodian astronomers and astrologers have long tracked the position of heavenly bodies to make complex calendrical calculations. The earth, personified as the goddess Nāṅ Gaṅhīṅ Braḥ Dharaṇī, is also a major vessel of *guṇ*, an idea emphasized in "In Praise of the Earth" (#19). According to Southeast Asian Buddhist narratives, including "The Defeat of Mara" (#12), it is the Earth Goddess who sweeps away the armies of Māra as the Buddha-to-be sits under the Bodhi tree. Having witnessed the Bodhisattva's countless acts of merit over the eons, symbolized by drops of water poured onto the ground, the Earth wrings out her hair, flooding the Evil One's troops and bearing witness to Siddhartha's right to seek enlightenment.[31]

Traditional Khmer texts follow the Buddhist map of the world, with Mount Meru at the center.[32] The foothills of Meru include the Himavant forest, home of myriad creatures and magical beings, including ascetic seers (Pali: *isī*) and sorcerers (*vijjādhara*). As described in "Hymn to the Buddha's Feet" (#43), the central mountain is surrounded by seven rings of lesser mountains and seas, and finally the great ocean and the four continents, ours being known as Jambudvīpa. The ideal ruler of the continent is a *cakkavatti*, a wheel-turning king or universal monarch, a model constantly referenced in religious and royal contexts. In Cambodian thought, the traditional cosmology of Jambudvīpa is merged with a more recognizable geography of Asia informed by Buddhist history, including the pilgrimage sites across South Asia where the relics or footprints of the Buddha are said to reside. Pre-twentieth-century Khmer poets were well aware of their position on the edge of the Theravada Buddhist world; they knew such sites could only be worshipped from afar.[33] Both "Relics of the Buddha" (#18) and "The Dharma of Union" (#44) reflect this perspective.

The Buddhist conception of the world is often juxtaposed with local religious beliefs about the earth and its inhabitants. One figure who appears prominently in Cambodian texts and rituals is Kruṅ Bālī, the serpent king believed to be the original ruler of the waters and the land. Rites to appease Kruṅ Bālī are often conducted prior to Buddhist ceremonies, to acknowledge his presence as the soil's true owner and to ask for his blessing.[34] The Cambodian landscape is populated with countless local tutelary deities (*anak tā*), worshipped in small altars in villages, among rice fields, and atop hills and natural mounds.[35] There are a plethora of local goddesses who may be petitioned for boons or to protect the country from invasion and disaster.[36] While these tutelary deities are only rarely encountered in the explicitly Buddhist poems gathered in this book, they are key entities in Khmer religious life.

Such gods and goddesses are connected to death as well. Local deities are often understood as powerful ghosts of the deceased, and the danger the dead pose to the living is a subject of much concern and ritual intervention. In response to potential havoc wreaked by the dead, Cambodian beliefs, rituals, and narratives concerning ghosts and spirits are particularly vivid. These include the hungry ghosts (Khmer: *pret*) referenced in Buddhist cosmology but also a variety of local ghouls and specters.[37] Such departed beings play a significant role in "Hungry Ghosts' Lament" (#26) and "This Heap Called a Body" (#33). Even living human beings are thought to be inhabited by nineteen spirits, or *bralịṅ*, which some Khmer texts tie to Buddhist concepts of the four elements, the five aggregates, and the ten doors of the human body.[38] These beneficial spirits have a tendency to wander off from us at moments of transition or crisis and must be ritually called back into the body.[39] Unable to transmigrate in samsara, they abandon us once and for all at the moment of death to return to their natural abode in the mountains and forests.

The doctrinal and cosmological world of Cambodian Buddhism is complex, composed of many historical, cultural, and ideological layers. Many of the figures and concepts summarized here appear throughout the corpus of translated poems. Dharma songs are grounded in traditional forms of Cambodian Buddhism, particularly the texts, rituals, and narratives that circulated prior to the modernist reforms of the twentieth century. Though their core themes of death, gratitude, and spiritual transformation speak to us all, these compositions also reflect the distinct way Buddhist compositions are composed, transmitted, and performed in Cambodia.

The Ritual Life of Dharma Songs

The forty-five songs translated in this book may be performed at a range of rituals; only a few of the poems are recited exclusively at one ceremony or the other. Yet there are long-standing traditions that connect many of the songs to particular rites. At the broadest level, songs from the first and last cycles are recited at rituals of celebration and consecration, while the middle two are chanted for the dying and the dead. More specifically, the songs of the Narrating Lives cycle are particularly appropriate for Vesak, the annual ceremony to mark the Buddha's birth, enlightenment, and passing away. The songs in Befriending Death are recited in deathbed rites, while those from Repaying Debts may be sung in memorials for the dead. Finally, the songs in Chasing Peace include both daily prayers as well as texts recited for the consecration of new Buddha images. This essay outlines the role of Dharma songs in each of these rituals: Vesak, deathbed rites, memorials, and consecrations.

Vesak (Khmer: *visākhapūjā*) became an official feature in the Khmer ritual calendar in the mid-nineteenth century.[1] It is celebrated on the full moon day of Visākha, the sixth lunar month, and usually falls in May. According to Theravada sources, the Buddha was born in Lumbini, reached enlightenment in Bodh Gaya, and entered nirvana in Kusinagara all on the same lunar date, the fifteenth waxing day of the sixth month. Many Cambodian Buddhist festivals began on the evening of the full moon and continue through the following morning. Buddhists may gather at their local temple for Vesak to chant Pali texts, listen to sermons, and recite Dharma songs. In some temples, monastic and lay devotees will take turns reciting poems about the Buddha's life throughout the night until daybreak. The songs in the Narrating Lives cycle are representative of the compositions selected for recitation in such annual ceremonies. "Indra's Lute" (#11), "Mourning the Buddha's Demise" (#16), and "The Cremation of the Buddha" (#17) were all composed with Vesak or post-Vesak ceremonies specifically in mind. Sermons on Vesak and other occasions are almost always preceded by the recital of "Invitation to Preach the Dharma" (#13).[2] Selected texts from Chasing Peace are popular in Vesak rites as well, including "The Homage Octet" (#40) and "Hymn to the Buddha's Feet" (#43).

Deathbed rites are generally conducted only for those of advanced age who are suffering from a terminal illness. Ideally the dying person is at home, in a clean, freshly painted or wallpapered room. Woven tapestries or painted banners of the Buddha's life may be hung from the walls or suspended from the ceiling. A small Buddha image is placed near the patient, along with a modest altar adorned with flowers, incense, candles, and other offerings. The altar is visible to the dying person, and easily accessible to family members, monastics, and other visitors. A space is prepared for monks, nuns, or laypeople to chant Buddhist texts or Dharma songs. People are most often invited to chant from the early evening onward. They may stop after a few hours or continue all night long.[3]

The songs from Befriending Death are among the most popular for recitation at such occasions. "This Life Is Short" (#30), "The Four Thieves" (#31), "The True Fate of Flesh" (#32), "This Heap Called a Body" (#33), "Song for the Hour of Death" (#34), "A Lesson in Meditation" (#35), and "The Fortunate Eon" (#36) are all found in bark-paper manuscripts created for use in deathbed rites. Selected Pali texts, including the *Ākāravattā*, the *Girimānanda Sutta*, the *Ratanamālā*, and various excerpts from the Abhidhamma, are also recited at such rituals, often with exceptionally elaborate melodies.[4] Various Khmer songs on the Buddha's life may be chanted as well, along with selected texts from the Repaying Debts cycle, especially "In Praise of the Earth" (#19), "The Twenty-Four Vowels" (#20), "The Thirty-Three Consonants" (#21), and "Absolving All Faults" (#22). The chants are intended to accompany the dying on their journey from life to death and may be recited until the person draws their last breath or even after they have passed away. In some Khmer traditions, as death approaches, the dying might be instructed to recite a short mantra, such as *buddho* or *arahaṃ*.[5] If they are no longer breathing, a lay priest might recite such mantras on their behalf. After death is confirmed and a set of final rites are performed, the body is washed, wrapped in a white shroud, and the funeral begins.

Cambodian memorials for the dead include the multiday funeral itself; memorial rites held at seven days, one hundred days, and sometimes a full year after death; and annual rites of making offerings to ancestors, the most important of which is Pchum Ben (*bhjuṃ piṇḍ*). A Cambodian funeral may last several days, depending on the nature of death, the time required for relatives to travel, and the astrological calculation of the ideal cremation date. Prior to cremation, which marks the end of the funeral rites, family members and friends gather near the shrouded body, either at home or at a temple.[6] During the evenings prior to cremation, monastics or laypeople may be invited to recite Dharma songs. Songs of lamentation and mourning from Narrating Lives are popular, including "Chaddanta's Lament" (#1), "Subhadra's Lament" (#2), "Parika's Lament" (#3), "Suvannasama's Lament" (#4), "Madri's Lament" (#5), "Maya's Lament" (#10), "The Buddha's Last Words" (#14), and "The Buddha's Passing Away" (#15). The seven-day, hundred-day, and one-year memorials likewise gather friends and family of the deceased to sit, eat, and listen to the Dharma together. Daytime recitation of Dharma songs is common, particularly "Filial Debts" (#23), "Asking for Mother's Forgiveness" (#24), and "Orphan's Lament" (#25) from the Repaying Debts cycle.

The dead continue to be memorialized through the annual Pchum Ben ceremony, which takes place during the dark half of the tenth lunar month (*bhadrapad*), typically in late September or early October. During this period, laypeople gather at the temple in the very early morning hours, well before sunrise, to make offerings of rice balls and other sweets to hungry ghosts (Sanskrit: *preta*;

Khmer: *pret*). In Buddhist cosmology, *preta* are depicted as miserable beings who have been reborn in a state of constant pain and hunger on account of their karma. Cambodian Buddhists believe that the two-week period leading up to the final day of Pchum Ben, which falls on the fifteenth waning day of the tenth lunar month, is ideal for making offerings to departed ancestors who may have been reborn as hungry ghosts. Laypeople also make direct offerings of food to monastics, asking them to transfer merit to their deceased relatives in return.[7] Dharma songs in Repaying Debts specifically composed for recitation at Pchum Ben include "Hungry Ghosts' Lament" (#26) and "Offerings for Monks and Ancestors" (#27). The transference of boons to ancestors may be sealed with the chanting of "Dedication of Merit" (#28).

Many of the poems in Chasing Peace are used for daily worship or across a wide range of rituals. These include "A Prayer for the People" (#38), "Homage to the Three Jewels" (#39), and "Homage to All Holy Sites" (#42). Others are specifically tied to the consecration of a new Buddha image. Such ceremonies typically take place between March and July.[8] In some cases, they may be tied to rituals of honoring the dead, including funerals, one-year memorials, or the annual Pchum Ben festival.[9] Either way, the traditional ritual follows the same general pattern.[10] The ceremony begins in the evening, and monks are invited to chant Pali texts to begin the process of empowering the image. This is followed by the recitation of "The Dharma of Union" (#44) to invite the Buddha's perfected powers (Pali: *pāramī*) and holy relics (*sārīrikadhātu*) to take up residence in the new icon.

"The Dharma of Union" is followed by a chanted performance of "The Defeat of Māra" (#12), the full version of which recounts the Buddha's defeat of Māra, Sujātā's offering of milk-rice, and the Buddha's final awakening under the Bodhi tree. Such recitations may be accompanied by a theatrical staging of these events in front of the Buddha image.[11] Deep into the night, or before dawn the next morning, the marks (Pali: *lakkhaṇa*) that connect the physical image with the spiritual body of the Buddha, or *dhammakāya*, are liturgically implanted on the statue, and the eyes of the image are ritually opened.[12] The central image is now consecrated as a "living Buddha" (Khmer: *braḥ jī(v)*) or "sacred ancestor" (*braḥ jī*). After sunrise, the image is then worshipped with lotus flowers and other offerings. "Lotus Offering to Reach Nirvana" (#37) or "Lotus Offering to Realize Awakening" (#45) may be recited at this time. Such poems from Chasing Peace are essential to the consecration process, binding reverence for the Buddha as an abstract, timeless figure with the specific qualities of the new wood, stone, or metal image.

The four cycles presented in this book cover a broad range of Cambodian rituals. Some were composed with specific rites in mind, while others were created for recitation across a range of ceremonies. Since Dharma songs are a living practice in Khmer communities, their ritual use is constantly changing. Older, longer chants, particularly those that take hours to perform, are more rarely heard today, while some shorter poems are gaining in popularity. The increased share of deaths occurring in hospitals, rather than at home, has meant that traditional deathbed rites are in decline. By contrast, rites for the dead and for deceased ancestors, especially Pchum Ben, appear to get more elaborate every year. All-night Dharma song vigils for Vesak remain common, particularly in the countryside. Traditional consecration rites, including a full complement of Dharma songs, are maintained at some temples, but many urban temples have adopted much shorter rituals in their place. All these developments are evidence of growth, change, and creative adaptation to the constraints of modern life. The four cycles are a snapshot of a ritual tradition in motion.

Oral and Written Transmission

Cambodian Dharma songs have been passed down through oral traditions as well as on written documents. This essay reflects on the mechanisms behind these two modes of transmission, including issues of language, pedagogy, scribal practices, and authorship. How were these poems composed, revised, and passed down for generations in Cambodia? To address this central question of how Dharma songs have survived to the present, we have to begin with language. If Cambodians are Theravada Buddhists, why are the songs in this book translated from Khmer? What about Pali?

For over seven hundred years, Khmer Buddhists in what is now Cambodia, northeastern Thailand, and southern Vietnam have used Pali as their language of ritual, traced their sacred writings back to the Pali Tipiṭaka, and supported monks who follow the Pali code of discipline. Though Khmer Buddhists hardly ever uttered the term "Theravada" prior to the mid-twentieth century, their adoption of Pali connects them to Burmese, Lao, Sinhala, and Thai Theravadins who share the same liturgical, scriptural, and monastic tradition.[1]

Pali and Khmer are strikingly different languages. Pali is an Indic language of the Indo-European family closely related to Sanskrit. Its grammatical structure favors long compounds and complex systems of declension and conjugation, being distantly related to French, Greek, Latin, Persian, Russian, and even English. Khmer comes from the completely unrelated Austroasiatic family. It shares many grammatical features with Vietnamese, its closest major relative. Like many mainland Southeast Asian languages, Khmer prefers short, one- or two-syllable words. Unlike most Indo-European languages, Khmer words do not vary by tense, mood, person, or number, so their grammatical relationships must be conveyed through subtle conventions of word order and sentence structure. Like English, the vocabulary of Khmer is drawn from diverse sources. Just as many words of Greek and Latin origin have been borrowed into English, Khmer has adopted many Pali and Sanskrit words, yet the underlying grammatical structure remains distinctly Southeast Asian.

Despite the importance of Pali as a source for Buddhist technical terms, very few Cambodian writers over the centuries composed exclusively in Pali.[2] Most authors preferred to write in bilingual Pali-Khmer prose or in monolingual Khmer verse.[3] Before the mid-twentieth century, the former was used for doctrinal treatises and public sermons, while the latter encompassed a range of didactic poems, epic narratives, and ritual chants.[4] Prior to widespread adoption of modern printed books in the early 1900s,[5] both Pali-Khmer prose and Khmer verse texts were recorded on traditional manuscripts fashioned from incised palm leaves or bark-pulp paper. Many of the verse texts were short enough to be learned by heart and therefore passed down through oral transmission. Neither the written nor the oral dimensions of Dharma songs should be neglected.

On the oral side, the poems in this collection are rooted in chanted performance. Cambodians today and throughout history are much more likely to hear Dharma songs than to read them. Performers are expected to memorize most of the texts they recite. The dense rhyme structures of Khmer poetry facilitate their memorization. Some of the most talented reciters of Cambodian Dharma songs are blind or illiterate but have nonetheless committed an impressive repertoire of songs to memory.[6] Other performers use books or manuscripts, either as tools for learning or as memory aids during recitation. Most performers learn the proper vocal techniques under the guidance of a lay or monastic teacher. Without the aid of a recognized musical notation system, students of Dharma songs cannot rely on visual cues but instead must learn the melodies and vocal styles through a long process of listening, imitation, and correction.[7] The rigorous process of oral transmission expresses core Buddhist values of patience, concentration, and devotion to one's teacher.

In terms of their written transmission, most of the forty-five poems gathered here were passed down in manuscript form between the seventeenth and nineteenth centuries. Some of the more recent examples first appeared in printed books from the twentieth century. All were written down in Khmer script. Scripts, like languages, are part of families, but script families and language families are typically unrelated. Khmer script is part of the larger Brahmi family that encompasses almost all of the traditional writing systems of South and Southeast Asia, except those based on Arabic, Chinese, or Roman script. The Brahmi family traces its origins to the script of the Ashokan inscriptions of the third century B.C.E. A south Indian variant of Brahmi script was first used to write a Khmer-language inscription in the sixth or seventh century C.E., gradually developing into the form familiar to Cambodians today.[8]

Along the way, Cambodian scribes expanded the linguistic and orthographic possibilities of Khmer script. They greatly enriched its vowel inventory to better record the exceptionally wide range of sounds in the Khmer language.[9] The Indic origins of Khmer script make it possible to record words or texts in Pali and Sanskrit as well. This orthographic flexibility applies to the many Indic Buddhist terms borrowed into the vernacular language. Cambodian scribes, when writing in Khmer, can write such words exactly as they would be spelled in Pali or Sanskrit.

Though the oldest surviving records of Khmer writing are on stone, we know that Cambodian scribes have long used palm-leaf manuscripts to record religious texts.[10] At some point in the past millennium, bark-paper manuscripts came into fashion. This accordion-folded manuscript format, also known as the leporello format, is the most important traditional medium for the written transmission of Cambodian Dharma songs. All but a handful of the poems translated in this book still circulate on leporellos in Cambodia.

While based in Cambodia in 2016 and 2017, I documented seventy such leporellos and the 653 chanted texts they contained, including 195 distinct compositions.[11] Surviving leporellos date from the mid-nineteenth century to the present, though the texts they record are often centuries older, being the products of a continuous scribal tradition.[12] Scribes frequently recopy older, deteriorating manuscripts onto fresh bark-pulp paper or modern substitutes, such as repurposed cement bags. This means that newer manuscripts often preserve much older texts. Prior to the mid-twentieth century, Cambodian manuscripts rarely followed a standard orthography, and the decentralized processes of written and oral transmission encouraged the proliferation of textual variants.

Some of the Khmer poems found on more recent leporellos were directly copied by scribes from books printed in the early to mid-twentieth century. For these texts, the original printed volume is the most reliable source. Most compositions, however, were composed long before the widespread adoption of print in the 1920s. For these texts, I relied on leporellos as well as a few palm-leaf manuscripts to establish a reliable reading of the original poem.

For twenty-five of the poems in this book, I created standardized editions of the Khmer texts on the basis of one or more manuscript sources. This process involved transcribing the text from the manuscripts, arranging each variant into a proper metrical structure, comparing the points of convergence and divergence, selecting the phrasing that appears closest to the now-lost original, and finally standardizing the spelling of the edited text.[13] For those who read Khmer, these standardized editions, along with complete digital images of the original leporello manuscripts I worked from, are freely accessible online from my dissertation website.[14]

I transcribed the remaining twenty texts from the oldest known non-manuscript sources: ten from printed books, six from handwritten notebooks, and four directly from audio recordings. Khmer-script versions for all but four of these twenty texts are available on either my dissertation website or my free online multimedia book, *Stirring and Stilling: A Liturgy of Cambodian Dharma Songs*.[15] A list of all the Khmer sources I used, both written and oral, appears in the notes for each poem.

My sources reflect the diverse ways Dharma songs are transmitted: Inked leporello manuscripts, made of fragile bark-pulp paper or refurbished cement bags, folded into an accordion format. Incised stacks of carefully prepared palm leaves, bound together as long, slim manuscripts between polished wood boards. Handwritten European-style lined notebooks, typically for private use but sometimes photocopied for wide distribution. Printed books from the late 1920s onward, often on brittle, yellowed paper, containing original poems or revised editions of older material. Audio recordings on vinyl, cassette, compact disc, and purely digital formats, produced in the field or in a professional studio.

Most Dharma songs are not limited to just one of these sources; a single text may appear across many manuscripts, notebooks, and printed books, as well as in the audio recordings of multiple performers. In editing the Khmer version of each text, I focused on the oldest sources available to me in an attempt to respect the original poets. In doing so, I was aware of the unfortunate risk of obscuring the complex layers of transmission that continue to shape Dharma songs up to the present.

This multiplicity of oral and written transmission is magnified by the fact that very few Dharma songs can be reliably attributed to known authors. Only eleven compositions in this book are tied to specific authorial identities. Two compositions indicate they were composed by Suvaṇṇakesar (late eighteenth or early nineteenth century) and Braḥ Dhammalikhit (flourished in the 1860s). But these are monastic titles, not personal names, and we know very little about the monks in question. The remaining nine texts are the work of seven better-known authors who largely wrote in the twentieth century, almost all of them monks or former monks.

In rough chronological order, these poets are Suttantaprījā Ind (1859–1924),[16] Juon Ṇāt (1883–1969),[17] Jăy M"ai (early 1900s–1975?), Miev Nand (early 1900s–1975?), Sandhar Jā (early 1900s–1975?), Lī Suvīr (1928–2019), and Bejr Sukhā (1949–2010). The exact year of death is unknown for Jăy M"ai, Miev Nand, and Sandhar Jā, as they presumably perished during the brutal Khmer Rouge regime of the late 1970s, a period when eminent Buddhist monks and intellectuals were targeted for execution.[18] All of the known authors are men. While writings by high-ranking women survive from throughout Cambodian history, the particular genre of Dharma songs is dominated by male authors.[19] This stands in marked contrast to contemporary performance practice, in which women are more numerous as both performers and listeners of Khmer Buddhist poems.[20]

The very category "Khmer Buddhist poems" conceals many complications of language, transmission, and authorship. In the broadest terms, the poems in this book are the products of a male-centered Khmer monastic culture over the past four hundred years. Their continued existence as written texts and oral poetry has been secured for contemporary Cambodians through a wide variety of physical and audio formats. The social upheavals of Cambodia's recent history—destructive wars in the early nineteenth century, colonial antagonism against traditional Buddhist practices in the early twentieth, and the terror unleashed by the Khmer Rouge almost fifty years ago—have allowed only a small percentage of the poetry penned by Cambodian Buddhists over the centuries to survive. What does remain, however, is extraordinary for its directness, emotional depth, and luminous faith.

Meter, Melody, and Rhyme

The structural and performative qualities of Cambodian Buddhist poems make them particularly challenging to translate. The complex meters, soaring melodies, and interlocking rhymes found in Dharma songs have few natural parallels in English. This essay takes up each of these three aspects of Khmer poetry in turn. I begin with a survey of Cambodian metrical forms. I then discuss the relationship between meter and melody, and the intended emotional impact of different melodies. I conclude with a reflection on rhyme and the four approaches to translation I have taken in this book: rhymed, unrhymed, extended, and free.

Meter

Cambodian poets have developed a range of intricate meters, six of which are represented here.[1] The earliest datable layers of Khmer vernacular literature are composed in three primary meters: *kākagati* ("crow's gait"), *brahmagīti* ("Brahma's song"), and *baṃnol* ("narration"). All three were in use by the sixteenth or early seventeenth century.[2] Twelve poems are written in the *kākagati* meter, each stanza of which consists of seven lines of four syllables each: "Leaving the Palace" (#9), "The Defeat of Mara" (#12), "The Relics of the Buddha" (#18), "In Praise of the Earth" (#19), "Absolving All Faults" (#22), "Dedication of Merit" (#28), "The True Fate of Flesh" (#32), "This Heap Called a Body" (#33), "Song for the Hour of Death" (#34), "A Lesson in Meditation" (#35), "The Fortunate Eon" (#36), and "Hymn to the Buddha's Feet" (#43). Another twelve use the *brahmagīti* meter, with four lines per stanza and the lines alternating between five and six syllables each: "Invitation to Preach the Dharma" (#13), "The Buddha's Last Words" (#14), "Mourning the Buddha's Demise" (#16), "The Twenty-Four Vowels" (#20), "The Thirty-Three Consonants" (#21), "Offerings for Monks and Ancestors" (#27), "The Four Thieves" (#31), "Lotus Offering to Reach Nirvana" (#37), "Homage to the Three Jewels" (#39), "The Buddha's Eightfold Array" (#41), "Homage to All Holy Sites" (#42), and "Lotus Offering to Realize Awakening" (#45). Only one poem, "The Dharma of Union" (#44), is composed entirely in the *baṃnol* meter, which follows a six-four-six syllable pattern for its three-line stanzas.

By the nineteenth century, a variety of newer meters had developed. The most popular of these is *bāky 7* (*bāky prāṃbīr*, "seven syllables"), consisting of four-line stanzas of seven syllables each. Fifteen compositions feature this meter: "Chaddanta's Lament" (#1), "Subhadra's Lament" (#2), "Parika's Lament" (#3), "Suvannasama's Lament" (#4), "Madri's Lament" (#5), "Maya's Guidance for Gotami" (#7), "Divine Messengers" (#8), "Maya's Lament" (#10), "The Buddha's Passing Away" (#15), "Filial Debts" (#23), "Asking for Mother's Forgiveness" (#24), "Orphan's Lament" (#25), "Hungry Ghosts' Lament" (#26), "This Life Is Short" (#30), and "A Prayer for the People" (#38). Another meter that gained popularity in the nineteenth century is *paṭhyāvatt* (from Pali *pathyāvatta*, a variant of the basic Indic *śloka* meter), consisting of four lines of eight syllables each. Each *paṭhyāvatt* stanza is actually comprised of two stanzas of *bāky 4* (*bāky puon*, "four syllables," also known as *me puon*), a simple and likely very old meter common in folk songs. Three poems follow the *paṭhyāvatt* structure: "The Cremation of the Buddha" (#17), "Funeral March" (#29), and "The Homage Octet" (#40). The sixth meter represented in this book is *bāky 9* (*bāky prāṃpuon*, "nine syllables"). True to its name, each stanza in this meter uses four lines of nine syllables each. Only one text in the collection adopts this meter, "Indra's Lute" (#11). Finally, one poem, "Lullaby of the Gods" (#6), does not follow a specific meter, belonging to a class of nonstandard Khmer poetry known as *kaṃraṅ kèv* ("garlands of gems"). Yet even this poem can be divided into identically structured stanzas.

The stanza (Khmer: *pad* or *lpaḥ*) is the basic unit of Khmer poetry. The stanza count provides a convenient way to measure the length of a particular text; poems in this collection range between three and more than one hundred stanzas. The longest poems in Khmer literature may be several thousand stanzas long, but most Buddhist compositions intended for ritual performance are considerably shorter, typically a few dozen stanzas, and certainly no longer than a few hundred. The corpus of Khmer texts gathered in this book comprises almost one thousand stanzas in total.

Melody

The stanza is also the basic unit for the chanted performance of Dharma songs. In most modern performance styles, the chosen melody is repeated exactly from stanza to stanza. In some older performance styles, including that taught by my first teacher, Prum Ut (1945–2009), the melody varies slightly from stanza to stanza, allowing the musical emphasis to fall on particular words. Either way, however, the stanza forms the basic written and melodic unit.

At least sixty different melodies, plus a range of variations, may be used to perform Khmer poetry.[3] Each meter has a set of melodies proper to it; melodies are generally tied to particular meters and may not be freely applied across meters. Secular poetry in romantic, didactic, or narrative genres tends to use short, simple melodies. The Buddhist works represented in this book often require long and musically complex melodies, demanding exceptional vocal technique and breath control. In the notes, I include the name of the melody used to perform each text, if known, following the conventions established by my teacher Yan Borin and his colleagues.[4]

The melodic aspects of Dharma songs shape the way they are composed and serve as a key link between the words of the text and the emotional impact they have on listeners.

The affective dimensions of Dharma song melodies include the emotional responses of *saṃvega* and *pasāda*. Put simply, certain songs may stir us from our complacency, while others may still us into a state of bliss. Cambodian Buddhists frequently articulate the purpose of Dharma songs as either to rouse and frighten us ("stirring"; Pali: *saṃvega*; Khmer: *saṅveg*) or calm and gladden us ("stilling"; Pali: *pasāda*; Khmer: *jraḥ thlā*).[5] Some Dharma song melodies are primarily used with texts intended to arouse stirring or *saṃvega*, while other melodies are associated with texts intended to evoke stilling or *pasāda*, an insight I learned from my teacher Koet Ran.

Both *saṃvega* and *pasāda* melodies feature similar vocal techniques: long phrases, intricate vocal ornamentation, register breaks, and extended melismatic passages, in which single syllables are stretched over many notes. The key difference between *saṃvega-* and *pasāda*-evoking melodies lies in their musical modes or scales. In the language of Western music theory, most melodies selected for performance in *saṃvega*-eliciting texts use five-, six-, and seven-note scales, with either a major third, a minor third, or both. If we take the note C as a fundamental pitch, these scales include: C-E-F-G-B♭, C-D-E♭-F-G-B♭, C-E♭-F-G-A-B♭, C-D-E-F-G-B♭, and C-E♭-E-F-G-B♭. *Pasāda* texts usually use an alternate set of five-, six-, and seven-note scales, always with a major third (E) and a major sixth (A): C-D-E-G-A, C-E-F-G-A-B♭, C-D-E-F-G-A-B).[6] These notes are only approximations, as Khmer music does not follow Western tuning systems exactly. Nevertheless, Western scales provide a convenient basis for understanding the divergent way that emotions are communicated through Dharma song melodies.

In translating Cambodian Dharma songs, I strive to keep these musical and affective dimensions in mind. Thirty-three of the forty-five translations maintain the syllabic structures of the original Khmer stanzas so that they can be performed in English using their traditional melodies. For the twelve translations that do not maintain the Khmer syllabic structure, I take two approaches: extended and free. By "extended," I mean maintaining the stanza and line structure of the original but lengthening the number of syllables per line to better suit English conventions. Such extensions are not without precedent: Cambodian poets regularly exceed the syllable counts of Khmer meters by inserting extra unstressed syllables, as such hypermetrical lines can be smoothed over in melodic performance.[7] Ten of my translations are extended in similar ways: "Indra's Lute" (#11), "Invitation to Preach the Dharma" (#13), "Mourning the Buddha's Demise" (#16), "The Twenty-Four Vowels" (#20), "The Thirty-Three Consonants" (#21), "Absolving All Faults" (#22), "Offerings for Monks and Ancestors" (#27), "The Four Thieves" (#31), "The Fortunate Eon" (#36), "Lotus Offering to Realize Awakening" (#45). By "free," I mean breaking the metrical structure of the Khmer completely in order to more dynamically capture its content in English. Just two of my translations take this approach: "This Heap Called a Body" (#33) and "Song for the Hour of Death" (#34).

Rhyme

For the thirty-three translations that maintain the original stanza, line, and syllable patterns of the Khmer, I have adopted two approaches: rhymed and unrhymed. Khmer poems feature intricate rhyme patterns, both within and between stanzas. These rhymes, which are considerably denser than those found in most English poetry, pose a special challenge in translation. With four exceptions—"Parika's Lament" (#3), "Suvannasama's Lament" (#4), "Orphan's Lament" (#25), and "This Life Is Short" (#32)—I do not replicate these rhyme patterns into English. This is because the rhymes pose too much strain on translating thematically or doctrinally complex poems. However, for some of the simpler texts, rhymed translations can be effective and have the added benefit of making the Khmer rhyme structure transparent to the English reader.

Take, for example, the last two stanzas of "Suvannasama's Lament." The left column shows the rhyme pattern in algebraic notation, the middle column shows the original Khmer in transliteration, and the right column shows the English translation, which matches the syllable and rhyme structure of the Khmer exactly:

1 2 3 4 5 6 A	dhvö mtec pān ghöñ nau mukh m"è	How can I see your sweet face?
1 2 3 A 5 6 B	kūn sūm lā m"è thṅai neḥ höy	Here in this place . . . I leave you.
1 2 3 4 5 6 B	kūn cpās' jā slāp' min khān ḷöy	Mother, come here, help me through,
1 2 3 B 5 6 C	o braḥ me öy mak juoy kūn phaṅ	like drops of dew . . . I vanish . . .
1 2 3 4 5 6 D	kūn sūm uddis ṭal' devatā	May all the gods hear my plea:
1 2 3 D 5 6 C	sūm prāp' mātāpitā phaṅ	the king shot me . . . I vanish . . .
1 2 3 4 5 6 C	piliyakkh pāñ' khñuṃ jhị̄ kanlaṅ	tell my parents . . . I anguish . . .
1 2 3 C 5 6 E	sūm devatā phaṅ prāp' jā ṭaṃṇịṅ	a humble wish . . . please tell them . . .

Of the thirty-three syllable-matching translations, the other twenty-nine are unrhymed. These maintain the metrical structure of the originals, including the melodic rules that divide lines into smaller groups of syllables but do not reproduce the Khmer rhyme schemes. Even without the rhyme patterns, the syllabic structures of Cambodian poetry carry over into English quite well. Part of the elegance of Khmer poems lies in their ability to compress complex ideas into very short lines, an effect that suits English better than most other European languages.

The first two stanzas of "The Buddha's Last Words" (#14) illustrate this kind of expressive and metrical alignment between Khmer and English:

1 2 3 4 A	yo vo ānand öy	YO VO Ananda!
1 2 A 4 5 B	nè pā röy mak āy r"ā	Come here now; don't delay.
1 2 3 4 B	tathāgat nịṅ maraṇā	I'll soon pass away,
1 2 B 4 5 C	cāk col pā min khān ḷöy	leaving you all alone.
1 2 3 4 D	cūr pā nau oy sukh	O friend, please be well.
1 2 D 4 5 C	kuṃ jā dukkh ṇā pā röy	Don't suffer needlessly,
1 2 3 4 C	tathāgat lā pā höy	for I must leave you.
1 2 C 4 5 E	kuṃ sok ḷöy ṇā ānand	Don't you grieve, Ananda!

The Khmer text is composed in the *brahmagīti* meter, with alternating lines of five and six syllables each, grouped into four-line stanzas and linked through an interlocking rhyme pattern. Melodic conventions demand a short pause, or caesura, before the last three syllables of each line. The English follows this structure exactly, with the exception of the rhymes themselves. The result is an unrhymed translation that maintains the compressed style of the Khmer and can still be performed with the original melody.

The *kākagati* meter may also be carried over into unrhymed English verse. Each stanza consists of seven groups of four syllables each. Though these groups are conventionally called "lines" (Khmer: *ghlā*), in modern Khmer printed books they are rarely given their own line. One common arrangement visually divides the seven groups into three lines. The first two stanzas of "The Fortunate Eon" (#36) would thus appear in this format:

<table>
<tr><td>1 2 3 A | 1 2 3 A | 1 2 3 B</td><td>rūpaṃ dukkhaṃ | dukkh öy dukkh khlāṃṅ | dukkh ban' pramāṇ</td></tr>
<tr><td>1 2 3 C | 1 C 3 B | 1 2 3 B</td><td>bī tūc ṭal' dhaṃ | dukkh ṅaṃ knuṅ prāṇ | dukkh it srāk srānt</td></tr>
<tr><td>1 2 3 D</td><td>dukkh ṭal' khluon ksăy</td></tr>
<tr><td>1 2 3 E | 1 2 3 E | 1 2 3 D</td><td>aniccaṃ buṃ ṭhit | buṃ ther nau nity | yīṇ yūr ḷöy nai</td></tr>
<tr><td>1 2 3 F | 1 F 3 D | 1 2 3 D</td><td>slāp' dau jā khmoc | asoc bek krai | ch-iṅ sāc' sar-sai</td></tr>
<tr><td>1 2 3 G</td><td>jā braḥ dharaṇī</td></tr>
</table>

I follow a similar format in most of my English translations: two lines of twelve syllables, composed of three groups of four syllables each, followed by a third line of four syllables. Just like in the Khmer, the metrical structure is iambic, meaning that it alternates between unstressed and stressed syllables:

RŪPAṂ DUKKHAṂ—such agony, endless, untold!
For young and old, pain boils within without relief,
  till death ends all.

ANICCAṂ—not fixed, not firm, not prone to last for long.
Once dead, only your corpse remains. All turns to soil:
  flesh, bone, sinew.

The *kākagati* meter, with its asymmetrical seven-group, three-line design, is markedly different than existing forms of English poetry. But like the sonnet or the haiku, which are long-established in English, *kākagati* is a well-traveled form: born in Cambodia, it was adopted by Siamese poets hundreds of years ago in Thailand, where it is known as *kāby surāṅganāṅg 28* ("kap surangkhanang yi sip paet," meaning "the 'body of a goddess' meter, twenty-eight syllables").[8] For the poems translated here, the unrhymed *kākagati* structure brings out the voices of the Khmer authors in English in a way that conserves their precise, aphoristic style.

The four translation methods I adopt in this book—rhymed, unrhymed, extended, and free—allow different facets of the Khmer poems to shine through. Each comes with advantages and drawbacks. The rhymed translations allow readers to experience how Cambodian poetry works in English at the expense of minor textual details. The unrhymed translations lose the intricate rhyme patterns yet can keep the tight structure and traditional melodic patterns of the originals. The extended translations sometimes break the metrical structure enough to compromise musical performance, though the extra syllables in English allow for a more precise rendering of the meaning. The free translations obscure the underlying metrical structure but make it easier for the content of the source text to speak directly to the reader. The poems in this book are not entirely consistent in how they look or sound; this is a conscious choice, for translation is always a compromise, an attempt to grasp the ungraspable. The combination of the four approaches makes it possible to take different angles on the Cambodian originals, to see these poems in the round, as living, breathing expressions of Buddhist practice.

PART THREE

Notes on the Songs

Unfolding Sources, Revealing Meanings

Each song included in this book traveled a unique arc across time. Skilled scribes and chanting masters left their mark on these poems, binding them to specific eras, melodies, and understandings of the Dharma. Here, in the third part of the book, I provide a more detailed look at the forty-five songs. For each text, I tabulate basic information, including the original title, poetic meter, performance style, and the author and date, if known. Along with relevant printed material, I also provide citations to the bark-paper and palm-leaf manuscript sources I used in compiling the Khmer-language comparative editions translated into English for this book. For more detail, see the key below.

For each song, this information on titles, meters, melodies, and sources is followed by a series of interpretative notes. My commentaries reveal some of the narratives, hidden meanings, and intertextual references that lie behind the poems. Many of the songs are connected to Pali sources, a selection of which I have translated in full. May these notes guide your journeys through the myriad passageways that Cambodian Dharma songs open for us.

Key

Title: Standardized title in romanized Khmer, as found in Walker's "Unfolding Buddhism" or in the original Khmer printed book. For titles shared across multiple texts, the title is followed by the first line in guillemets (« »).

Literal: Literal English translation of standardized title, if different than the title used in this book. For titles shared across multiple texts, the first line is translated as well, preceded by "beginning with."

Meter: Name of meter in romanized Khmer, followed by syllable counts per line.

Form: Meter used in English translation, whether the same as or different from the original Khmer.

Melody: Name of melody, with scale and tonality. Melody names are based on V"èn Sun and Y"ān' Pūrin, *Rapāyakāra(ṇ) pūk sarup laddhaphal*; and Walker, "Saṃvega and Pasāda." Scale and tonality based on Walker, "Saṃvega and Pasāda."

Stanzas: Number of stanzas.

Author: Name of author in romanized Khmer, if known; otherwise anonymous.

Date: Date of composition, if known; in most cases a range of centuries is given.

Khmer: Earliest printed Khmer version.

English: Previous English translations.

French: Previous French translations.

Edition: Edition of Khmer text used for this book.

Sources: Leporello manuscripts, palm-leaf manuscripts, and private notebooks used in edition. Leporellos are cited according to their manuscript codes from Walker, "Unfolding Buddhism," along with page numbers and the title and other paratextual information provided in the manuscript. Palm-leaf manuscripts are cited according to their Fonds pour l'Édition des Manuscrits du Cambodge (FEMC) codes. Handwritten notebooks are cited by owner and title.

1. Chaddanta's Lament

Title: daṃnuoñ chaddant
Meter: *bāky 7* (7-7-7-7)
Form: Unrhymed *bāky 7* (7-7-7-7)
Melody: *mahāmāyā* (C-E-F-G-B♭ = C^7)
Stanzas: 6
Author: Anonymous
Date: Mid-twentieth century
English: Walker, "Unfolding Buddhism," 1420–22.
Edition: Walker, "Unfolding Buddhism," 1420–22.
Sources: UB018, 48a–49b, daṃnuoñ stec ṭaṃrī sar; UB019, 38a–39b, daṃnuoñ stec ṭaṃrī sar; Ḍuk Ât, *Prajuṃ dhamma-saṅveg nānā* [notebook], 66.

This is a retelling of the Chaddanta Jātaka. In a distant past life, the Buddha-to-be was born as a six-tusked elephant, Chaddanta ("six-tusked" in Pali or *stec ṭaṃrī sa*, "the white elephant king," in Khmer), who lived with his two wives in the wilderness. After the younger wife becomes upset when her husband accidentally causes a shower of ants to fall on her, she wanders off, dies, and is reborn as a powerful human queen. Eager to exact revenge on Chaddanta, she sends a hunter to retrieve his distinctive ivory. When the hunter is not strong enough to cut through the thick tusks, the elephant grasps the saw with his own trunk and slices them off himself.[1]

2. Subhadra's Lament

Title: daṃnuoñ subhadrā
Meter: *bāky 7* (7-7-7-7)
Form: Unrhymed *bāky 7* (7-7-7-7)
Melody: *mahāmāyā* (C-E-F-G-B♭ = C^7)
Stanzas: 6

Author: Anonymous
Date: Mid-twentieth century
English: Walker, "Unfolding Buddhism," 1429–30.
Edition: Walker, "Unfolding Buddhism," 1429–30.
Sources: UB018, 63b–65a, daṃnuoñ braḥ nāṅ sabbadrā; Ḍuk Ât, *Prajuṃ dhammasaṅveg nānā* [notebook], 67.

This is a continuation of the narrative from the previous poem. Princess Yasodharā Bimbā, the Buddha's consort in his final birth as Siddhartha Gautama, follows him throughout countless lifetimes. In Cambodia, she is revered as the "Consort of the Omniscient One" (Khmer: *kansai sarabejñ*) and the Buddha's true "partner in samsara" (*gū saṅsār*, modern Khmer for "boyfriend" or "girlfriend"). Their long journey together is far from easy. Yasodhara recounts her many shared lives with the Buddha-to-be in a Southeast Asian Pali narrative, the *Bimbānibbāna*.[2]

3. Parika's Lament

Title: daṃnuoñ mtāy suvaṇṇasām
Literal: Suvaṇṇasāma's mother's lament
Meter: *bāky 7* (7-7-7-7)
Form: Rhymed *bāky 7* (7-7-7-7)
Melody: *madrī* (C-D-E♭-E-F-G-B♭= Cm^7-C^7)
Stanzas: 5
Author: Anonymous
Date: Mid-twentieth century
English: Walker, "How Sophea Lost Her Sight," 526–27 [excerpt]; Walker, "Unfolding Buddhism," 1428–29.
Edition: Walker, "Unfolding Buddhism," 1428–29.
Sources: UB018, 37a–38a, daṃnuoñ mātā braḥ suvaṇṇasām; Ḍuk Ât, *Prajuṃ dhammasaṅveg nānā* [notebook], 69.

A retelling of the Suvaṇṇasāma Jātaka, this poem recounts the tale of an ascetic couple, Dukūlaka and Pārikā, who dwell in the forest along with their son Suvaṇṇasāma, the Buddha-to-be. One day, a startled snake sprays venom on the couple, blinding them.[3]

4. Suvannasama's Lament

Title: daṃnuoñ suvaṇṇasām
Meter: *bāky 7* (7-7-7-7)
Form: Rhymed *bāky 7* (7-7-7-7)
Melody: *madrī* (C-D-E♭-E-F-G-B♭= Cm^7-C^7)
Stanzas: 6
Author: Anonymous
Date: Mid-twentieth century
English: Walker, "Stirring and Stilling," 23–24.
Edition: Walker, "Stirring and Stilling," 23–24.
Sources: UB018, 62a–63b, daṃnuoñ braḥ suvaṇṇasām; Ḍuk Ât, *Prajuṃ dhammasaṅveg nānā* [notebook], 68.

This is a continuation of the narrative from the previous poem. Suvaṇṇasāma, perfecting the practice of kindness (*mettā*) toward his parents, serves them daily after they lose their sight. But one day, while out on a hunting trip, King Piliyakkha accidentally shoots the Buddha-to-be with a poisoned arrow. Suvaṇṇasāma is eventually revived by a god, but not before sharing this lament.

5. Madri's Lament

Title: daṃnuoñ madrī
Meter: *bāky 7* (7-7-7-7)
Form: Unrhymed *bāky 7* (7-7-7-7)
Melody: *madrī* (C-D-E♭-E-F-G-B♭= Cm^7-C^7)
Stanzas: 35
Author: Sandhar Jā

Date: 1960
Khmer: Sandhar Jā, *Lpök madrī*. Reproduced in Som Suvaṇṇ, *Prajuṃ māghapūjā niṅ visākhapūjā*, 53–57.
English: Walker, "Framing the Sacred," 21–23 [excerpt].

The poem is a retelling of the Vessantara Jātaka, excerpted from a verse version focused on Madrī by the Khmer poet Sandhar Jā. It recounts a key episode from the Buddha-to-be's antepenultimate life as Prince Vessantara. After giving away a rainmaking elephant to a rival kingdom, Vessantara, his wife Madrī (Pali: Maddī), and their two children, Jāli and Kṛṣṇā (Pali: Kaṇhājinā), are banished by their subjects to the forests of Mount Vaṅkata. There Vessantara takes his obsession with generosity to new extremes, giving away Jāli and Kṛṣṇā to a cruel brahman, Jūjaka. The gods aid Vessantara's quest for perfection by transforming themselves into wild beasts to prevent Madrī from interfering with her husband relinquishing their children to Jūjaka.[4]

6. Lullaby of the Gods

Title: devatā paṃbe kūn
Literal: The gods sing a lullaby to [Vessantara's] children
Meter: *kaṃraṅ kèv*
Form: Unrhymed, but otherwise strict representation of the *kaṃraṅ kèv* structure.
Melody: *devatā paṃbe kūn* (C-E♭-E-F-G-B♭= Cm^7-C^7)
Stanzas: 3
Author: Anonymous
Date: Late nineteenth or early twentieth centuries
Khmer: V"èn Sun and Y"ān' Pūrin, *Rapāyakāra(ṇ) pūk sarup laddhaphal*, 59.
English: Walker, "Stirring and Stilling," 24–25.
Edition: Walker, "Stirring and Stilling," 24–25.

Source: Transcribed from a recorded performance by Y"ān' Pūrin (Yan Borin), 2003.

This song recounts a later episode from the Vessantara Jātaka. Two deities from the heavens above take pity on the plight of Jāli and Kṛṣṇā. They transform themselves to look like Madrī and Vessantara and sing the children to sleep as Jūjaka slumbers nearby. The metrical and melodic structure of this piece imitates traditional Khmer lullabies.

7. Maya's Guidance for Gotami

Title: paṇṭāṃ mahāmāyā
Literal: Mahāmāyā's admonitions
Meter: *bāky* 7 (7-7-7-7)
Form: Unrhymed *bāky* 7 (7-7-7-7)
Melody: *mahāmāyā* (C-E-F-G-B♭ = C^7)
Stanzas: 7
Author: Anonymous
Date: Late nineteenth or early twentieth centuries
English: Walker, "Stirring and Stilling," 26–27.
Edition: Walker, "Stirring and Stilling," 26–27.
Sources: Kaṅ Phū, Untitled [notebook], 7; Ḍuk Ât, *Prajuṃ dhammasaṅveg nānā* [notebook], 23.

Prince Siddhartha's mother, Queen Māyā, dies seven days after his birth. This poem imagines her words to her younger sister Mahāpajāpatī Gotamī, the Buddha's aunt, asking her to raise him after she dies.[5] The version translated here is one of several that circulate in Cambodia.[6]

8. Divine Messengers

Title: draṅ' ceñ dat suon udyān
Literal: [The Bodhisattva] leaves to see the gardens.
Meter: *bāky 7* (7-7-7-7)
Form: Unrhymed *bāky 7* (7-7-7-7)
Melody: *sāṅ braḥ phnuos* (C-E-F-G-B♭ = C^7)
Stanzas: 9
Author: Anonymous
Date: Twentieth century
English: Walker, "Stirring and Stilling," 28–29.
Edition: Walker, "Stirring and Stilling," 28–29.
Sources: Kaṅ Phū, Untitled [notebook], 9; Ḍuk Ât, *Prajuṃ dhammasaṅveg nānā* [notebook], 13–14.

This is the Buddha-to-be's first encounter with the "divine messengers" (Pali: *devadūta*) of an old person, a sick person, a corpse, and a monastic, leading to his decision to give up his life of luxury in the palace.

9. Leaving the Palace

Title: phcāñ' mār «nā kāl adhrātr»
Literal: Defeat of Māra, beginning with "At midnight's hour."
Meter: *kākagati* (4-4-4-4-4-4-4)
Form: Unrhymed *kākagati*, presented in three lines (12-12-4).
Melody: *phcāñ' mār* (C-E-F-G-B♭ = C^7)
Stanzas: 7
Author: Anonymous
Date: Nineteenth or early twentieth century
English: Walker, "Stirring and Stilling," 30–32.
Khmer: Gaṅ' V"ān'-nuon, *Prajuṃ kauvatār*, 86–87.
Edition: Walker, "Stirring and Stilling," 30–32.
Sources: UB016, 28a–29a; UB038, 20a–20b, braḥ aṅg ceñ pab-

bajjā; UB038, 76a–77b, pad phcāñ' mār kāl braḥ aṅg ceñ pabbajjā; UB047, 62a–62b, phcāñ' mār kāl braḥ aṅg ceñ sāṅ pabbajjā.

Here, the Bodhisattva departs from the palace in the middle of the night, giving voice to his admonitions to his just-born son, Rāhula. This poem is known as "The Defeat of Māra" in Khmer for two reasons. One, the meter and melody are drawn from an an older text also included in this book, "The Defeat of Māra" (#12). Two, the Buddha defeated Māra, or the personification of evil and temptation, as various junctures along his journey to enlightenment. The painful choice to leave his wife and newborn son behind was such a juncture.

10. Maya's Lament

Title:	daṃnuoñ mahāmāyā
Literal:	Mahāmāyā's lament
Meter:	*bāky* 7 (7-7-7-7)
Form:	Unrhymed *bāky* 7 (7-7-7-7)
Melody:	*mahāmāyā* (C-E-F-G-B♭ = C^7)
Stanzas:	14 (only 1–11 are translated)
Author:	Jăy M"ai
Date:	1942
English:	Walker, "Unfolding Buddhism," 1424–27.
Khmer:	Jăy M"ai, *Nānādhammasaṅveg*, 14–15.
Edition:	Walker, "Unfolding Buddhism," 1424–27.
Sources:	UB018, 54a–56a, braḥ nāṅ sirimahāmāyā; UB019, 21b–23b, daṃnuoñ braḥ nāṅ sirimahāmāyā; UB027, 67a–68b; UB038, 25b–27a, daṃnuoñ nāṅ sirimahāmāyā; UB047, 68a–69b, braḥ aṅg dhvö dukkharakiriyā; UB049, 3a–6a, dukkhara:kiriyā; UB062, 74b–75b, pruḥ banlak.

This is a conversation between the Buddha's mother, Queen Māyā, and the emaciated Bodhisattva during his practice of austerities. The final three stanzas, not included here, note that the author, Jăy M"ai, created this poem on the basis of several unnamed Pali and Sanskrit texts.

11. Indra's Lute

Title:	*buddhapravatti bāky kāby*
Literal	The Buddha's life in verse
Meter:	*bāky 9* (9-9-9-9)
Form	Extended into four-line free verse (X-X-X-X)
Melody:	*rās'* (C-D-E-F-G-A-B♭ = C^7)
Stanzas:	6-stanza excerpt of ~600-stanza work
Author:	Miev Nand
Date:	1951
Khmer:	Miev Nand, *Buddhapravatti bāky kāby*, 32 (excerpt; complete text on pages 1–72).
English:	Walker, "Framing the Sacred," 25.

The Bodhisattva's practice of austerities comes to an end when Indra descends from Trāyastriṃśa Heaven to play a song on a lute to teach the middle way between hedonism and asceticism. Most Cambodian depictions of this episode show Indra playing a traditional Khmer long-necked lute (*cāp"ī ṭaṅ vèṅ*, "chapei dang veng"). This poem is excerpted from Miev Nand's *Buddhapravatti bāky kāby*, one of the finest twentieth-century verse versions of the Buddha's life from birth to nirvana.

12. The Defeat of Mara

Title:	phcāñ' mār «yŏṅ khñuṃ paṅgaṃ»
Literal:	Defeat of Māra, beginning with "We bow down."
Meter:	*kākagati* (4-4-4-4-4-4-4)

Form: Unrhymed *kākagati*, presented in seven lines (4-4-4-4-4-4-4)

Melody: *phcāñ' mār* (C-E-F-G-B♭ = C^7)

Stanzas: 26-stanza excerpt (124–149) of a 149-stanza work.

Author: Anonymous

Date: Eighteenth or nineteenth century

Khmer: Lī Suvīr, *Bidhī dhvö puṇy buddhābhisek*, 4–22; Preap Chanmara, "Phcāñ' mār," 2–26.

French: Giteau, *Le bornage rituel des temples*, 73–99.

Edition: Giteau, *Le bornage rituel des temples*, 73–99.

Sources: UB002, 61b–77a, braḥ dhaŕm phcāñ' mār, with food offering instructions on 68b and a short Pali portion on 80a: *pañcamāri canināththo puttosambodhī muttamaṃ catusaccaṃ mārasenaṃ phall"āyanti*; UB003, 34a–40 and 42b–49a, phcāñ mār; UB007, 27a–35b; UB008, 16a–33b, phcāñ mār; UB009, 28a–38a; UB010, 48b–63b; UB011, 49b–53b and 54a–65b, phcāñ' mā/phcāñ mār; UB012, 51a–65a [no title given, but last line of text reads mahāmār vijăy]; UB017, 44a–58b, phcāñ' mār, with final note: *nīṅ saṃḍèṅ knuṅ dhaŕm y"ok phcāñ' mār tè puṇṇèḥ*; UB021, 12b–40a; UB035 33a–50a and 52a–52b, phcāñ mār; UB039, 26a–39b; UB041, 25b–38b, dhaŕm phcāñ' mār, with the incipit *namatthu* (explicit missing); UB046, 16a–33b, phcāñ' mār; UB048, 73a–55b, pad phcāñ' mā/pchāñ mār; UB051, 17b–30b, braḥ phcāñ mmār; UB062, 53b–61b, pad phcāñ' mār/phcāñ' mār/thvāy madhupāyās, with the incipit *namo tassa namatthu*; UB065, 70a–81b, phcāñ' mār, draṅ ceñ braḥ bhnuos, thvāy madhupāyās/abhisek/dhaŕm yog; UB067, 73a–86b.

One of the longest and most celebrated Dharma songs, "The Defeat of Mara" narrates the Buddha's journey to awakening as a series of battles against Māra. Only the final twenty-six stanzas are translated here; the full poem runs to 149 stanzas and takes nearly three hours to recite. The poem begins with an account of the four *devadūta*, similar to "Divine Messengers" (poem #8 in this book). Next the Bodhisattva decides to leave behind his son and his wife but is challenged by Māra, who tries to prevent him from leaving the palace. The text then describes the Buddha-to-be's disgust with the woman of the harem, his departure from the palace on his horse, Kanthaka, accompanied by his horseman, Channa, and an entourage of deities. Siddhartha cuts off his hair and vows to reach awakening, and the gods carry his topknot to the Cūḷamaṇī stupa in Trāyastriṃśa Heaven.

The poem continues with a brief account of his six years of ascetic practice, followed by Sujātā's offering of milk-rice. The king of the nāgas warns Māra about Siddhartha's impending awakening, so Māra sends his three young daughters to seduce the Bodhisattva. Unfazed, the Buddha-to-be transforms them into old women. Māra, in anger, assembles a vast army of gods and ferocious beasts—but the Bodhisattva's perfections (*pāramī*) join the fray, bringing Māra's armies to a standstill.

The final portion of the text, translated here, begins at this point, with the Bodhisattva transforming all projectiles flung at him into flowers. "Baldy," "hermit," and "smooth-head" translate Khmer *sramaṇ*, from Sanskrit *śramaṇa*, "striver; renunciate wanderer." Māra uses this as a derisive term of address for the Bodhisattva. The Earth Goddess is Nāṅ Gaṅhīṅ Braḥ Dharaṇī, whose role in the Buddha's enlightenment is distinct to Khmer, Lao, and Thai Buddhist traditions. After Māra and his armies are washed away by the water in the Earth Goddess' hair, the Prince Siddhartha finally becomes the Buddha. Along the way, he predicts that Māra, his longtime foe, will eventually reach nirvana as a "lone buddha," or *paccekabuddha* (someone who attains nirvana on their own but declines to teach).

13. Invitation to Preach the Dharma

Title:	ārādhanā dhammadesanā
Literal:	Invitation to Preach the Dhamma
Meter:	*brahmagīti* (5-6-5-6)
Form:	Extended into four-line free verse (X-X-X-X)
Melody:	*ārādhanā* (C-D-E-F-G-A-B = C^{Δ})
Stanzas:	22
Author:	Suttantaprījā Ind
Date:	Late nineteenth or early twentieth century
Khmer:	Ind, "Ārādhanā dhammakathik," 34–37.
English:	Walker, "A Chant Has Nine Lives," 57–62.
French:	San Sarin, "Les textes liturgiques fondamentaux," 69–78.
Edition:	Walker, "A Chant Has Nine Lives," 57–62.
Sources:	UB009, 9a–10a, pad brahm ārādhanā dhaŕm desanā; UB036, 56a–58a, bāky ārādhanā dhaŕm desanā pad brahmagit.

Suttantaprījā Ind was one of Cambodia's leading poets and intellectuals from the late nineteenth and early twentieth centuries. This poem of his stands in the middle of a complex intertextual history of Pali, Thai, Khmer, and Vietnamese chants for inviting a monk to give a sermon.[7] Out of several Khmer and Pali versions known in Cambodia, Ind's "Invitation to Preach the Dharma" is by far the most widely recited today. Almost all contemporary sermons are preceded by a layperson reciting Ind's text, though often just the final eight stanzas.

The first ten stanzas translate a modified version of the opening verse of the *Buddhavaṃsa*:

> Brahmā Sahampati, Lord of the World,
> palms folded together, beseeched the Unexcelled One:

> "There exist, here below, beings with minor defilements—
> preach the Dhamma; have mercy for this generation."[8]

Ind's version, particularly in the sixth through tenth stanzas, expands significantly on the original Pali. "Worldly realms are fleeting wastes" is literally "the Three Realms [of desire, form, and formlessness] are the arid land of the Three Marks [of impermanence, suffering, and not-self]" (*trailok gok trailakkha(ṇ)*). "Ignorance is the fundamental cause / that sets in motion a chain of effects" is literally "ignorance is the root, / the condition for [the arising of] of mental formations" (*avijjā jā ṛs gal' / jā paccăy nai saṅkhār*), a reference to the twelve links of dependent origination (Pali: *paṭicca samuppāda*). "The Five Māras" (*pañcamāra*) refers to a late commentarial interpretation of Māra as the aggregates, the defilements, karmic formations, a deity, and death itself.[9]

The next four stanzas are translated from a Pali stanza of unknown origin:

> The drum of the true Dhamma, whose frame is the Vinaya,
> whose straps are the Sutta, whose leather head is the
> Abhidhamma—
> striking [this drum], whose mallet is the Four Truths,
> awaken those fit to be led in the midst of the assembly.[10]

Ind's version expands on the Pali term *neyye* ("those fit to be led"), interpreting it as one of "The Four Assemblies" (*catuparisā*): those who understand the Dharma immediately, those who understand after detailed explanation, those who need further training, and those who must learn by rote (*ugghaṭitaññū*, *vipañcitaññū*, *neyya*, and *padaparama*), explained in the *Puggalappaññatti* as referring to beings with different innate capacities for the Buddha's teachings. He then links these assemblies to four kinds of "lotus buds in the water," a simile found in Buddhaghosa's commentary to the *Dīgha Nikāya*, the *Sumaṅgalavilāsinī*.[11]

The final eight stanzas describe the Buddha's assent to Sahampati Brahmā's request, a summary of the Blessed One's teaching career, and a direct invitation for monastics to preach the Dharma on the model of the Buddha. No Pali originals may have existed for these stanzas, so Ind appears to have composed four Pali verses of his own to match this portion of his Khmer poem:

> Thus the Brahmā Sahampatī
> requested the Blessed One.
> By means of silence, the Buddha,
> having resorted to compassion,
>
> from that spot arose and by foot
> went to the Deer Park.
> As for those to be led, starting with the Group of Five,
> he had them drink of the Deathless, naturally.
>
> From that complete beginning, the Perfect Buddha
> for forty-five rainy seasons
> preached sermons on the Dhamma
> to fulfill the aims of living beings.
>
> Hence, it would be excellent, O Venerable,
> were you to preach a sermon on the Dhamma—
> please have mercy
> on the assembly gathered here.[12]

The "Group of Five" (Pali: *pañcavaggiya*) refers to the five monks the Buddha practiced austerities with prior to his awakening. After shunning the Buddha when he gave up on extreme asceticism, they became the audience for his first sermon at the Deer Park of Isipatana. Ind's use of Pali in these stanzas showcases his exceptional facility in the language: "forty-five rainy seasons" (*māghavassāni*) is an exceedingly rare Pali usage of the *kaṭapayādi* system of numerals, and "to fulfill the aims of living beings" (*sattānaṃ atthasiddhakaṃ*) is a clever pun on Siddhartha (Sanskrit *siddhārtha*; Pali *siddhattha*), "he whose aims are fulfilled."

14. The Buddha's Last Words

Title: pacchimabuddhavacana
Literal: The final words of the Buddha
Meter: *brahmagīti* (5-6-5-6)
Form: Unrhymed *brahmagīti* (5-6-5-6)
Melody: *yo vo* (C-D-E♭-F-G-B♭ = Cm^7)
Stanzas: 7
Author: Unknown
Date: Nineteenth or early twentieth century
Khmer: Jăy M"ai, *Nānādhammasaṅveg*, 27.
English: Walker, "Stirring and Stilling," 32–34.
Edition: Walker, "Stirring and Stilling," 32–34.
Sources: UB018, 65b–66b, paṇtāṃ braḥ bodhisatv; UB019, 29a–30a, paṇtāṃ braḥ bodhiñāṇ; UB047, 84b–85b, yo vo ānand/parinibbānakathā; UB065, 20a, pacchimabuddhavacana.

This is one of several anonymous Khmer poems that bring the Buddha's last words (Pali: *pacchimabuddhavana*) to life. Most Cambodians know this text by the name "Yo vo," which are the two Pali words that open the poem. This phrase is a reference to a famous line in the *Mahāparinibbāna Sutta* uttered by the Buddha shortly before he passes into nirvana:

> Ānanda, the Dharma and Vinaya I have taught and declared to you shall be your Teacher after I pass away (*yo vo ānanda mayā dhammo ca vinayo ca desito paññatto so vo mam'accayena satthā*).[13]

15. The Buddha's Passing Away

Title: parinibbānakathā
Literal: The story of the Buddha's final nirvana
Meter: *bāky 7* (7-7-7-7)
Form: Unrhymed *bāky 7* (7-7-7-7)
Melody: *sāṅ braḥ phnuos* (C-E-F-G-B♭ = C^7)
Stanzas: 11
Author: Jăy M"ai
Date: 1942
Khmer: Jăy M"ai, *Nānādhammasaṅveg*, 31–32.
English: Walker, "Unfolding Buddhism," 1434–36.
Edition: Walker, "Unfolding Buddhism," 1434–36.
Sources: UB018, 56b–58b, nibbānasūtr; UB019, 30b–32b, bodhiñāṇ yāṅ cūl nibbān; UB027, 69a–70b; UB047, 85b–86b, braḥ buddh yāṅ cūl nibbān/parinibbān; UB057, 152a–154a; UB062, 75b–76b, nibbānasūtr; UB065, 20b–21a, parinibbānakathā.

This poem narrates Ānanda's encounter with a group of laypeople who hadn't yet been informed about the Buddha's final nirvana, a scene that first appears in Buddhaghosa's introduction to the *Sumaṅgalavilāsinī* (see Shulman, *Visions*, 115). "A snake year, ending in five" refers to the traditional date for the Buddha's final nirvana, namely 544 B.C.E., which was indeed a snake year (albeit not one ending in five in any Cambodian calendar).

16. Mourning the Buddha's Demise

Title: sira: on
Literal: Bowing my head
Meter: *brahmagīti* (5-6-5-6)
Form: Extended into unrhymed *paṭhyāvatt* (8-8-8-8)

Melody: *saṃbau thay* (C-D-E♭-F-G-B♭ = Cm^7)
Stanzas: 11
Author: Unknown
Date: Nineteenth or early twentieth century
Khmer: Jăy M"ai, *Nānādhammasaṅveg*, 30.
English: Walker, "Unfolding Buddhism," 1293–95.
Edition: Walker, "Unfolding Buddhism," 1293–95.
Sources: UB038, 58a–59a, sira: on; UB065, 51a–51b, sira: on; Kaṅ Phū, Untitled [notebook], 60.

This is a lamentation on the Buddha's passing into nirvana, one of the "four pivots in our Lord's life" celebrated on Vesak, the full moon of the sixth lunar month, Visākha. The others are his birth, departure from the palace, and enlightenment under the Bodhi tree. The poem adopts a wide range of epithets for the Blessed One, including "the Chief Sage" (*braḥ munind*), "the World's Crown" (*bin lokā*), "Self-Arisen" (*braḥ sayambhū*), "Lord of Lords" (*braḥ jā mcās'*), and "the Teacher" (*braḥ sāstā*). "Our ark, our anchor throughout time" is literally "[he whom] living beings must rely on to secure karmic affinity" (*satv trūv bịṅ yak nissăy*).

17. The Cremation of the Buddha

Title: aṭṭhamīpūjā gāthā samrāy
Literal: Stanzas for Aṭṭhamīpūjā, translated into Khmer.
Meter: *paṭhyāvatt* (8-8-8-8)
Form: Unrhymed *paṭhyāvatt* (8-8-8-8)
Melody: *samrāy* (C-D-E-G-A = C^6)
Stanzas: 8
Author: Unknown
Date: Nineteenth or early twentieth century
Khmer: Ñāṇ Jhīṇ, *Visākhapūjā*, 33–34.
English: Walker, "Unfolding Buddhism," 1386–88.
Edition: Walker, "Unfolding Buddhism," 1386–88.

Sources: UB066, 18a–18b and 20a, visākhapūjā; Kaṅ Phū, Untitled [notebook], 59.

This is one of several Khmer verse translations of the *Aṭṭhamīpūjā Gāthā*, a set of Pali verses in the *anuṭṭhubha* meter composed by King Mongkut (Rama IV) of Siam for recitation in the annual celebration of the eighth (*aṭṭhamī*) day after Vesak. This occasion marks the day when the monarchs of the Malla kingdom cremated the Buddha. The original, translated from the Pali, begins:

> Today is the eighth day after the full moon of Visākha. On such a day, the funeral pyre that the faithful Mallas had made from all kinds of fragrant things for the deceased Realized One, the Lord of Men, manifested a miracle: it burst into flames of its own accord. The final body of the Great Sage, with its thirty-two marks, burned up by means of the element of fire. Now, just like that time, a distinguished occasion has arrived. This moment is recognized as most auspicious, a lucky constellation.[14]

18. The Relics of the Buddha

Title: caṅkūm kèv
Literal: The jewel canine relics
Meter: *kākagati* (4-4-4-4-4-4-4)
Form: Unrhymed *kākagati*, presented in three lines (12-12-4).
Melody: Unknown
Stanzas: 35
Author: Suvaṇṇakesar
Date: Eighteenth or nineteenth centuries
English: Walker, "Unfolding Buddhism," 1094–1102.
Edition: Walker, "Unfolding Buddhism," 1094–1102.
Sources: UB059, 30b–34a, dhaŕrm braḥ caṅkom kèv.

This poem was penned by a certain Suvaṇṇakesar of Jhūk Sa ("White Lotus") monastery, located in Oudong (*uṭtuṅg*) village, Veang Chas (*vāṃṅ cās'*) commune, Oudong district, Kampong Speu province, Cambodia, near the site of the royal palace in the seventeenth through nineteenth centuries. Only one manuscript survives, and unfortunately there are two largely illegible stanzas between "twelve yojanas tall" and "the upper robe of the Buddha."

Suvaṇṇakesar's Khmer text is based on a set of Pali verses, likely of Southeast Asian origin, that describe the division and distribution of the Buddha's relics after his nirvana. The first five stanzas of the original read:

> The great Buddha, Gautama,
> entered nirvana in Kusinara,
> from where his relics were spread
> to various different places.
>
> His crown, four canine teeth,
> and two clavicles, seven in all:
> these relics remained intact.
> The remaining ones broke in pieces.
>
> The large pieces filled five bamboo tubes,
> the medium pieces filled seven,
> the small pieces another five:
> like so, the pieces were divided.
>
> The large pieces: split mung beans.
> The medium pieces: split rice grains.
> The small pieces: mustard seeds.
> Thus were the sizes of the relics.
>
> The large ones were the color of gold.
> The medium ones the radiance of crystal.

The small ones the hue of bakula flowers.
To all these relics, I pay homage.[15]

"Bamboo tube" translates *nāḷi*, a measure of capacity in Pali. In Khmer, the term (usually spelled *nāli*) is used as a measure of both capacity and weight for grain, equivalent to six hundred grams. "Sprouts of buddhas" is a literal rendering of *braḥ buddh banlak*, a synonym for bodhisattva.

19. In Praise of the Earth

Title: sarasör pr̥ithabī
Meter: *kākagati* (4-4-4-4-4-4-4)
Form: Unrhymed *kākagati*, presented in three lines (12-12-4).
Melody: Unknown
Stanzas: 42
Author: Anonymous
Date: Seventeenth or eighteenth century
English: Walker, "Unfolding Buddhism," 1235–44.
Edition: Walker, "Unfolding Buddhism," 1235–44.
Sources: UB011, 72a–73b, dhaŕm (ra)pā; FEMC d.122, lpök pr̥ithabī.

This is an old text, offering praise to the virtues, or *guṇ*, of the Earth, other deities, our parents, and the Three Jewels, as well as specific instructions for what texts to chant and what rituals to perform to repay our debts to each. The poem is remarkable for the way it weaves together various Cambodian beliefs and practices around *guṇ* into a coherent whole.

A yojana is a traditional Indian measurement of distance, equivalent to between eight and fifteen kilometers, depending on the estimate. Vaiśravaṇa is another name for Kubera, the Hindu-Buddhist god of wealth. In Cambodia, Vaiśravaṇa (*braḥ baisraba(ṇ)*) eventually became recognized as the god of paddy, that is, of rice as a crop.[16] As the poem indicates ("a mother to all, a father too"), Vaiśravaṇa's gender is ambiguous in Cambodia. Cooked rice, or sometimes rice in all stages of its production, is known as "Holy Mother" (*braḥ me*).[17]

The phrases "The Blessed One," "Well-expounded," and "Well-practiced is the Lord's Sangha" are abbreviations for standard Pali descriptions of the virtues of the Buddha (*iti pi so . . . bhagavā ti*), the Dharma (*svākkhāto . . . viññūhī ti*), and the Sangha (*supaṭipanno . . . lokassā ti*). These are found in the *Dhajagga Sutta*, among other places in the Pali canon, and are foundational to a range of Cambodian meditation practices.[18]

The Cambodian tradition emphasizes how the Buddha repaid his debt to his mother Māyā through preaching the Abhidhamma to her in Trāyastriṃśa Heaven and to his father by returning to his homeland to preach the *Vessantara Jātaka*. Both the Abhidhamma and the *Vessantara Jātaka* have been prominent in bilingual Pali-Khmer sermons since the sixteenth and seventeenth centuries.[19] The noncanonical *Ākāravattā*[20] and *Paññāsajātaka*[21] are likewise essential in traditional Cambodian practice.

Building small mounds or stupas out of sand, a long-standing practice in Laos and Thailand,[22] has been attested in Cambodia since the seventeenth century.[23] The five-mound model mentioned in the poem remains current today, including in some funeral rites in Cambodia.[24] In addition to the Buddhist valences of building sand stupas as an act of merit, Ang Choulean points out that such mounds amount to making the world anew in the face of old age, death, and the cyclic rotation of time.[25] For the author of "In Praise of the Earth," piling sand into stupas has the primary function of repaying our debts to the deities of earth, rain, wind, fire, and rice.

The poem mentions the construction of sand stupas during the fourth lunar month of Phalguna (February/March) or during "the three days of the New Year," a solar-calendar event that happens in mid-April, usually near the end of the fifth lunar month, Caitra. During the New Year, water plays a key role in ritual renewal, including respectfully pouring water on Buddha images, monastics, and elders.

The *Mahāmetrī*, or *Mahāmetti Sutta*, is a noncanonical Pali text recited in Cambodia.[26] The "Sun Sutta" (*Suriyaparitta* or *Suriya Sutta*) and "Moon Sutta" (*Candaparitta* or *Candima Sutta*) are canonical texts from the *Saṃyutta Nikāya* that have been incorporated into the monastic chanting curriculum.[27] Rāhu is the deity believed to swallow the sun during eclipses.

20. The Twenty-Four Vowels

Title: namo namassakār
Literal: With [the syllables] "namo" I pay homage.
Meter: *brahmagīti* (5-6-5-6)
Form: Extended into unrhymed *paṭhyāvatt* (8-8-8-8)
Melody: Unknown
Stanzas: 10
Author: Anonymous
Date: Eighteenth or nineteenth century
English: Walker, "Unfolding Buddhism," 1272–73.
Edition: Walker, "Unfolding Buddhism," 1272–73.
Source: UB042, 47a–48a, namo namassakār.

There are two main sets of vowels in Khmer, dependent and independent. The dependent vowels form a larger set and can only appear in conjunction with a consonant. The independent vowels, of which there are fewer, can stand on their own. Only consonants and independent vowels are used as heart syllables in Cambodian practices. This text presents twenty-four independent vowels as standing in for the *guṇ* of various entities, including parents, relatives, teachers, and many aspects of the Buddha and his Dharma.

Indian alphabets often begin with *siddhaṃ* ("Success!"). Traditional Khmer thought extends this by adding *namo buddhāya* ("Homage to the Buddha!") prior to *siddhaṃ*. The poem translated here presents one of several Cambodian conceptions of the correct alphabetic order for the independent vowels: NA, MO, BU, DDHĀ, YA, SI, DDHAṂ, A, Ā, I, Ī, U, Ū, UV, Ṛ, Ṝ, Ḷ, Ḹ, E, AI, O, AU, AṂ, ĀṂ, AḤ. Other texts in the esoteric tradition provide different lists for the independent vowels.[28]

21. The Thirty-Three Consonants

Title: akkharā 33
Meter: *brahmagīti* (5-6-5-6)
Form: Extended into four-line free verse (X-X-X-X), with some stanzas combined.
Melody: Unknown
Stanzas: 46
Author: Anonymous
Date: Eighteenth or nineteenth century
English: Walker, "Unfolding Buddhism," 1295–1302.
Edition: Walker, "Unfolding Buddhism," 1295–1302.
Sources: UB060, 33b–35b, akkharā 33; FEMC 1017-B.01.06.01.I.3, lpök akkharā sām sip pī; Kaṅ Phū, Untitled [notebook], 51–52.

In the suttas and in the *Visuddhimagga*, thirty-one parts of the body are listed.[29] In later Pali texts this is expanded to thirty-two by adding the phrase "the brain within the skull" (*matthake matthaluṅgaṃ*.) A Southeast Asian tradition expands this to thirty-three by taking *matthake* and *matthaluṅgaṃ* separately, resulting in "the skull" and "the brain."[30]

The poem "The Thirty-Three Consonants" follows this tradition, connecting twelve liquid parts of the body to the *guṇ* of our mothers and twenty-one to that of our fathers. This reckoning aligns precisely with the number of consonants in the Khmer alphabet: KA, KHA, GA, GHA, ṄA, CA, CHA, JA, JHA, ÑA, ṬA, ṬHA, ḌA, ḌHA, ṆA, TA, THA, DA, DHA, NA, PA, PHA, BA,

BHA, MA, YA, RA, LA, VA, SA, HA, ḶA, and A (the lattermost representing a glottal stop in Khmer).

The Pali phrase cited in the poem, *imasmiṃ kāye*, is a reference to the canonical formula for meditation on the parts of the body: "in this body, there are head hairs, body hairs, nails, teeth, skin, . . ." (*atthi imasmiṃ kāye kesā lomā nakhā dantā taco*).

22. Absolving All Faults

Title: lā pāp «bhante bhagavā»
Literal: Taking leave of sins, beginning with "O Blessed One."
Meter: *kākagati* (4-4-4-4-4-4-4)
Form: Extended unrhymed *kākagati*, presented in three lines (12+, 12+, 4+).
Melody: *trailakkha(ṇ)* (C-E♭-E-F-A-B♭ = C, F^7)
Stanzas: 72
Author: Anonymous
Date: Seventeenth or eighteenth centuries
Khmer: Nuon Saṃ-ân, *Gihippatipatti gharāvāsadharm* (2544), 104–10; Nuon Saṃ-ân, *Gihippatipatti gharāvāsadharm* (2547), 56–62.
English: Walker, "Unfolding Buddhism," 1215–32.
French: Bernon, "Le manuel des maîtres," 757–60 [25-stanza recension].
Edition: Walker, "Unfolding Buddhism," 1215–32.
Sources: UB005, 45a–49a, dharm lā pāp; UB011, 79b–81b, dharm (ra)pā; UB015, 45a–53b, lpār [cap' lpār lvĕḥ]; UB016, 12b–16b and 18a–19b; UB020, 92a–99b (explicit missing); UB025, 23a–27b and 28b–31b, rapā sūtr smā lā dos; UB028, 51a–55a, dharm smā lā, with extra verse at incipit but much shorter overall; UB029, 15b–16b, lpā smā lā pāp lā doḥ lā pramād satv tūc ddhaṃ niṅ māṭāpīṭā grū ācāry braḥ ādit braḥ cand' braḥ agī gaṅgā ṭī dik (explicit missing); UB031, 23–34a; UB033, 34a–42b and 43b–45b (middle missing); UB034, 28a–35b, bhantè bhaggavār

(explicit missing); UB034, 56a–64b, dhamm bhantèr; UB037, 31a–32b, 34b–36a, and 36b (incipit and middle missing); UB042, 43a–45b, lpā lā pāp, with the incipit *namo tassa bhagavato arahato sammāsambuddhassa* (short version); UB052, 2–8b (incipit missing); UB053 30b (explicit missing); UB055, 58a–67a, sūt smār lā dos°; UB060, 49a–54b, khñuṃ sūm lā pāp, with the incipit *namo tassa*; UB065, 47a–49a, dhaŕm lā pāp; UB067, 39b–47b lpār.

This poem is a long prayer for absolution from karmic faults and their consequences. The title itself merits detailed reflection. In Khmer, this text is known by a variety of different names, the most common of which is simply *lā pāp*, literally "taking leave (*lā*) of sins (*pāp*; from Pali *pāpa*)." The word *lā* can also be translated as "goodbye" and appears in a variety of formal and informal Khmer phrases for bidding farewell to someone. To say goodbye to our sins means to aspire to never encounter them or their karmic consequences again.

Some manuscripts add additional words to the basic title of *lā pāp* or *lā dos* ("taking leaving of faults," from Pali *dosa*, "fault"). One such word is *lpā* (sometimes spelled *rapā*). As a nominal derivation of *lā*, *lpā* means "renunciation" or "absolution," that is, giving up, taking leave of, and seeking absolution from karmic faults. Another such word is *smā*. Though not recognized in Khmer dictionaries as such, *smā* (also spelled *samā* or *smār*) appears to be derived from Pali *khamā* or Sanskrit *kṣamā* (cf. Thai *samā/ṣamā*; Lao *saḥmā*), with the sense "to forgive/absolve" or "to seek forgiveness/absolution."

One manuscript combines several of these terms together into one long title: "Prayer of absolution to seek forgiveness and take leave of sins, faults, and carelessness toward creatures great and small, parents, teachers, the Sun, the Moon, the God of Fire, the Goddess of Water, the earth, and the water [sic]" (*lpā smā lā pāp lā doḥ lā pramād satv tūc ddhaṃ niṅ māṭāpīṭā grū ācāry braḥ ādit braḥ cand' braḥ agī gaṅgā ṭī dik*). This version of the title, though slightly convoluted at the end, conveniently summarizes what the poem is about: acknowledging all of the possible ways we have harmed others, seeking forgiveness from those we have harmed, and wishing to be freed from any possible karmic effects of our negative actions. When recited in a deathbed context, the list of sins in "Absolving All Faults" enacts a kind of life review for the dying. It offers a final chance to reflect back on any harmful actions taken in the course of one's life that could lead to karmic retribution in the future.

Many of the sins described in "Absolving All Faults" seem impossible to avoid. Some lie beyond conscious control, such as hurting our mothers during pregnancy or infancy. Other sins may be hard to avoid given the norms of Cambodian culture at the time the poem was composed: killing animals for food, beating troublesome cats and dogs, shouting at one's students, erecting shrines to non-Buddhist deities, consulting astrologers, and drinking liquor to ward off evil spirits. The text asks for absolution from these acts but does not ask people to stop eating meat, refrain from berating their pupils, disrespect tutelary deities, or contravene traditional practices for averting malevolent ghosts.

Part of the genius of "Absolving All Faults" is the recognition that being human entails some degree of violence to the natural world, animals, and other people. We cannot live a blameless life, entirely free of harm to fellow human beings, plant and animal food sources, and the earth, air, and water that sustain us. The poem makes clear that all such forms of violence are reprehensible, and indeed have grave karmic consequences. But by acknowledging that we have caused harm and vowing to "take leave" of all such sins—that is, to never commit them again—we can repair ourselves and the world.

The opening phrase of the text, "O Venerable Blessed One!" (*bhante bhagavā*), signals that the poem is a prayer addressed to the Buddha. While this phrase occurs occasionally in the Tipiṭaka and the commentaries, in the Cambodian context, *bhante bhagavā* is more likely to be a direct reference to a noncanonical Pali repentance chant intoned in ordination ceremonies as well as daily rituals of worship:

> Permit me, O Venerable Blessed One, I pay homage! O Venerable, absolve all of my faults. Whatever merit has been done by me should be rejoiced in by my Master. Whatever merit has been done by my Master should be given to me. Excellent, excellent, I rejoice![31]

After this opening invocation to the Buddha, the text asks for absolution of any sins incurred in utero or shortly after birth. Buddhist texts describe the experience of gestation and parturition as painful and distressing for the fetus as well as the mother.[32] "Ten lunar months" is considered a typical pregnancy. "A fierce wind blew: / the force of fate" refers to the Pali term *kammajavāta*, the "wind born of karma," which means the movements within the mother's body that reposition the fetus's head and initiate labor. "The final wall that rings the world" translates *cakkavāḷa*, a term used in Pali cosmologies to refer to a circular wall at the edge of the universe. "A blazing fire for nine full days" invokes a Southeast Asian practice of postpartum healing known as "roasting over the fire" (*āṃṅ bhlöṅ* in Khmer), in which a new mother is expected to recover on a bed with burning coals placed underneath.[33]

"Absolving All Faults" then details sins committed during childhood and as a young monk. "Vengeance" and "Karmic traces, wanting revenge" refer to Khmer concepts of *verā*, *bier*, or *kamm bier* (from Pali *vera* and Sanskrit *vaira*), all of which mean "rancor" or "hostility." The basic idea is that actions that harm others leave behind traces that can ripen into unpleasant consequences. In the Cambodian context, this kind of vile karma is personalized, being projected onto specific beings who have been hurt by our actions and therefore seek revenge, perpetuating a cyclic sequence of violence that can last several lifetimes. To take leave of all such rancor and hostility means to acknowledge the pain we have caused, ask for forgiveness, and make a firm intention to end the round of revenge.

After describing faults committed against animals and drinking alcohol in violation of Buddhist law, the author lists several dozen disfiguring illnesses, skin diseases, and congenital abnormalities, all of which are thought to be the result of having harmed others in a previous existence. Not all of the terms used to describe these medical conditions are still in use today, and they pose multiple challenges in translation. Further comparative work is necessary to determine the precise referents of the illnesses enumerated in the poem.

After asking to be absolved from violating the five precepts—killing, stealing, sexual misconduct, lying, and using intoxicants—the text gives a detailed account of the various ways people misbehave at Buddhist monasteries. These include activities that violate the sanctity of the temple ("cart races and elephant rides"), wearing inappropriate dress ("hair in a turban, shoes on my feet"), or simply failing to show proper respect ("Chin in my palm, I chatted with my neighbors, / thinking of other places"). A "shrine for a tutelary spirit" refers to a small religious building erected for *anak tā* or other local spirits.

The text closes with a short set of aspirations. The phrase "may I forsake a monarch's crown, / even my spouse, even our children" invokes the bodhisattva path of extreme generosity, necessary for fulfilling the perfections required for buddhahood, as practiced by the Buddha in his life as Prince Vessantara and in many other previous births.

23. Filial Debts

Title: raṃḷk guṇ mātāpitā-7
Literal: Recollection of the Virtues of Parents
Meter: *bāky 7* (7-7-7-7)

Meter: Unrhymed *bāky 7* (7-7-7-7)
Melody: *raṃḷk guṇ* (C-E♭-E-F-G-B♭ = Cm^7-C^7)
Stanzas: 8
Author: Anonymous
Date: Nineteenth or early twentieth century
Khmer: Nuon Saṃ-ân, *Gihippatipatti gharāvāsadharm* (2547), 62–63.
English: Walker, "Unfolding Buddhism," 1442–43.
French: Bernon, "Le rituel de la « grande probation annuelle »," 499–500 [12-stanza version].
Edition: Walker, "Unfolding Buddhism," 1442–43.
Sources: UB038, 77b–79b, raḷik guṇ mātāpitā; UB065, 34b–35a, sūm raṃḷk mātāpitā ṭèl mān guṇ dhṅan'; Kaṅ Phū, Untitled [notebook], 83.

The eight-stanza version translated here is the most commonly recited version in Cambodia. An older twelve-stanza version includes the memorable line: the debts we owe our parents are "heavier than the unweighable earth / taller than the summit of the world" (*dhṅan' lös pṛthabī it upameyy / phut huos visăy sumerā*).[34]

"Giving, ethics, and meditation" (*dāna sīla bhāvanā*) refer to the three foundations of merit-making for laypeople.

24. Asking for Mother's Forgiveness

Title: khamā dos aubuk mtāy
Literal: Asking for parents' forgiveness from faults
Meter: *bāky 7* (7-7-7-7)
Meter: Unrhymed *bāky 7* (7-7-7-7)
Melody: *sāṅ braḥ phnuos* (C-E-F-G-B♭ = C^7)
Stanzas: 8
Author: Anonymous
Date: Twentieth century
English: Walker, "Stirring and Stilling," 21–22.

Edition: Walker, "Stirring and Stilling," 21–22.
Source: Transcribed from a recorded performance by Ṇet M''aṃ (Net Mom), 2008.

Like "Absolving All Sins" (#22), this text references a traditional Cambodian understanding of pregnancy, namely that food that is too "salty, spicy, hot, or cold" can disturb the growing fetus. The three treasures, or *sampatti*, refer to the fortunate attainments of the human world, the heavens, and nirvana.

25. Orphan's Lament

Title: daṃnuoñ kūn kaṃbrā
Meter: *bāky 7* (4-4-4-4)
Meter: Rhymed *bāky 7* (4-4-4-4)
Melody: *daṃnuoñ* (C-E♭-F-G-B♭ = Cm^7)
Stanzas: 9
Author: Anonymous
Date: Twentieth century
English: Walker, "Stirring and Stilling," 19–20.
Edition: Walker, "Stirring and Stilling," 19–20.
Source: Transcribed from a recorded performance by Köt R''ān (Koet Ran), 2011.

The word for orphan in Khmer, *kūn kaṃbrā*, can refer to those who have lost one or both parents.

26. Hungry Ghosts' Lament

Title: daṃnuoñ pret raṅ kamm
Meter: *bāky 7* (4-4-4-4)
Form: Unrhymed *bāky 7* (4-4-4-4)
Melody: *daṃnuoñ pret* (C-E-F-G-A-B♭ = C^7add^6)

Stanzas: 28
Author: Bejr Sukhā (1949–2010)
Date: 1980s or 1990s, no later than 2001
English: Walker, "Quaking and Clarity," 45–46 (excerpt).
Source: Transcribed from a recorded performance by Bejr Sukhā (Pech Sokha), 2001.

Bejr Sukhā's iconic performance of "Hungry Ghosts' Lament" has been broadcast on national radio every Pchum Ben for at least the past two decades. Penned in the 1980s or 1990s, it has since become a staple of Pchum Ben rituals throughout Cambodia and the diaspora. In his most widely distributed recording, from 2001, Bejr Sukhā is accompanied by an unknown musician on the *dra so* ("tro sao"), a two-string fiddle related to the Chinese *erhu*. The author reads the first three stanzas out loud, recites the next ten (from "Parents live for their children" until "bitter, lonely, miserable") in an elaborate *smūtr* melody, and then returns to a normal reading voice for the remainder of the poem.

"Making merit can't beat wine" translates a line that means literally "festivals for making offerings are not delicious; only alcohol is delicious" (*puṇy dān min chṅāñ' chṅāñ' tè srā*). This prefigures a line near the end of the text: "Don't make offerings at the bar!", which is literally "don't take a liquor shop as a field for making merit" (*kuṃ yak tiem srā dhvö srè puṇy*).

The wretched lives of hungry ghosts, or *pret*, depicted in the poem may be found throughout Buddhist literature: "Only eating pus, blood, and shit, / walking alone, with a hideous face." A distinct Khmer emphasis, however, is the notion that *pret* suffer in this way because they killed animals to feed their own children: "This is what comes to parents / who harm others to feed their kids"; "Your parents killed and harmed creatures / to find you food and nourish your life." No traditional Cambodian texts advocate vegetarianism; the sin of killing animals is considered an inevitable part of life. Thus "Hungry Ghosts' Lament" portrays rebirth as a *pret* as a potentially unavoidable consequence of loving one's own children. The responsibility falls to children to save their deceased relatives through performing acts of merit.

According to Khmer belief, during the two-week period leading up to Pchum Ben, Yama lets the *pret* leave their miserable realm to find their families. Many Cambodians believe that in order to maximize their chances of feeding unseen relatives who have been reborn as hungry ghosts, they should visit seven temples with offerings of handmade rice balls and other snacks.[35] These ideas are referenced when the *pret* complains, "I've gone to all the temples, / but you've never come at all" (*ilūv ṭör rak grap' tė vatt / min ghöñ mak soḥ kūn bisī*).

27. Offerings for Monks and Ancestors

Title: thvāy pāy piṇḍ
Literal: Offering rice balls
Meter: *brahmagīti* (5-6-5-6)
Form: Extended into unrhymed *paṭhyāvatt* (8-8-8-8)
Melody: Unknown
Stanzas: 11 (stanzas 10–20 of the 21-stanza text)
Author: Anonymous
Date: Eighteenth or nineteenth century
English: Walker, "Unfolding Buddhism," 1263–66.
Edition: Walker, "Unfolding Buddhism," 1263–66.
Sources: UB003, 6a–8a, dharm sūtr thvāy pāy piṇḍ.

The first ten stanzas of this poem, not translated here, list symbols on the Buddha's feet, similar to "Hymn to the Buddha's Feet" (#43). The translated portion describes a bounty of offerings made to the Sangha on Pchum Ben for the sake of transferring merit to ancestors. The transference involves several elements: a "secure resolution" on the part of the donors to dedicate the merit, an invitation to all deities to "rejoice in our dedication," and a request to the monks to redirect "the swift stream of our merit" to flow to the departed.

The final stanza, not included in my translation, is written in a local form of Pali that loosely translates as:

By this, this charity,
and by this, this morality,
may I realize nirvana
as a leading disciple [of a future Buddha].[36]

28. Dedication of Merit

Title: tejaḥ khñuṃ sāṅ
Literal: By grace of what I've built
Meter: *kākagati* (4-4-4-4-4-4-4)
Form: Unrhymed *kākagati* (4-4-4-4-4-4-4)
Melody: *sūtr rāy* (C-D-B♭ = C)
Stanzas: 4
Author: Anonymous
Date: Seventeenth or eighteenth centuries
Khmer: Ras' Kèv, *Gihipratipatti bises bistār*, 193.
French: San Sarin, "Les textes liturgiques fondamentaux," 126; Bernon, "Le manuel des maîtres," 577.
Edition: San Sarin "Les textes liturgiques fondamentaux," 125.
Sources: Kaṅ Phū, Untitled [notebook], 4.

This old dedication poem, found in various versions, is recited frequently in Buddhist rituals. Many older Cambodians know it by heart.

"May all my vows / be soon realized" translates a line that is literally "[when] my thoughts arise / [may they] be my success" (*gaṃnit khñuṃ köt / kaṃṇöt khñuṃ mān*). *Kaṃnöt*, which usually means "birth," here takes on an extended meaning of "fortune," "success," or "capability."[37] The phase "there is thought [but] no success" (*mān gaṃnit it kaṃṇöt*) means "the inability to bring one's ideas to fruition."[38] The poem suggests the opposite condition, in which all of one's wholesome aspirations come true.

"Gone and to come" is literally "seven generations" (*prāṃbīr santān*). This is most commonly understood as one's own generation plus three older generations (ending with great-grandparents) and three younger generations (ending with great-grandchildren).

29. Funeral March

Title: saṃleṅ klaṅ khèk
Literal: The sound of *klong khaek*
Meter: *paṭhyāvatt* (8-8-8-8)
Form: Unrhymed *paṭhyāvatt* (8-8-8-8)
Melody: *parābhavasūtr* (C-E♭-F-G-A-B♭ = Cm^7)
Stanzas: 5
Author: Lī Suvīr
Date: 1991
Khmer: Lī Suvīr, *Maṙtak braḥ buddhasāsanā khmèr*, 49–50.
English: Walker, "Stirring and Stilling," 16–17.
Edition: Lī Suvīr, *Maṙtak braḥ buddhasāsanā khmèr*, 49–50.

Lī Suvīr's "Funeral March" invokes the power of music for the dead to inspire the living. A "drum-and-oboe dirge" refers to the music of the *klaṅ khèk* ("klong khaek") ensemble, consisting of several long, India-style drums (the Khmer name comes from Thai *klaaṅ khèk*, meaning "Indian drum") and a multi-reed, oboe-like woodwind instrument. Also known in Khmer as "victory drum" (*sgar jhnaḥ*), this ensemble is synonymous with funeral processions in Cambodia. Its repertoire features slow, wailing melodies from the high-pitched oboe punctuated by sparse beats on the drums.[39]

30. This Life Is Short

Title: trailakkha(ṇ) «aniccā saṅkhār»
Literal: The Three Marks, beginning with "This Life Is Short."
Meter: *bāky* 7 (7-7-7-7)
Form: Rhymed *bāky* 7 (7-7-7-7)
Melody: *mahāmāyā* (C-E-F-G-B♭ = C^7)
Stanzas: 10
Author: Ek Ñịm (revising an older, anonymous text)
Date: 1933 (revision; original from late nineteenth or early twentieth century)
English: Walker, "Stirring and Stilling," 13–15.
Khmer: Ek Ñịm, *Girimāmanadasūtr prè jā bāky*, 17–18.
Edition: Walker, "Unfolding Buddhism," 1409–11.
Sources: UB005, 49b–51a, dhaŕm aniccā rūp; UB006, 61a–61b; UB014, 68b–70b, dha'mmasaṅvèk; UB016, 27a–28a; UB016, 31a–32b; UB018, 46a–48a, braḥ dhaŕm saṅkhār min dieṅ; UB019, 5a–6b, braḥ dhaŕm saṅkhār min dieṅ; UB020, 37b–39b, braḥ trai lakkha(ṇ) ṭoy saṅkhèpp khlīy°; UB025, 53a–54b; UB036, 50b–51b, braḥ trai lakkha(ṇ) saṅkhep pad bāky prāṃbīr; UB038, 51a–52a, braḥ trai lakkha(ṇ); UB039, 80a–81b, trai lakkha(ṇ)/ trai lakkha(ṇ) ṭoy saṅkhep; UB043, 66b–67b, trai lakkha(ṇ) pad bāky prāṃbīr; UB044, 39a–40b, trai lakkha(ṇ) dī 1; UB057, 123b–125a; UB060 38a–39a, aniccā saṅkhār; UB065, 38b–39a, braḥ trai lakkha(ṇ) saṅkhep.

The title and opening phrase of this poem (*aniccā saṅkhār*, "Conditioned Things Are Impermenent," or "This Life Is Short") recalls a famous Pali verse:

> Impermanent, alas, are all conditioned things.
> They have the nature to arise and pass away.

Having arisen, they disappear.
Their complete stilling is bliss.[40]

This verse, drawn from the *Dīgha Nikāya*, among other canonical sources, is one of the most important Pali stanzas recited in Cambodian funeral rituals. The climax of the funeral involves a monastic rolling up and removing a white shroud from the corpse while intoning this verse. This is known as the *paṅsukūl* rite, from the Pali for "rag-robe" (*paṃsukūla*). The basic idea is that Buddhist renunciates should make their own robes from discarded cloth, including shrouds for corpses. They should wash, dye, and sew these scraps into proper robes. When a monastic removes the shroud for this purpose, the dead person may gain great merit. The shroud stands in for the skin of the deceased, and thus their final gift is also symbolically a gift of the body (Pali: *ajjhattikadāna*, "internal gift"), one of the most celebrated donations in Buddhist texts.[41]

"This Life Is Short," along with "This Heap Called a Body" (#33) and "Song for the Hour of Death" (#34), evoke a Cambodian mortuary practice from the eighteenth and nineteenth centuries: the disposal of bodies in charnel grounds or deep in the forest. While cremation is the norm for Khmer Buddhists today, these poems describe how corpses were once hauled off to the woods to be feasted on by birds and beasts. The message to the living is simple: one day we too will be shouldered off to the jungle.

31. The Four Thieves

Title: aciraṃ vata yaṃ kāyo-gāthā samrāy
Literal: Bilingual version of Pali stanza beginning with "Soon, alas, this body."
Meter: *brahmagīti* (5-6-5-6)
Form: Extended into unrhymed *paṭhyāvatt* (8-8-8-8)
Stanzas: 49 (fragment); only stanzas 35–48 translated.

Melody: Unknown
Author: Anonymous
Date: Eighteenth or nineteenth century
English: Walker, "Unfolding Buddhism," 1309–16.
Edition: Walker, "Unfolding Buddhism," 1302–09.
Sources: UB006, 59b–60b; UB020, 41b–47b.

The translated text is just a portion of the original poem, which does not survive in full in any manuscript known to me. The first sixteen stanzas offer a bilingual Pali-Khmer unpacking of the key terms relevant to the suffering of birth (Pali: *jāti*), old age (*jarā*), sickness (*byādhi*), and death (*maraṇa*). The following eighteen stanzas perform a similar bilingual analysis and commentary on a Pali verse about the inevitability of death:

> Soon, alas, this body
> will lie on the earth,
> thrown away, unconscious,
> useless as a rotting log.[42]

This is followed by the thirteen stanzas included in this book. The selected excerpt begins with an exhortation to study meditation (Khmer: *kammaṭṭhān vipassanā*), including the recitation of preparatory mantras (*parikamm cāṃ bhāvanā*). To my knowledge, the simile on the four thieves that follows does not appear elsewhere in Pali Buddhist literature, despite the poet's claim to the contrary.

32. The True Fate of Flesh

Title: *trailakkha(ṇ) «rāl' rūp dāṃṅ as'»*
Literal: The Three Marks, beginning with "All you people."
Meter: *kākagati* (4-4-4-4-4-4-4)
Form: Unrhymed *kākagati* (4-4-4-4-4-4-4)
Melody: *trailakkha(ṇ)* (C-E♭-E-F-A-B♭ = C, F^7)

Stanzas: 13
Author: Anonymous
Date: Nineteenth or early twentieth century
English: Walker, "Unfolding Buddhism," 1102–5.
Edition: Walker, "Unfolding Buddhism," 1102–5.
Source: UB033, 57a–59b, braḥ lakhañāṇ/braḥ traiy° lakkhañāṇ ṭoy° saṅkhep.

This poem turns around the Khmer term *rūp* (Pali: *rūpa*), which in Cambodian conception includes the body but also materiality, embodiment, and even humanity itself. It is translated here in many different ways: "bodies," "this body," "your body," "people" (in the sense of "everybody"), "human life," "flesh and bones," and "carnality." Cambodian texts distinguish the physical body from the multiple "souls" (Khmer: *braliṅ*) of a person, here translated as "spirits."[43] The *braliṅ* animate beings during their lives but are generally not believed to be involved in the process of rebirth. After the body dies and decays, the *braliṅ* are left to fend for themselves; only the mind, or consciousness in a Buddhist sense (*viññāṇa*), is understood to continue into the next life. In "The True Fate of Flesh," the spirits are said to seek refuge in the Dharma after the death of the body, though what this means is not specified.

The phrase "Count your merit; pray drop by drop" is literally "meditate and dedicate [merit by intoning the chant that begins with] *iminā* and pouring water" (*bhāvanā pañjūn / iminā crūc dịk*). This refers to a widespread Theravada practice of slowly pouring out water from a small vessel, either onto the ground or into a different container, while chanting a Pali verse for dedicating the merit of one's good deeds to all beings. The *iminā* chant, as found in Cambodian manuscripts, goes as follows:

By this act of merit,
may all those of great virtue—
preceptors, masters,

supporters, parents, relatives,
the Sun, the Moon, the King,
and all people I owe a debt;
Brahmas, Māras, Indras,
World-Guardians, and other deities;
Yama, friendly people
neutral people, and enemies—
may all beings rejoice
in the merits I've made.
May you win threefold bliss
and swiftly attain the Deathless.[44]

In the Pali verses, as understood in Cambodia, the words *guṇuttarā* and *guṇavantā* can either be construed as "those endowed with virtue" or "those owed a debt of gratitude," both in reference to the central notion of *guṇ*.

33. This Heap Called a Body

Title: trailakkha(ṇ) «rūpakkhandho»
Literal: The Three Marks, beginning with "This Heap Called a Body."
Meter: *kākagati* (4-4-4-4-4-4-4)
Form: Each *kākagati* stanza translated as five lines of free verse (X-X-X-X-X)
Melody: *trailakkha(ṇ)* (C-E♭-E-F-A-B♭ = C, F^7) or *buddhapād prāṃ ṭhān* (C-E-F-G-A-B♭ = C^7add^6)
Stanzas: 34
Author: Anonymous
Date: Eighteenth or nineteenth century
Khmer: Lī Suvīr, *Maŕtak braḥ buddhasāsanā khmèr*, 51–52 [short excerpt].
English: Walker, "This Heap Called a Body"; Walker, "Unfolding Buddhism," 1106–14.
Edition: Walker, "Unfolding Buddhism," 1106–14.

Sources: UB020, 85b–92a, rūppakhandh; UB033, 52a–55a and 56a–57a, braḥ lakhañāṇ/braḥ traiy° lakkhañāṇ ṭoy° saṅkhep (middle missing); UB060, 26a–28b, accīraṃ prè; UB065, 39b–41b, o! rūpakkhandho; Ḍuk Ât, *Prajuṃ dhammasaṅveg nānā* [notebook], 221–25 [incomplete].

"This Heap Called a Body" offers a detailed portrait of the process of death, from horrific pain on the deathbed to the gruesome decay of the body. The poet imagines the inner experience of the dying, as they are slowly bound and pummeled by the minions of Death himself, and the lonely regrets of the departed ghost, permanently severed from its now-defunct corpse.

Many Dharma songs are referred to by their first line in Khmer. "This Heap Called a Body" follows this pattern. The English title translates the phrase that opens the poem, the inflected Pali compound *rūpakkhandho* (from Pali *rūpakkhandha*). Literally "the aggregate of form," *rūpakkhandha* covers the physical aspect of the human person as well as materiality in its broadest sense. Early Buddhist texts divide our experience of the world into five "heaps" (Pali: *khandha*): form, feeling, perception, formations, and consciousness. Our physical bodies and the material world they interact with belong to the first heap.

The remainder of the first stanza, composed in a mix of Khmer and inflected Pali, goes on to mention three of the elements (water, earth, and fire; Pali: *dhātu*) that comprise the body and its various sense faculties (*indriya*), including the ears, the eyes, and the tongue. Other Pali phrases appear throughout the text, including "Soon this body / shall be cast away / or so the scriptures say" (*ayaṃ kāyo / duraṃ gato*), which recalls the Pali verse unpacked in "The Four Thieves" (#31, *aciraṃ vat'ayaṃ kāyo . . .*).

The opening eleven stanzas describe the internal workings of death. First, Yama's henchmen ("Death's little men" or "Death's minions"; Khmer: *pamrö braḥ yam* or *yamapāl*) tie us down and seal the sense doors. Only seeking "the path of saints" can bring deliverance at this point, namely finding the crystal spheres (Khmer: *ṭuoṅ kèv*) that mark the stages leading to arhatship. Then the wind element, carried by the breath, slowly drains from the body. "In, out, held" refers to three modes of breathing or three kinds of wind important in esoteric meditation practices: inhalation (*assāsavāta*), exhalation (*passāsavāta*), and the held breath (*nisvāsavāta*), restrained in the abdomen by the diaphragm (Bizot, *Le figuier à cinq branches*, 129; note that the terms for exhalation and inhalation are sometimes switched). Some esoteric texts call these the winds (*khyal'*) of the Vinaya (inhalation), Sutta (exhalation), and Abhidhamma (held) (Walker, "Unfolding Buddhism," 493). At the end of life, these winds can reverse direction in painful, contorted ways, suffocating the dying person. Such an interpretation appears in a poem of a similar genre called "The Three Marks, beginning with 'Form is painful, form is impermanent'" (*trailakkha(ṇ) «rūpaṃ dukkhaṃ rūpaṃ aniccaṃ»*):[45]

Here I'll explain
what's natural for all,
ourselves and others,
at the time of death.
As death awaits,
the bodies of beings
are battered by winds.

The Vinaya winds
blow up the abdomen,
rushing into the belly.
Fire burns the heart,
flipping it over.
How painful, near death,
and miserable thereafter!

The Abhidhamma winds,
having gathered above,

blow down as one,
crushing the heart
within the chest.
How pained the heart
when these winds unite![46]

Thus the natural processes of the breath turn against us at the end of life: "You gasp for air. Your body goes slack / as you lay weak, helpless on your bed." Once breathing stops, family members may place a piece of silver in the corpse's mouth ("They slot a coin through your lips"). A serving of betel leaf and areca nut, prepared with lime, may also be slid between the teeth of the deceased.

This description of the process of death is followed by an account of the ghost after death. The term used in the text is *bhūt* (from Pali *bhūta*, "existed" or "has-been"). This term commonly means a malevolent wandering ghost in Khmer.[47] In a Buddhist context, *bhūt* is understood more specifically as the remnants of the corpse's four basic elements of earth, water, fire, and wind (*catubhūta*), which may continue to haunt the living.[48] To prevent the *bhūt* from returning from the forest to the village, some Cambodians will score a cross in the dirt or block the trails with thorns.

The description of the decaying corpse in "This Heap Called a Body" draws on Pali meditations on the foul (*asubhakammaṭṭhāna*), as detailed in the *Visuddhimagga* and other classical treatises.[49] The lines "Study the virtues within your body / that lead to freedom from pain" refer to esoteric meditation on various *guṇ* inside our bodies as a path to reach liberation.

34. Song for the Hour of Death

Title: trailakkha(ṇ) «rūpaṃ dukkhaṃ dukkh rūp ruom khlāṃṅ»
Literal: The Three Marks, beginning with "Pain binds your body, intensifying."
Meter: *kākagati* (4-4-4-4-4-4-4)

Form: Free verse
Melody: *trailakkha(ṇ)* (C-E♭-E-F-A-B♭ = C, F^7)
Stanzas: 60
Author: Anonymous
Date: Eighteenth–nineteenth century
Khmer: Unknown publication by Cāp Bin, dating to 1962, referenced in UB026 (partial; stanzas 3–4 and 6–38 only)
English: Walker, "Unfolding Buddhism," 1148–62.
Edition: Walker, "Unfolding Buddhism," 1148–62.
Sources: UB001, 27b–36a, braḥ trailakkh pūr"āṇ; UB014, 107b–118b, lākkh'ñāṇ; UB015, 107b–99a; UB016, 22b–27a; UB026, 44a–47a, dhaŕm sāvapād pad kākagati/ dhaŕm trăy lakkhaṇ, with the note: khñuṃ pān ṭak sraṅ bī krāṃṅ pūrāṇ jā yūr aṅvèṅ mak höy _ lok ṭāk' jhmoḥ hau thā (dhaŕm sāvapād) tè binity rien sūtr dau _ hau dhaŕm trăy lakkhaṇ _ ká pān.

"Song for the Hour of Death" parallels and expands upon the core themes of "This Heap Called a Body" (#33). Both texts are intended to be recited for the dying as well as for those who are caring for them. "Song for the Hour of Death" places a greater emphasis on the principle of not-self: this body isn't ours, so how can we wrest it from the powerful cycles of life and death?

The phrase "the thirty-two vessels" (*sar-sai dāṃṅ sām sip saṅ*) appears in several older Khmer poems. The word for "vessel," *sar-sai*, is multivalent: it can mean our arteries, veins, nerves, tendons, sinews, or fibers. The number thirty-two appears to refer to a long-forgotten anatomical understanding of how to count the fibrous or tubular parts of the human body.

References to "a lace-hemmed skirt, / an embroidered silk blouse, a blended scarf" reflect fashion trends from eighteenth- and nineteenth-century Cambodia. Close-cropped hair, often dramatically shaved in an undercut style, was in vogue for elite women:

"You trim your hair, massage it with oil, and shave the sides so you can show off."

The lines "Such attachments bind your neck, waist, and ankles, / your whole body shackled like a thrice-bound corpse" refer to a funerary custom that survives to the present. The three ropes (Khmer: *khsè pās*) used to bind the body are symbolically conceived as our attachments to our children, our spouse, and our possessions.[50]

The phrase "forty-five subjects / the masters selected for meditation" is a reference to traditional *kammaṭṭhān* meditation, though it is not clear which practices count among these forty-five. In the *Visuddhimagga*, only forty subjects of meditation are listed; Cambodian manuals often list upward of sixty topics.[51] Further references to meditation in the text include "all five of the obstacles" (the five *nīvaraṇa* that impede progress in meditation) and the "jewels of virtue" (Khmer: *guṇ kèv*), the crystal spheres that secure the attainment of the various stages of sainthood (*magg phal*).

The closing section on proper decorum ("Learn to speak softly; keep your voice reined in") recalls a genre of Khmer didactic poetry known as *cpāp'*.[52]

35. A Lesson in Meditation

Title: kāyagatā
Literal: Body-connected [awareness]
Meter: *kākagati* (4-4-4-4-4-4-4)
Form: Unrhymed *kākagati*, presented in three lines (12-12-4)
Melody: Unknown
Stanzas: 55
Author: Anonymous
Date: Eighteenth or nineteenth century
English: Walker, "Unfolding Buddhism," 1081–94.
Edition: Walker, "Unfolding Buddhism," 1081–94.
Sources: UB014, 98a–107b, braḥ kāyagatā; UB015, 1 and 115b–107b, braḥ kāyyagatār.

This poem offers the most in-depth description of esoteric meditation in this book. As a Dharma song recited in deathbed rites, "A Lesson in Meditation" helps dying practitioners recall the four foundations of awareness (Pali: *satipaṭṭhāna*)—body, feelings, mind, and mental factors—and their associated signs (*nimitta*) and counterpart images (*paṭibhāganimitta*).

After an initial exposition of the four foundations, the text articulates an opening propitiation (*ārādhanā*, literally "invitation"): "May I commence with a firm vow to develop / wisdom and faith within this life to grasp the objects / of meditation." This is a crucial first step in esoteric meditation systems in Southeast Asia and Sri Lanka.[53]

The poem invokes the heart syllables NA MA BA DA, connecting them to the four foundations of awareness. These same syllables can stand in for a range of other meanings in esoteric practice. The most common sense is the four elements (water, earth, fire, and wind). In the Khmer tradition, these are considered the inner virtues or qualities of human beings (*guṇ khāṅ knuṅ*) in contrast to NA MO BU DDHĀ YA, cited in "The Twenty-Four Vowels" (#20), which stand for the five qualities of the external world (the four elements plus space).[54]

"A Lesson in Meditation" invokes two more sets of heart syllables, NA MA ARAHAṂ and U Ū ARAHAṂ. The first set is connected to the *guṇ* of our mothers: "short syllables fixed as letters / for the virtues of the bright jewel inherited / from our mother." Since mothers are connected to the water element, their *guṇ* is "like the ocean." The second set of syllables is the legacy of our fathers. The earth element's association with paternal *guṇ* means that these syllables embody "the earth disc in all four realms."

The poem links the maternal and paternal *guṇ* of NA MA ARAHAṂ and U Ū ARAHAṂ to two different jewels (Khmer: *kèv*) that abide within our bodies, the *maṇijoti* and *maṇiratana* jewels, respectively. Together with the *maṇipaduma* and *vaiḍūrya* jewels, they comprise four jewels: one from our mother; one from our father; one from the *Paṭṭhāna*, the last book of the Abhidhamma, also described as "a Buddha's sprout" (Khmer: *banlak*; cf. Pali *buddhaṅkura*, "a bodhisattva or nascent Buddha"); and one from the Buddha himself. These jewels or crystal spheres presumably represent the four stages of awakening in the Southeast Asian esoteric meditation systems, which culminate in arhatship or buddhahood.

The "city of the body" (Pali: *kāyanagara*) is a common image in Khmer, Lao, and Thai meditation texts.[55] "A Lesson in Meditation" combines this image with the idea of the body as a tree. The "two round bushes" are our eyes; the "two gates," our nostrils; the "gate made for the lord of the realm," our mouth; the two "bushes . . . on the sides," our ears; and the "the forest of Himavant," our hair.[56] The text also describes the body as the city of Ayudhyā, Rāma's capital in the *Rāmakerti* (the title used for Khmer versions of the *Rāmāyaṇa*). Ayudhyā is symbolically understood as the seat of the meditator's mind.[57] The poem calls the mind itself "Prince [and/or] Princess Mind," the hero or heroine of many allegorical narratives in traditional meditation texts.[58]

The middle portion of the poem, from "The first foundation of awareness centers the body" to "it takes its gem atop the city / of Ayudhya," summarizes the signs and counterpart signs that are supposed to arise during meditation on the four foundations of awareness. While signs and counterpart signs are described in the *Visuddhimagga* and other Pali sources, they are interpreted and developed in distinctive ways in the esoteric Theravada meditation manuals. In these systems, the signs and counterpart signs usually take the form of colors and/or spheres of light.[59] In "A Lesson in Meditation," the signs and counterpart signs are unusually vivid and detailed, incorporating colored rays, complex shapes in motion, cosmological metaphors, and physical sensations.

The above is only a partial guide to this challenging, multilayered poem. Not all aspects can be satisfactorily explained, for "A Lesson in Meditation" belongs to a tradition in which secrets, lineages, and initiations are highly valued. The text itself alludes to confidential instructions from one's teacher: "The concentrated meditator knows these [four] letters / in secret ways but establishes just three of them / as instructed."

36. THE FORTUNATE EON

Title: trailakkha(ṇ) «rūpaṃ dukkhaṃ» purāṇ
Literal: The Three Marks, beginning with "Rūpaṃ dukkhaṃ," old version.
Meter: *kākagati* (4-4-4-4-4-4-4)
Form: Extended unrhymed *kākagati*, presented in three lines (12+, 12+, 4+).
Melody: *trailakkha(ṇ)* (C-E♭-E-F-A-B♭ = C, F⁷)
Stanzas: 116
Author: Anonymous
Date: 1832
Khmer: Sèm Sūr, *Prajuṃ dhaŕm pad*, 86–105.
English: Walker, "Unfolding Buddhism," 1117–46.
Edition: Walker, "Unfolding Buddhism," 1117–46.
Sources: UB005, 31b–44b, braḥ trailakkha(ṇ); UB015, 67a–86a, braḥ traiy lā'kkh saṅkhèp pakaraṇ; UB018, 50a–53b, dhaŕm braḥ trailakkha(ṇ) (explicit missing); UB023, 29a–34b (explicit missing), with final note: *sleḥ tè puṇṇeḥ sin evāṃṅ*; UB025, 20a–23a (explicit missing); UB027, 49a–50a and 50b–60b, braḥ trai lakkha(ṇ)/ lakkhaṇañāṇ (explicit missing); UB030, 1–13b and 14 (incipit and explicit missing); UB031, 34a–40b, 42, 43, 45–58b, braḥ traiy° lakkh (lvèv) (middle missing), with opening *namo tassa bhagavato arahato sammāsambuddhassa*; UB034, 36–52b, braḥ traiy° lakkhañān/braḥ traiy° lakkh (incipit missing); UB036, 13a–22b, braḥ trai lakkha(ṇ) rapiep samǎy jān' ṭöm; UB042, 19a–24b, braḥ trai lǎkkkh(ṇ)/lakkhaṇañāṇ, with the incipit *namo tassa bhagavato arahato sammāsambuddhassa* (explicit missing); UB047, 2b–17b, dhammasaṅvek; UB048, 14a–

26b, braḥ trai lakkh rapiep samăy jān' ṭöm/trailakkha(ṇ); UB052, 32b–41a, with incipit *pad kākkati* (explicit missing); UB055, 7b–18b, trai lakkh; UB057, 27a–51b, braḥ traiy° lăkkh/braḥ traiy° lăkkh'; UB060, 40a–49a, trai lakkha(ṇ); UB068, 1–8a (severe water damage; almost entirely illegible) (incipit and explicit missing); FEMC d.620, lpök daṃnāy braḥ buddh trās' 5 braḥ aṅg knuṅ bhaddakapp.

The longest poem translated in this book, "The Fortunate Eon," usually known as *trailakkha(ṇ)* or "The Three Marks" in Khmer, is one of most frequently recopied chants in Cambodian leporello manuscripts. It offers an extended meditation on the passing of time, from the impermanence of our bodies to the flourishing and decay of the Buddhist religion.

The opening stanzas describe the Three Marks of impermanence, suffering, and not-self, though the order is changed to read "form is suffering" (*rūpaṃ dukkhaṃ*), "impermanent" (*aniccaṃ*), and "not the self" (*anattā*).

The first part of the poem recounts the five buddhas of our present "fortunate eon" (*bhaddakappa*), which followed from the previous "empty eon" (*suññakappa*), a period in which neither buddhas nor Buddhist teachings are present. We are briefly introduced to the three buddhas before Gautama, or Shakyamuni, the historical Buddha and the fourth Awakened One of our age. The fifth Buddha, Maitreya, is given special emphasis as our hope for the future. These buddhas gather together in the magnificent city of nirvana, the goal of the practice.

These buddhas, as vessels to help living beings reach the far shore, are described as "five great ships, blazing with jewels." Their destination is the city of nirvana, where "all the buddhas, in vast numbers, uncountable, / resort together in the crystal city, the realm of peace, / incomparable." This description of nirvana echos that found in the noncanonical *Nibbāna Sutta*.[60] Other lines from "The Fortunate Eon" would not be out of place as Mahayana descriptions of Sukhāvatī: "The crystal city resounds in song, with tender tones: / bliss beyond bliss, suffering long gone."

The middle section of the poem emphasizes the dangers of samsara and the importance of cultivating the mind. The meditation instructions provided match those of the esoteric tradition, with lines such as "Make your mind bright as the sun's orb, suffused with light," "Keep your heart bright as the Moon," and "When inner winds are clear and at ease, the centered mind / attains the goal." Other stanzas encourage reflection on the lives of deities and universal monarchs, similar to the *devānussati* practice described briefly in the *Visuddhimagga*.[61]

The final section continues the overall meditation on time through a brief recounting of the history of Buddhism, including the third-century B.C.E. Indian emperor Ashoka; his son, Mahinda, credited with bringing Buddhism to Sri Lanka; the second-century B.C.E. Indo-Greek king Milinda (Menander I), remembered for his debates with the monk Nāgasena, as recorded in the *Milindapañha*; the second-century B.C.E. Sinhala king Duṭṭhagāminī Abhaya (Dutugamunu); and finally the fifth-century Indian exegete Buddhaghosa, known for his travels to Sri Lanka to translate the commentaries from Sinhala to Pali. The dates cited in the poem roughly follow this chronology but are often off by several centuries from what we now know of these historical figures. Moreover, in a Cambodian twist, the poem includes a scene of Buddhaghosa visiting Phnom Penh to translate the Tipiṭaka and its commentaries into Khmer. Though modern historians have no reason to believe such an event ever occurred, the legend reveals much about local conceptions of Buddhist history in nineteenth-century Cambodia.

Likely penned in 1832 C.E. (2375 of the Buddhist era), in the midst of a period of intense warfare and destruction, "The Fortunate Eon" closes with a series of predictions and warnings on further dangers to come as well as the future arrival of a "person of merit" (Khmer: *anak mān puṇy*), a messianic figure who will glorify the teachings of the Buddha once more and usher in an era of peace. This portion of the text varies considerably between different recensions; my presentation here relies on the witness of FEMC d.620, a palm-leaf manuscript held today by the National Museum of Cambodia. As commonly witnessed in Khmer prophetic texts, the predictions are based on the twelve-year cycle of animal years and thus are not always connected to specific calendar years. Moreover, not all of the animal years mentioned in the poem accord with the proper decade years, making the time line hard to interpret. I hope additional manuscripts of "The Fortunate Eon" will eventually be found to help clarify the author's intention in this passage.

37. Lotus Offering to Reach Nirvana

Title: padum thvāy phkā «yöṅ khñuṃ mān citt trek»
Literal: Lotus flower offering, beginning with "Our hearts brim with joy."
Meter: *brahmagīti* (5-6-5-6)
Form: Unrhymed *brahmagīti* (5-6-5-6)
Melody: *laṃ-on* (C-D-E-G-A = C^6)
Stanzas: 9
Author: Anonymous
Date: Nineteenth or early twentieth century
English: Walker, "Unfolding Buddhism," 1287–89.
Edition: Walker, "Unfolding Buddhism," 1287–89.
Sources: UB066, 35a–35b, pūjā phkā caṃboḥ braḥ ratana:trăy.

This poem is a modern adaptation of the much longer and older chant "Lotus Offering to Realize Awakening" (#45). In the original text, the offering of flowers is symbolic; our cupped hands take the form of a lotus. In the new version, the floral gift is specific and concrete: "We take these blossoms / weave them into garlands, / fragrant rings and wreaths." The final goal referenced in the text is the "real bliss" of nirvana. "Step by step" translates *magg phal*, literally "the [four] paths and the [four] fruits," the stages of sainthood that culminate in arhatship.

38. A Prayer for the People

Title: pad sarabhaññ
Literal: Chant in the *sarabhañña* style
Meter: *bāky 7* (7-7-7-7)
Form: Unrhymed *bāky 7* (7-7-7-7)
Melody: *sarabhaññ* (C-E♭-F-G-A♭-B♭ = Cm)
Stanzas: 6
Author: Juon Ṇāt
Date: 1965
Khmer: Jhịm Ŝum, *Pad sarabhaññ*, 8.
English: Walker, "Stirring and Stilling," 10–11.
Edition: Walker, "Stirring and Stilling," 10–11.

Juon Ṇāt, the most celebrated scholar-monk of twentieth-century Cambodia, penned this poem in 1965. It was adopted by the government for use in official ceremonies shortly thereafter, beginning with the Vesak ceremony held at a reliquary in front of the Phnom Penh railway station in 1966.[62] This site, where precious relics from Sri Lanka were installed in 1957 to mark the 2,500th year since the Buddha's nirvana, was the main location for the Cambodian government's celebration of Vesak until 1975.[63]

Today Juon Ṇāt's poem is recited by schoolchildren, adult laypeople, and monastics alike for a variety of school, government, and temple ceremonies. The simple, somber melody, unique to this text, was perfected in 1966 by a group of musicians from the Ministry of Education, in consultation with Juon Ṇāt.[64] The Khmer title comes from the Pali term *sarabhañña*, meaning "vocalic recitation." In the Pali Vinaya, this refers to a recitation style explicitly permitted by the Buddha that preserves the distinctions between long and short vowels.[65]

39. Homage to the Three Jewels

Title: samantapāsādikā-gāthā samrāy
Literal: Stanzas from the Samantapāsādikā, translated into Khmer.
Meter: *brahmagīti* (5-6-5-6)
Form: Unrhymed *brahmagīti* (5-6-5-6)
Melody: *sūtr rāy* (C-D-B♭ = C)
Stanzas: 15
Author: Unknown
Date: Eighteenth or nineteenth centuries
Khmer: Som Suvaṇṇ, *Prajuṃ māghapūjā niṅ visākhapūjā*, 1–4; Ras' Kèv, *Gihipratipatti bises bistār*, 42–44.
English: Walker, "Unfolding Buddhism," 1044–47.
French: San Sarin, "Les textes liturgiques fondamentaux," 171–74.
Edition: Walker, "Unfolding Buddhism," 1044–47.
Sources: UB026, 24b–25b and 27b, trairatanappaṇāma buddharatanappaṇāma, with the note: *pālī pad indavajīr _ samrāy pad brahmagīti* (Pali stanzas 1-3), bāky prakās sūm sec ktī sukh, with the note: *pālī pad indavajīr _ samrāy pad brahmagīti* (Pali stanza 4); UB044, 76b–79a, namaskār braḥ ratanatrăy yokappakoṭīhi pi prè jā kāby 1 piep diet.

An old, anonymous Khmer translation of the first four stanzas of the *Samantapāsādikā*, Buddhaghosa's commentary on the Vinaya, which reads:

> He who for measureless billions of eons
> practiced severe austerities and toiled
> for the sake of the world, our Protector:
> Homage to him of great compassion!

Unawakened to the Dharma of the buddhas,
living beings cycle through various worlds:
Homage to that excellent Dharma, which cuts
the net of defilements, starting with ignorance.

I bow my head to the Sangha of the Noble Ones,
endowed with conduct, concentration, wisdom,
freedom, knowledge, and illumination,
the field for all those who seek the good.

Worshipping the Three Jewels,
always to be worshipped in this way,
I receive a vast stream of merit:
May all calamities be destroyed![66]

The Pali stanzas are written in the *indavajirā* meter, featuring eleven syllables per line. The Khmer translation is composed in the twenty-two-syllable *brahmagīti* meter and matches the pattern of short and long syllables found in the Pali. Cambodians often recite the Pali and Khmer versions together in sequence, maintaining the same melody and rhythm throughout.

40. The Homage Octet

Title:	namo-aṭṭhaka-gāthā samrāy
Literal:	Stanzas of the homage octet, translated into Khmer.
Meter:	*paṭhyāvatt* (8-8-8-8)
Form:	Unrhymed *paṭhyāvatt* (8-8-8-8)
Melody:	*samrāy* (C-D-E-G-A = C^6)
Stanzas:	7 (the translation expands stanza 6 into 2 stanzas, for a total of of 8)
Author:	Anonymous
Date:	Nineteenth or twentieth century
Khmer:	Ñāṇ Jhīn, *Visākhapūjā*, 5–6.

English: Walker, "Unfolding Buddhism," 1377–79.
Edition: Walker, "Unfolding Buddhism," 1377–79.
Sources: UB027, 35a–35b, prè ghloṅ 8 bāky.

One of several Khmer verse translations of the *Namo Aṭṭhaka Gāthā*, a Pali composition by King Mongkut (Rama IV) of Siam, composed in eight half-stanzas (sixteen lines) of the *anuṭṭhubha* meter, which reads:

> Homage to him, the Worthy One,
> to the Buddha, the Great Seer.
> Homage to the highest Teaching,
> well-proclaimed here by the Buddha.
> Homage to the great Disciples,
> flawless in their virtue and view.
> Homage to all of the Three Jewels,
> beginning with the sacred AUM.
> Homage to all of the Three Jewels,
> far beyond the things of the world.
> By the power of this homage,
> may misfortunes now disappear.
> By the power of this homage,
> may there always be well-being.
> By the power of this homage,
> may I thrive in this liturgy.[67]

The phrases "The sublime union of three letters: A, U, and M" (Khmer) or "beginning with the sacred AUM" (Pali *omātyārad-dhassa*) refer to an acrostic for the Three Jewels: *Arahant* ["the Worthy One"], *Uttaradhamma* ["the highest Teaching"], and *Mahāsaṅgha* ["the great Disciples"]. When the initial letters of these epithets combine, they form AUM, the sacred sound OṂ.

41. The Buddha's Eightfold Array

Title: sabbadisabuddhamaṅgal
Literal: Blessings of the buddhas in all directions
Meter: *brahmagīti* (5-6-5-6)
Form: Unrhymed *brahmagīti* (5-6-5-6)
Melody: Unknown
Stanzas: 10
Author: Anonymous
Date: Eighteenth or nineteenth century
English: Walker, "Unfolding Buddhism," 1316–17.
Edition: Walker, "Unfolding Buddhism," 1316–17.
Sources: UB042, 46a–47a, braḥ buddhamaṅgal pūjā astādịs; Kaṅ Phū, Untitled [notebook], 125, dhaŕm buddhamaṅgal purāṇ.

This poem is based on a short Pali protective text, the "Protective Chant on the Blessings of the Buddhas in All Directions" (*Sabbadisabuddhamaṅgala Paritta*).[68] Its stanzas are also included in a larger collection known as the *Mahādibbamanta* in Thailand.[69] The relevant passage is as follows:

> The supreme Buddha in the center,
> Sāriputta in the south,
> Ānanda in the west,
> Moggallāna in the north,
> Koṇḍañña in the east,
> Gavampati in the northwest,
> Upāli in the southwest,
> Kassapa in the southeast,
> Rāhula in the northeast:
> all these are blessings of the buddhas.
> May those who know them be honored in the world,
> free from pain, free from calamity.

May they achieve great power
and may all success arise for them.[70]

Note that Kaccāyana is another name for Gavampati in Southeast Asia.[71]

Some Cambodian temples, including Vatt Sārāvăn Tejo (Wat Saravan Techo) and Vatt Gien Ghlāṃṅ (Wat Kien Khleang) in Phnom Penh, still feature inscriptions that reference this eightfold array of disciples. The inscriptions are placed around the outside of the central *vihāra*, the principal sacred space of the temple, often on eight *sīmā* stones or boundary markers, one in each of the cardinal and intermediary directions.[72] Before entering the *vihāra*, monks and laypeople were traditionally expected to offer a stick of incense at each *sīmā* stone and intone the heart syllable corresponding to the respective disciple.[73]

42. Homage to All Holy Sites

Title:	cetiyavandana-gāthā samrāy
Literal:	Stanzas in homage of *cetiyas*, translated into Khmer.
Meter:	*brahmagīti* (5-6-5-6)
Form:	Unrhymed *brahmagīti* (5-6-5-6)
Melody:	*sūtr rāy* (C-D-B♭ = C)
Stanzas:	6
Author:	Anonymous
Date:	Eighteenth or nineteenth centuries
Khmer:	Som Suvaṇṇ, *Prajuṃ māghapūjā niṅ visākhapūjā*, 4–5.
English:	Walker, "Unfolding Buddhism," 1034–35.
Edition:	Walker, "Unfolding Buddhism," 1034–35.
Sources:	UB044, 76a–76b, namaskār pūjanīyavatthu jā dī gorab.

A Khmer translation and expansion of a Pali verse of unknown origin for honoring sacred places, including stupas (*cetiya*), Bodhi trees, Buddha images, and relics. The Pali original reads:

I bow down to the holy stupas
well-established in all places,
and to all relics, Bodhi trees,
and Buddha images for all time.[74]

43. Hymn to the Buddha's Feet

Title: sarasör braḥ pād stāṃ
Literal: In praise of the holy right foot
Meter: *kākagati* (4-4-4-4-4-4-4)
Form: Unrhymed *kākagati* (4-4-4-4-4-4-4)
Melody: *buddhapād prāṃ ṭhān* (C-E-F-G-A-B♭ = $C^{7}\text{add}^{6}$)
Stanzas: 41
Author: Anonymous
Date: Eighteenth or nineteenth centuries
Khmer: Som Suvaṇṇ, *Prajuṃ māghapūjā niṅ visākhapūjā*, 38–45; Jhịm Ŝum, *Pad sarabhaññ*, 27–33.
English: Walker, "Unfolding Buddhism," 1245–54.
French: Bizot, "La figuration des pieds," 411–14 (partial); San Sarin, "Les textes liturgiques fondamentaux," 189–97.
Edition: Walker, "Unfolding Buddhism," 1245–54.
Sources: UB022, 56b–62a, braḥ pād khāṅ stām (lev°); UB025, 48a–53a, panlèr aṭṭhuttarasatamaṅgal; UB041, 62a–62b, buddhapād 5 ṭhān pad kākagati (short version); UB044, 87a–88a, buddhapād prāṃ thān (short version); FEMC d.500; FEMC a.472, sar-sör braḥ pād chveṅ stāṃ nūv braḥ caṅkūm kèv.

This paean in praise of the Buddha's feet is an eighteenth- or nineteenth-century Khmer translation of a Siamese original.[75] The Khmer translation generally keeps close to the Siamese in both content and style, with the exception of the concluding section on the benefits of reciting the text, which is greatly expanded in the Khmer.

The Pali opening line, "Permit me! To his two feet I bow in praise" (*ukāsa pādayugalaṃ namāmi'haṃ*), is only found in the Khmer. The passage that follows describes a set of symbolic offerings created through the body and mind of the devotee, echoing similar passages in "The Relics of the Buddha" (#18) and "Lotus Offering to Realize Awakening" (#45).

After this initial offering, the text provides a summary list of the 108 auspicious symbols on the Buddha's feet.[76] One example where the Khmer poet followed Cambodian convention instead of the Siamese text concerns the symbol known in Pali as *sirivaccha*. In Thailand, this symbol is depicted as a polished oval mirror,[77] a choice reflected in the Siamese version of the poem, "there are maidens lifting mirrors" (*mī nāṅ jū vèn*$_{1}$).[78] The Khmer text, however, reads "maidens clutching [lovely] candleholders" (*dhītā ṭai kān' / babil sobhăṇ*), which reflects the Khmer interpretation of the *sirivaccha* symbol.[79] A *babil* is an oval-shaped metal Khmer ritual object, to which candles may be affixed during ceremonial use.[80]

Another passage where the Khmer poet diverges from the Siamese version concerns the five places where the Buddha's footprints are supposed to remain today. The Siamese text lists one of these footprints as enshrined in Ayutthaya and another in Chiang Mai, both part of modern Thailand. The Khmer text replaces these toponyms with Suvaṇṇapabbata and Saccabandha, respectively, removing a Siamese geographic interpretation from the poem. Moreover, while the Siamese suggests that the footprints are active sites of worship, the Khmer text denies this, saying they are too far away and therefore impossible to venerate in person ("We can't even reach / those distant shrines."). This change speaks to a Khmer sensibility, common in eighteenth- and nineteenth-century texts, that Cambodia was located on the very edge of the Buddhist world.[81]

One common Khmer title for this poem, *sarasör braḥ pād stāṃ* ("In praise of the holy right foot"), points to a local distinction between the symbols on the left and right feet of the Buddha.[82]

44. The Dharma of Union

Title: dhaŕm yog
Meter: *baṃnol* (6-4-6)
Form: Unrhymed *baṃnol* (6-4-6)
Melody: *dhaŕm yog* (C-D-E-G-A-B♭ = C^7add^6)
Stanzas: 71
Author: Braḥ Dhammalikhit
Date: 1869
Khmer: Lī Suvīr, *Bidhī dhvö puṇy buddhābhisek*, 11–14.
English: Walker, "Unfolding Buddhism," 1349–58.
French : Giteau, *Le bornage rituel des temples*, 73–79.
Edition: Walker, "Unfolding Buddhism," 1349–58.
Sources: UB002, 55a–61a, braḥ dhaŕm yok; UB003, 63b–68b dhaŕm yok; UB010, 43a–48b, dhaŕm yokkh; UB011, 41b–45b and 47a–49b, dhaŕm y"ok/dhaŕm yok; UB012, 45a–50b [no title given, but last line of text reads *braḥ dhaŕmmapattimārayoggā*]; UB017, 34b–40b, dharaŕmm yok; UB021, 2b–9a; UB035, 21b–29a, braḥ dhaŕmm yok; UB039, 20a–25b; UB041, 18a–25a, dhaŕm y"ok, with the incipit *namatthu*; UB046, 9b–16a, dhaŕm y"ok; UB048, 84a, 82b–82a, and 80b–80a, pad y"ok [blue pen] (explicit missing); UB048, 79a–73a, pad yog/dhaŕm yog; UB051, 7b–12b, braḥ dhaŕmm yokk; UB062, 50a–53a, dhaŕm y"ok, with the incipit *namattha namo tassa*; UB065, 66b–69b, abhisek, añjöñ braḥ dhātu; UB067, 65a–70a.

"The Dharma of Union" translates the common name of this poem, *dhaŕm yog*, pronounced as if written *dhaŕm y"og* ("thoa yaok"). The "union" invoked here is the ritual union between a new Buddha image and all of the relics, radiance, perfections, and Dharmas invited into it. A more formal, if less grammatically sensible, Pali name appears in some manuscripts: *dhammapaṭiyogā vaṇṇanā*, roughly meaning "commentary on the union with the Dharmas."

This poem is one of the few pre-twentieth-century Dharma songs for which a clear textual history can be established. The Khmer version of "The Dharma of Union," translated here, is itself a translation of an earlier Siamese text of the same name.[83] The Siamese text has been recited in Cambodia since at least the early eighteenth century, being cited in a 1747 C.E. inscription from Angkor Wat.[84] A colophon surviving in an early twentieth-century manuscript from Kampong Cham province, UB051, relates the year, place, and reason the Siamese version was translated into Khmer.[85] After stating the date, equivalent to November 18, 1869 C.E., the colophon provides the following information in verse:

> We decided to translate "The Dharma of Union"
> clearly and correctly in keeping with
> the letter, meaning, and meter of the ancients,
>
> since that of olden times
> was now incomprehensible,
> mixed with Khmer, Lao, and Siamese,
>
> with the words no longer clear at all.
> We sought to compose a poem
> in Khmer that could be understood,
>
> with Braḥ Dhammalikhit as our leader,
> residing at that time
> at Vatt Uṇṇālom in Phnom Penh,
>
> who had the compassionate idea
> to translate it into verse,
> elucidating both its substance and style,
>
> so that the public
> might chant it as an offering
> to consecrate images of the Glorious Victor.[86]

The translation itself is quite faithful to the original Siamese, changing only a few toponyms to better suit the Cambodian context.[87]

The poem begins with an opening homage to the Three Jewels. The word "poets" (*kavī*) here is perhaps an error for *kinnarī*: half-bird, half-woman creatures who feature prominently in Southeast Asian Buddhist art. The "nine stages" are the four paths, the four fruits, and nirvana. In most Khmer manuscripts, the phrase "his Sons / and his Daughters" reads "the Buddha-mouth of the Teacher" (*buddha-oṣṭh sāstā*), but this is surely an error for "the children of the Buddha, the Teacher" (*buddha-oras sāstā*), as given in the Siamese.[88] "Give alms, keep rules, / and fill our minds with love" is literally "make merit, give donations, uphold the precepts, and practice the meditation on goodwill" (*dhvö puṇy oyº dān / cāṃ sīl mettā bhāvanā*).

An extensive ritual invitation follows, beginning with the relics of the Buddha. The geography mentioned is identical to that in "The Relics of the Buddha" (#18). The brilliant rays of the Buddha and various aspects of his wisdom and teachings are then invited into the body and monastic garments of the new image.

After the invitation portion is complete, the poem enumerates a set of elaborate offerings to present to the image being consecrated. These include *pāy sī* ("leafy towers, left and right / handmade with care), tiered offerings made of banana trunks and leaves, and *slā dhaŕm* ("coconuts adorned with leaves / and cigarettes"), conical offerings made of coconuts topped with various adornments, including betel nuts, areca leaves, incense sticks, and hand-rolled cigarettes.

45. Lotus Offering to Realize Awakening

Title: padum thvāy phkā «khñuṃ phguṃ amrām ṭap'»
Literal: Lotus flower offering, beginning with "I cup my palms in humble prayer."
Meter: *brahmagīti* (5-6-5-6)
Form: Extended into unrhymed *paṭhyāvatt* (8-8-8-8)

Melody: *laṃ-on* (C-D-E-G̣-A = C^6)
Stanzas: 39
Author: Anonymous
Date: Late sixteenth or early seventeenth century
English: Walker, "Unfolding Buddhism," 1282–87.
Edition: Walker, "Unfolding Buddhism," 1275–82.
Sources: UB003, 8b–12b, dhaŕm thvāy phkā; UB009, 38b, thvāy phkā padum caṃboḥ braḥ sammāsambuddh; UB011, 65b–69b, dhaŕm pūdaṃ/dhaŕm pūdaṃ thvāy phkār; UB017, 59a–63b, thvāy° phkār; UB041, 59a–60a, pūduṃ thvāy phkā (short version); UB046, 39b–42a, bidhī thvāy phkār pad braṃhmagit/bidhī thvāy phkār, with the incipit *namo tassa bhagavato arahato sammāsambuddhassa tāṅ namo pī pad*; UB066, 36a–36b, padum thvāy phkā (short version); FEMC 059; FEMC 95.B.04.03.03.

One of the oldest texts in this collection, this extensive prayer was excerpted in two stone inscriptions at Angkor Wat, IMA 31 of 1684 C.E. and IMA 38 of 1701 C.E.[89] It opens with a symbolic offering: cupped hands in the shape of a lotus flower. The praise of the Buddha that follows reflects the poem's use as the first chant recited to a newly sacralized icon in the early hours of the morning.

The remainder of the poem articulates an expansive set of aspirations. Some of the less familiar references include the wealthy merchant (*seṭṭhī*) Jotika from the *Dhammapada Aṭṭhakathā*,[90] the Buddha's past life as Prince Temiya,[91] and Viśvakarman (Vishvakarman), the divine architect known as *braḥ bisṇukār* in Khmer.[92]

The aspirations are adapted from an earlier source, though their ultimate origin is unclear. The closest surviving Pali parallel appears in a colophon appended to certain manuscripts of the *Hatthavanagallavihāravaṃsa*. The main text is a short chronicle of a monastery in Sri Lanka, composed between 1236 and 1266 C.E.[93] The colophon's date is uncertain, though likely prior to the sixteenth or early seventeenth century, when the Khmer poem was composed. Translated from the Pali, the colophon reads:

> By means of this merit, up until
> the point when I reach nirvana,
> may I be born into a good, pure,
> faithful, rich, and prosperous family.
>
> In the tongues of all regions,
> in all of the practical arts,
> in worldly wisdom, and in fooling
> the wicked, may I be skilled.
>
> In the Piṭakas, the Vedas,
> in the many grammars,
> and in the other sciences,
> such as logic, may I be confident.
>
> May I be a poet, an exegete, a preacher
> who wins over my opponents,
> and one who memorizes many
> thousands of stanzas upon a single hearing.
>
> May I bear in mind thousands of stanzas
> by merely listening to them,
> both in their literal meaning
> and their thousands of significations.
>
> Just as a lion's fat stored
> in a golden vessel or a stone
> inscription [is well-preserved],
> may I always retain what I hear.
>
> May I be mighty, powerful,
> grateful, skilled, strong,

brave, and of lofty birth
in all of my lives.

May no one harm me
and may I harm no one.
Without stick or sword,
may I subdue all living beings.

May I never be friends
with heretics or sinners.
May I never kill a living being,
no matter how small.

Whatever riddles, clever or
obscure, are posed to me,
may I resolve them instantly,
delighting all people.

With just a single glance,
may I cause all incurable
diseases to fall away,
like drops of water from a lotus.

Whatever things I own,
even as small as a thread,
may kings, thieves, enemies,
fire, and water

never destroy them, seize them,
burn them, or wash them away.
May diseases, illnesses, and dangers
never reach me.

May gods, humans, titans,
gandharvas, ogres, and demons

protect me during
my travels through samsara.

May I never steal, take others' spouses,
drink intoxicants, slay [living beings],
or speak falsehoods,
not even in a dream.

From now on, may I never
even think of committing
the five sins of immediate retribution
or the five types of misconduct.

May I never do, cause another to do,
or even think of committing
a sin, no matter how small,
that could harm a living being.

May I never be afflicted
by any of the suffering
in the four lower realms
of animals, ghosts, titans, and the hells.
Having fulfilled the merit for awakening,
may I become a Buddha in the future.[94]

Notes

The World of Cambodian Buddhism

1. Edwards, *Cambodge*; Hansen, *How to Behave*; Braun, *Birth of Insight*; Crosby, *Esoteric Theravada.*
2. On the modernist/traditionalist dichotomy in Cambodian Buddhism, see Harris, *Cambodian Buddhism*, 207–24; Kobayashi, "An Ethnographic Study"; Marston, "Reconstructing 'Ancient' Cambodian Buddhism."
3. In Laos and Thailand, *guṇ* ("khun") shares this same range of meanings. See Kourilsky, "Note sur la piété filiale"; and Kourilsky, "La place des ascendants familiaux," 497–519.
4. On the social meaning of *kataññū/katavedī* ("grateful one") and *pubbakārī* ("one owed a debt of gratitude") in Cambodia, particularly in the student-teacher context, see Hansen, "Buddhist Communities of Belonging," 70–71.
5. On these meditation systems, see Bizot, *Le figuier à cinq branches*; Crosby, "Tantric Theravāda;" Bernon, "Le manuel des maîtres"; Crosby, *Esoteric Theravada.*
6. Bernon, *Yantra et Mantra*, 54–55.
7. Bernon, "Le manuel des maîtres," 775–76; Kourilsky, "La place des ascendants familiaux," 506.
8. Siyonn Sophearith, *Pidan (Bitān) in Khmer Culture*, 35–36.
9. Bizot, *Le figuier à cinq branches*, 129–34; Crosby, *Esoteric Theravada*, 54–60.
10. Crosby, *Esoteric Theravada*, 33–36.
11. Pou, "Les inscriptions modernes d'Angkor Vat," 119–29; Thompson, "Mémoires du Cambodge," 180; Walker, "Carved Chants and Sermons on Stone," 65.
12. Ratnayaka, "The Bodhisattva Ideal of Theravāda"; Samuels, "The Bodhisattva Ideal in Theravāda Buddhist Theory and Practice."
13. Skilling, "Sambuddhe Verses"; Revire, "Back to the Future."
14. Bernon, "Des buddha aussi nombreux."
15. On the the iconographic realization of this quintet, see Thompson, "Future of Cambodia's Past."

16. For an intriguing local interpretation of the three *sampatti*, see Davis, *Deathpower*, 2–3.
17. For a fourteenth-century example, see Pou, "Les inscriptions modernes," 101–12; Thompson, *Engendering the Buddhist State*, 163–65.
18. On this conception of nirvana as a city, see Hallisey, "*Nibbānasutta.*"
19. For a traditional prose manual on this theme, see Cāp Bin, *Nagar kāy*.
20. Walker, "Unfolding Buddhism," 574–75.
21. Davis, *Deathpower*, 40.
22. This binding of the body is mirrored in Khmer funerary rituals as well. See Davis, *Deathpower*, 55; Lī Suvīr, *Bidhī dhvö puṇy khmoc*, 24–25.
23. Ang Choulean, "Saṅkhep jaṃnīö lö braḥ yamarāj."
24. On the Buddha's rays, see Reynolds and Reynolds, *Three Worlds*, 263–69.
25. Cicuzza, *A Mirror Reflecting the Entire World*, liii–lxiii.
26. The (1) path and (2) fruit of a stream-enterer, the (3) path and (4) fruit of a once-returner, the (5) path and (6) fruit of a non-returner, the (7) path and (8) fruit of an arhat or awakened saint, and (9) nirvana.
27. On the thirty-eight virtues of the Dharma, see Bizot and von Hinüber, *La guirlande de joyaux*, 36–37.
28. On noncanonical *paritta* in Cambodia, see Walker, "Echoes of a Sanskrit Past." On noncanonical *jātaka* in Southeast Asia, see Jaini, "Apocryphal Jātakas."
29. Bizot, *Le figuier à cinq branches*, 138–42.
30. For more on these figures, see Malalasekera, *Dictionary of Pāli Proper Names*; and Nyanaponika and Hecker, *Great Disciples of the Buddha*.
31. For more on the Earth Goddess in Cambodia and Thailand, see Guthrie, "A Study of the History."
32. For details of this cosmology in the Thai and Cambodian context, see Reynolds and Reynolds, *Three Worlds*.
33. For a rare exception, see Bernon, "Journeys to Jetavana."
34. Giteau, *Le bornage rituel des temples*, 64–73; Davis, *Deathpower*, 127–29.
35. Ang Choulean, *Les êtres surnaturels*, 201–22.
36. Mikaelian, "Recherches sur l'histoire," 474–526.
37. For more on *pret* and other ghosts, see Ang Choulean, *Les êtres surnaturels*.
38. The ten doors are the mouth, the two eyes, the two ears, the two nostrils, the urethra, the anus, and the fontanel; see Bizot, *Le figuier à cinq branches*, 101n2. Other interpretations include the ten perfections, the four paths, the four fruits, and nirvana; or the ten perfections, the five aggregates, and the four elements; see Lī Suvīr, *Bidhī dhvö puṇy buddhābhisek*, 2.
39. Ang Choulean, *Braḥ Liṅg*; Thompson, *Calling the Souls*.

The Ritual Life of Dharma Songs

1. Santi Pakdeekham, "Court Buddhism," 421–23.
2. Kun Sopheap, "Les rituels accompagnant," 98.
3. Sèm Sūr, *Prajuṃ dharm kāvatār*, 5–6 and 84–87; Walker, "Unfolding Buddhism," 235–46.
4. For the *Ākāravattā*, see Jaini, "*Ākāravattārasutta*"; for the *Ratanamālā*, see Bizot and von Hinüber, *La guirlande de joyaux*. On these and other Pali chants recited at Khmer deathbed rites, see Walker, "Unfolding Buddhism," 180–84.
5. Siyonn Sophearith, "Rak buddho"; Walker, "Unfolding Buddhism," 228–35.
6. Davis, *Deathpower*, 61–63.
7. For more on Pchum Ben, see Davis, *Deathpower*, 59–84; Holt, "Pchum Ben."
8. Bizot, "La consécration des statues," 108.
9. On the intersection of funerals and consecration rites, see Ang Choulean et al., *Ṭaṃṇör jīvit manuss khmèr*, 88; Walker "Unfolding Buddhism," 182–83.
10. For more on consecration rituals, see Giteau, *Le bornage rituel des temples*; Bizot, "La consécration des statues," 108–16; Lī Suvīr, *Bidhī dhvö puṇy buddhābhisek*.
11. Guthrie, "Performance of the Māravijaya."
12. Bizot, *Le chemin de Laṅkā*, 293–300.

Oral and Written Transmission

1. On the absence of the term "Theravada" in Cambodian discourse, see Hansen, "Buddhist Communities of Belonging," 65–68. On "Theravada" as a modern term in the Buddhist world writ large, see Perreira, "Whence Theravāda?"
2. Bernon, "The Status of Pāli in Cambodia."
3. On bilingual Pali-vernacular writing in Southeast Asia, see Walker, "Indic-Vernacular Bitexts" and "Bilingualism."
4. For extensive catalogs of surviving manuscripts of bilingual prose and Khmer verse in Cambodia, see Bernon et al., *Inventaire provisoire des manuscrits* (2004) and *Inventaire provisoire des manuscrits* (2018).
5. Edwards, *Cambodge*, 104–6.
6. Walker, "How Sophea Lost Her Sight."

7. This is true for the study of Pali chants in Cambodia as well. San Sarin, "Les textes liturgiques fondamentaux," i–ii.
8. Sanskrit-language inscriptions survive in the region from a few centuries earlier. The oldest dated inscription in the Khmer language is K.600 from 612 C.E. (Cœdès, *Inscriptions du Cambodge*, 21–23; Chhom "Le rôle du sanskrit," 265).
9. Antelme, "Inventaire provisoire des caractères," 12 and 29–39.
10. Goodall, "What Information Can Be Gleaned."
11. Details of these manuscripts are available in Walker, "Unfolding Buddhism," 656–844.
12. Walker, "Carved Chants and Sermons on Stone," 78–86.
13. Regarding the editing process, see Walker, "Unfolding Buddhism," 41–46.
14. https://www.trentwalker.org/unfolding-buddhism
15. https://www.stirringandstilling.org
16. For more on Ind's life and works, see Hansen, "Khmer Identity and Theravāda Buddhism," 55; Khing Hoc Dy, *Suttantaprījā ind niṅ snā ṭai*.
17. On Juon Ṇāt (Chuon Nath), see Huot Tāt, *Kalyāṇamitt rapas' khñuṃ*; Edwards, "Making a Religion," 69–75; Hansen, *How to Behave*, 101–6.
18. Harris, *Buddhism in a Dark Age*, 118–38.
19. For a remarkable twelfth-century example of female-authored Buddhist text from Cambodia, see Thompson, *Engendering the Buddhist State*, 120–35; Walker, "In Praise of Sister Queens," 4–5.
20. For perspectives of contemporary female Dharma song performers, see Walker, "How Sophea Lost Her Sight;" and Grant, "Social Shifts."

Meter, Melody, and Rhyme

1. For more details on Khmer meters, see Roeské, "Métrique Khmère"; Bernon, "Ieng Say"; Jacob, *Traditional Literature of Cambodia*, 53–64; Lī Sumunī, *Kaṃnāby khmèr*.
2. Jacob, *Traditional Literature of Cambodia*, 54.
3. V"èn Sun and Y"ān' Pūrin, *Rapāyakāra(ṇ) pūk sarup laddhaphal*; Walker, "Saṃvega and Pasāda," 301–11.
4. Twenty different melodies are named in the notes: *ārādhanā*, *buddhapād prāṃ ṭhān*, *daṃnuoṅ*, *daṃnuoṅ pret*, *devatā paṃbe kūn*, *dhaŕm yog*, *laṃ-on*, *madrī*, *mahāmāyā*, *parābhavasūtr*, *phcāñ' mār*, *raṃḷk guṇ*, *rās'*, *saṃbau thay*, *samrāy*, *sāṅ braḥ phnuos*, *sarabhaññ*, *sūtr rāy*, *trailakkha(ṇ)*, and *yo vo*.
5. Walker, "Stirring and Stilling" and "Saṃvega and Pasāda."

6. Walker, "Saṃvega and Pasāda," 312–15.
7. Jacob, "Some Features of Khmer Versification," 217–18.
8. Gedney, "Siamese Verse Forms," 65–75.

Notes on the Songs

1. For the full narrative, see Cowell, *Jātaka*, vv. 20–31.
2. For a Khmer verse version, see Nū Kan, *Bimbānibbān*.
3. For the full narrative, see Appleton and Shaw, *Ten Great Birth Stories of the Buddha*, 1:117–44.
4. For the full narrative, see Appleton and Shaw, *Ten Great Birth Stories of the Buddha*, 2:507–639.
5. For the context of this song within the broader narrative of Mahāpajāpatī's life, see Garling, *The Woman Who Raised the Buddha*, 49–51.
6. See also Siyonn Sophearith, "Smūt paṇṭāṃ nāṅ mahāmāyā;" and Jăy M"ai, *Nānādhammasaṅveg bistār*, 82–83; edition and translation in Walker, "Unfolding Buddhism," 1432–34.
7. For details of this history, see Walker, "A Chant Has Nine Lives."
8. Walker, "A Chant Has Nine Lives," 44. The original is as follows:

brahmā ca lokādhipatī sahampatī
katañjalī andhivaraṃ ayācatha
sant'īdha sattā 'pparajakkhajātikā
desetu dhammaṃ anukamp'imaṃ pajaṃ

9. Malalasekera, *Dictionary of Pāli Proper Names*, 2:611.
10. Walker, "A Chant Has Nine Lives," 48. The original is as follows:

saddhammabheriṃ vinayañ ca kāyaṃ
suttañ ca bandhaṃ abhidhammacammaṃ
ākoṭayanto catusaccadaṇḍaṃ
pabodha neyye parisāya majjhe

11. For more on these references, see Walker, "A Chant Has Nine Lives," 59–61.
12. Walker, "A Chant Has Nine Lives," 62. The original is as follows:

evaṃ sahampatī brahmā
bhagavantaṃ ayācatha
tuṇhībhāvena taṃ buddho
kāruññenādhivāsaya

tamhā vuṭṭhāya pādena
migadāyaṃ tato gato
pañcavagyādayo neyye
ama[ta]ṃ pāyesi dhammato

tato pabhūti sambuddho
anūnā dhammadesanaṃ
māghavassāni desesi
sattānaṃ atthasiddhakaṃ

tena sādhu ayyo bhante
desetu dhammadesanaṃ
sabbāyidha parisāya
anukampam'pi kātave

13. Ek Ñiṃ and Ras' Kèv, *Bhāṇavāra kiccavatt bṛik lṅāc*, 120; Kèv Ûc, *Parittasamodhān pālī*, 329; and Rhys Davids and Carpenter, *Dīgha Nikāya*, 2:154.
14. Ñāṇ Jhīn, *Visākhapūjā*, 33; Rama IV, *Ṕraḥjum braḥ rājaniban(dh) bhāṣā pālī*, 266. The original is as follows:

visākhapuṇṇamāy'ajja
divaso hoti aṭṭhamo
yādise naradevassa
sunibbutassa tādino
mallehi sabbagandhānaṃ
saddhehi katacītako
pāṭiheraṃ dassayanto
sayam eva apajjali
tass'antimadehabbhūtaṃ
battiṃsavaralakkhaṇaṃ
dhātubhūtena tejena
ajjhāyittha mahesino
tādiso va ayan dāni
sampatto abhilakkhito
iman dāni sunakkhattaṃ
abhimaṅgalasammataṃ

15. Ras' Kèv, *Gihipratipatti bises bistār*, 21–22 [full text on 21–26]. The original is as follows:

mahāgotamasambuddho
kusinārāya nibbuto

dhātuvitthārakaṃ katvā
tesu tesu visesato

uṇhīsaṃ catasso dāṭhā
akkhakā dve ca sattamo
asambhinnā va tā satta
sesā bhinnā va dhātuyo

mahantā pañca nāḷi ca
majjhimā ca cha nāḷiyo
khuddakā pañca nāḷi ca
sambhinnā tividhā matā

mahantā bhinnamuggā ca
majjhimā bhinnataṇḍulā
khuddakā sāsapamattā
evaṃ dhātuppamāṇikā

mahantā suvaṇṇavaṇṇā
majjhimā phalikappabhā
khuddakā bakulavaṇṇā
tā'pi vandāmi dhātuyo

16. Pou, "Notes on Brahmanic Gods," 347; Preap Chanmara, "Braḥ baisraba(ṇ) ṝ deb srūv."
17. Davis, *Deathpower*, 89.
18. Bizot and von Hinüber, *La guirlande de joyaux*, 21–25.
19. Walker, "Carved Chants and Sermons on Stone," 83–85.
20. Jaini, "*Ākāravattārasutta*"; Walker, "Unfolding Buddhism," 122–29.
21. Jaini, "The Apocryphal Jātakas."
22. Gabaude, *Les cetiya de sable*.
23. Walker, "Carved Chants and Sermons on Stone," 64.
24. Ang Choulean, "God of the Dead," 7.
25. Ang Choulean, "Saṅkhep jaṃnīö lö braḥ yamarāj," 29–32.
26. Walker, "Unfolding Buddhism," 298–304; Walker, "Echoes of a Sanskrit Past," 83–92.
27. Institut bouddhique, *Bhāṇavār pālī*, 141–44; Kèv Ûc, *Parittasamodhān pālī*, 291–94; Walker, "Unfolding Buddhism," 281.
28. Bizot and von Hinüber, *La guirlande de joyaux*, 195–99; Bernon, "Le manuel des maîtres," 388–92.
29. Ñāṇamoli, *Path of Purification*, 237.
30. Kourilsky, "La place des ascendants familiaux," 49n31.

31. Nuon Saṃ-ân, *Gihippatipatti gharāvāsadharm* (2547), 17. The original reads as follows:

> *ukāsa vandāmi bhante bhagavā. sabbaṃ aparādhaṃ khamatha me bhante. mayā kataṃ puññaṃ sāminā anumoditabbaṃ. sāminā kataṃ puññaṃ mayhaṃ dātabbaṃ. sādhu sādhu anumodāmi.*

32. Langenberg, *Birth in Buddhism.*
33. Ang Choulean et al., *Ṭaṃṇör jīvit manuss khmèr*, 64–65.
34. Bernon, "Le rituel de la « grande probation annuelle »," 500.
35. Davis, *Deathpower*, 169.
36. Walker, "Unfolding Buddhism," 1266. The original is as follows:

> *idan tena dānaṃ*
> *idan tena sīlaṃ*
> *aggasāvakañāṇaṃ*
> *yāva nibbānaṃ paccayo*

37. San Sarin, "Les textes liturgiques fondamentaux," 126n3.
38. Pou, *Un dictionnaire du khmer-moyen*, 86.
39. For more on this form of music, see Keo Narom, *Maratak tantrī khmèr*, 64–69.
40. Walker, "Unfolding Buddhism," 1060, citing Cāp Bin, *Trairăta(n) pūjā niṅ trairăta(n) praṇām*, 61. The original is as follows:

> *aniccā vata saṅkhārā*
> *uppādavayadhammino*
> *uppajjitvā nirujjhanti*
> *tesaṃ vūpasamo sukho*

41. For more on the *paṃsukūl* rite, see Bizot, *Le don de soi-même*; Davis, "Weaving Life out of Death"; and Davis, *Deathpower*, 138–56.
42. Walker, "Unfolding Buddhism," 906, citing *Dhammapada* 3.9. The original is as follows:

> *aciraṃ vat'ayaṃ kāyo*
> *paṭhaviṃ adhisessati*
> *chuddho apetaviññāṇo*
> *niratthaṃ va kaliṅgaraṃ*

43. On the *braḷiṅ*, see Ang Choulean, *Braḥ Liṅg*; and Thompson, *Calling the Souls.*

44. Walker, "Unfolding Buddhism," 1005–6. The original reads as follows:

iminā puññakammena
upajjhāyā guṇuttarā
ācariyūpakārā ca
mātāpitā ca ñātikā
suriyo candimā rājā
guṇavantā narāpi ca
brahmamārā ca indrā ca
lokapālā ca devatā
yamo mittā manussā ca
majjhattā verikāpi ca
sabbe sattā sukhī hontu
puññāni pakatāni me
sukhaṃ ca tividhaṃ dentu
khippaṃ pāpetha vo'mataṃ

45. Walker, "Unfolding Buddhism," 1162–73.
46. Walker, "Unfolding Buddhism," 1170–71. The original reads as follows:

neḥ nịṅ niyāy
dhammajāti dāṃṅ ḷāy
yöṅ ge grap' gnā
maraṇaṃ kāle
pö raṅ' slāp' noḥ
grap' rūp srī pruḥ
vāyo khyal' pak'.

khyal' braḥ vinăy
pak' ḷöṅ ṭal' phdai
udar prañāp'
bhlöṅ cheḥ dịk citt
dhlāk' citt ṭal' phkāp'
laṃpāk diep slāp'
slāp' höy vedanā.

khyal' braḥ abhidhamm
khāṅ lö prajuṃ
pak' cuḥ phsabv gnā
dhlāk' grap khdap' citt
ṭhit ṭhān hadayā
citt öy vedanā
kāl grā prajuṃ khyal'.

47. Saveros Pou and Ang Chouléan, "Vocabulaire khmer relatif au surnaturel," 80. *Bhūt* has a similar sense in some South Asian languages today.
48. Lī Suvīr, *Bidhī dhvö puṇy khmoc*, 51; Davis, *Deathpower*, 74.
49. See Ñāṇamoli, *Path of Purification*, 169–70.
50. Lī Suvīr, *Bidhī dhvö puṇy khmoc*, 24–25.
51. Bernon, "Le manuel des maîtres," 240–42.
52. Pou, "La littérature didactique khmère."
53. Bernon, "Le manuel des maîtres," 229–35.
54. Bernon, "Le manuel des maîtres," 387.
55. Cāp Bin, *Nagar kāy*; Bernon, "Le manuel des maîtres," 37.
56. For a strikingly different use of a tree image in this tradition, see Hallisey, "*Nibbānasutta*", 126–27.
57. Bizot, *Rāmaker*, 46.
58. Bizot, *Le figuier à cinq branches*, 112–15; Crosby, *Esoteric Theravada*, 69–71.
59. Bernon, "Le manuel des maîtres," 242–45; Phibul Choompolpaisal, "Nimitta and Visual Methods"; Crosby, *Esoteric Theravada*, 54–57.
60. Hallisey, "*Nibbānasutta*," 128.
61. Ñāṇamoli, *Path of Purification*, 221–22.
62. Jhịm Ŝum, *Pad sarabhaññ*, 5.
63. Marston, "El Buda Jayanti en Camboya," 23.
64. Jhịm Ŝum, *Pad sarabhaññ*, 5.
65. Walker, "Saṃvega and Pasāda," 272–73.
66. Ras' Kèv, *Gihipratipatti bises bistār*, 42–44. The original reads as follows:

yo kappakoṭīhi pi appameyyaṃ
kālaṃ karonto atidukkarāni
khedaṃ gato lokahitāya nātho
namo mahākāruṇikassa tassa

asambuddhaṃ buddhanisevitaṃ yaṃ
bhavābhavaṃ gacchati jīvaloko
namo avijjādikilesajālaṃ
viddhaṃsino dhammavarassa tassa

guṇehi yo sīlasamādhipaññā-
vimuttiñāṇappabhūtīhi yutto
khettañ janānaṃ kusalatthikānaṃ
tam ariyasaṅghaṃ sirasā namāmi

icc'evam accantanamassaneyyaṃ
namassamāno ratanattayaṃ yaṃ

puññābhisandaṃ vipulaṃ alatthaṃ
tassānubhāvena hatantarāyo

67. Pussadeva, *Svat man(t) chpăp hlvaṅ*, 4; Rama IV, *Ṕraḥjum braḥ rājaniban(dh) bhāṣā pālī*, 38–39. For the English, see Walker, "Stirring and Stilling," 9–10. The original reads as follows:

namo arahato sammā-
sambuddhassa mahesino
namo uttamadhammassa
svākkhātasseva tenidha
namo mahāsaṅghassāpi
visuddhasīladiṭṭhino
namo omātyāraddhassa
ratanattayassa sādhukaṃ
namo omakātītassa
tassa vatthuttayassa pi
namo kārappabhāvena
vigacchantu upaddavā
namo kārānubhāvena
suvatthi hotu sabbadā
namo kārassa tejena
vidhimhi homi tejavā

68. UB070, 6a; Bernon, "Le manuel des maîtres," 329.
69. Jaini, "Mahādibbamanta"; Walker, "Echoes of a Sanskrit Past," 93–102.
70. UB070, 6a, corrected on the basis of Damrong Rajanubhab, *Mahādibaman(t)*, 3–4; cf. Bernon, "Le manuel des maîtres," 329; Jaini, "Mahādibbamanta," 508. The original reads as follows:

buddho ca majjhimo seṭṭho
sāriput[t]o ca dakkh[i]ṇe
pacchime'pi ca ānando
uttare moggallānako
ko[ṇḍ]añ[ñ]o p[u]bbabhā[g]e ca
bāyabbe ca [g]avampati
upāli neharati[ṭṭh]āne
[ā]ganeyye ca kassapo
rāhulo c'eva īsāne
sabbe te buddhamaṅgalā
yo ñatvā pūjito loke
nidukkho nirupad[d]avo

mahātejo sadā hontu
sabbasotthī bhavantu [t]e

71. Lagirarde, "Gavampati in Southeast Asia."
72. Bernon, "Le manuel des maîtres," 790–96.
73. Bernon, "About Khmer Monasteries," 212–14.
74. Ras' Kèv, *Gihipratipatti bises bistār*, 36; Walker, "Unfolding Buddhism," 1034. This verse in the original language is as follows:

vandāmi cetiyaṃ sabbaṃ
sabbaṭṭhānesu patiṭṭhitaṃ
sārīrikadhātumahābodhiṃ
buddharūpaṃ sakalaṃ sadā

75. For an edition and translation of the Siamese version, see Walker, "Unfolding Buddhism," 1514–30.
76. For details on the items mentioned in this and other related lists, see Cicuzza, *A Mirror Reflecting the Entire World*.
77. Cicuzza, *A Mirror Reflecting the Entire World*, 119n38.
78. Walker, "Unfolding Buddhism," 1524.
79. Jhịm Ŝum, *Pad sarabhaññ*, 24; Walker, "Unfolding Buddhism," 410.
80. For more on the *babil*, see Thompson, *Engendering the Buddhist State*, 150–57.
81. Walker, "Unfolding Buddhism," 410–13.
82. For an edition and translation of the corresponding Khmer poem focused on the Buddha's left foot, see Walker, "Unfolding Buddhism," 1254–61.
83. For an edition and English translation of the Siamese text, see Walker, "Unfolding Buddhism," 1063–80.
84. Walker, "Carved Chants and Sermons on Stone," 85–86.
85. Walker, "Unfolding Buddhism," 788–91.
86. Standardized from UB051, 31a–31b; Walker, "Unfolding Buddhism," 418–19. The original reads as follows:

git prè dharm̐ yog oy° jăk'
oy° trūv tām akkha(r)
tām ār̐th tām pad purāṇ.

ṭpid purāṇ tè bī mun mān
sịṅ stāp' buṃ pān
lāy khmèr lāv siem phaṅ.

min cpās' as' bāky jā mtaṅ
git lök cèṅ caṅ

jā bāky khmèr oy° stāp' pān.

braḥ dhammalikhit ṭá pradhān
kāl gaṅ' nau sthān
nau vatt palom bhnaṃ beñ.

mān braḥ dăyahā sraḷāñ'
git lök prè ceñ
oy° cpās' as' ārth vohār.

duk oy° mahājan grap' gnā
sūtr thvāy pūjā
abhisek aṅg braḥ jinasrī.

87. Walker, "Unfolding Buddhism," 420–29.
88. Walker, "Unfolding Buddhism," 422.
89. Walker, "Unfolding Buddhism," 624–51; Walker, "Carved Chants and Sermons on Stone," 77–78.
90. Malalasekera, *Dictionary of Pāli Proper Names*, 1: 968–70; Skilling, "Some Literary References," 77–78.
91. Appleton and Shaw, *Ten Great Birth Stories of the Buddha*, 1:51–79.
92. Pou, "Notes on Brahmanic Gods," 344.
93. Gornall, *Rewriting Buddhism*, 55.
94. Walker, "Unfolding Buddhism," 634–37. The original Pali, adapted from Godakumbara, *Hatthavanagallavihāravaṃsa*, 33–34, is as follows:

puññen'ānena pappomi
nibbutiṃ yāva tāva'haṃ
uppajjeyaṃ kule suddhe
saddhe aḍḍhe mahaddhane

asesadesabhāsāsu
sakalāsu kalāsu ca
kusalo lokapaṇḍicce
caṇḍanimadane pi ca

piṭakesu ca vedesu
nekavyākaraṇesu ca
takk'ādisu pan'aññesu
satthesu ca visārado

kavī c'āgamako vādī
paravādappamaddano

ekassutidharo 'neka-
sahassānam pi ganthato

ganthasatasahassam pi
sutamattena dhāraye
atthavyañjanato vā pi
sahassanayato pi ca

vasāsīhassa pakkhittā
yathā kañcanapātiyā
silālekhe 'va me niccaṃ
sutaṃ sabbaṃ na nāsaye

mahiddhiko mahātejo
kataññū kusalo balī
dhitimā jātisampanno
bhaveyyaṃ jātijātiyaṃ

paro pi maṃ na hiṃseyya
na hiṃseyyaṃ paraṃ pi ca
adaṇḍena asatthena
dame 'haṃ sabbapāṇinaṃ

kudiṭṭhipāpamittañ ca
na seveyyaṃ kudācanaṃ
pāṇakaṃ aṇumattaṃ pi
na haṇeyyaṃ kadāci pi

nipuṇaṃ duddasaṃ pañhaṃ
yena kenaci pucchito
muhuttena pakāseyyaṃ
tosento sakalaṃ pajaṃ

atekicchā'pi ye rogā
te mayā pekkhitakkhaṇe
nissesā vyapagacchantu
udabindū va pokkharā

dasikasuttamattaṃ pi
yaṃ kiñci mama santakaṃ
rājacora'ppiyā sattā
agginā udakena vā

na vinassantu me bhogā
mā gayha ḍayha vuyhatu

rogavyādha'ntarāyā tu
na pappontu kadāci maṃ

devā manussā asurā
gandhabbā yakkharakkhasā
te pi maṃ parirakkhantu
bhave saṃsarato mama

adinnaṃ paradārañ ca
surāpānavihiṃsanaṃ
asaccaṃ supinenā'pi
na bhaṇeyyaṃ kudācanaṃ

pañc'ānantariyaṃ kammaṃ
pañcaduccaritaṃ pi ca
manasā pi na cinteyyaṃ
sabbakālam ito paraṃ

na kareyyaṃ na kāreyyaṃ
na cinteyyaṃ kudācanaṃ
pāpakaṃ aṇumattam pi
tathā dukkhañ ca pāṇinaṃ

niraye vā tiracchāne
pete asurayoniyaṃ
yaṃ yaṃ hi dukkhaṃ taṃ sabbaṃ
na phuseyyaṃ kudācanaṃ
pūretvā bodhisambhāre
buddho hessaṃ anāgate ti.

Bibliography

Abbreviations

EFEO	École française d'Extrême-Orient
FEMC	Fonds pour l'Édition des Manuscrits du Cambodge
UB	Leporello manuscripts cataloged in Walker, "Unfolding Buddhism."

1. Notebooks

Kaṅ Phū. Untitled. Handwritten collection of Dharma songs on a reused 1974 Banque Inadāna Jāti calendar. Phnom Penh: 1981 [scanned in 2006].

Ḍuk Ât. *Prajuṃ dhammasaṅveg nānā.* Handwritten collection of Dharma songs on lined paper. Battambang: 1998 [scanned in 2008].

2. Palm-Leaf Manuscripts

FEMC code	*Library and location*
FEMC a.472	Bibliothèque de la Pagode d'Argent (Phnom Penh)
FEMC d.122	Bibliothèque EFEO – Preah Vanarat Ken Vong (Phnom Penh)
FEMC d.620	Bibliothèque du Musée national (Phnom Penh)
FEMC 059	Hun Sen Library, Royal University of Phnom Penh
FEMC 1017-B.01.06.01	Vatt Bhūmi Thmī (Kampong Cham)
FEMC 095-B.04.03.03	Vatt Vālukārām (Kampong Cham)

3. Leporellos

UB Code	*FEMC or EFEO Code*	*Date*	*Library*	*Origin*
UB001	FEMC d.936	1979–2000 (?)	FEMC	Kandal
UB002		2005	Monastic	Siem Reap
UB003		2000–2010 (?)	Monastic	Siem Reap
UB005		2000–2010 (?)	Private	Kampong Speu
UB006		1996	Monastic	Surin (Thailand)
UB007		1993	Private	Tboung Khmum
UB008		1900–1925 (?)	Monastic	Tboung Khmum
UB009		2010	Monastic	Kampong Cham
UB010		2004	Monastic	Siem Reap
UB011		2004	Monastic	Siem Reap
UB012		2003	Monastic	Siem Reap
UB014	FEMC d.938	1925–1960 (?)	FEMC	Kampong Cham (?)
UB015	FEMC d.939	1875–1925 (?)	FEMC	Kampong Cham (?)
UB016		1979–2000 (?)	Monastic	Kampong Speu
UB017	FEMC 040-B.04.10.01	1900–1925 (?)	Monastic	Kampong Cham
UB018		1990–2005 (?)	Monastic	Kandal
UB019		1990–2005 (?)	Monastic	Kandal
UB020		1961–1962	Private	Kandal
UB021	EFEO CAMB. O. 353	1900–1925 (?)	EFEO-Paris	Unknown
UB022	EFEO CAMB. O. 404	1900–1925 (?)	EFEO-Paris	Unknown
UB023	FEMC d.940	1962	FEMC	Unknown
UB025	EFEO-FEMC Photocopy 56	1979–1990 (?)	Monastic	Phnom Penh
UB026	FEMC d.941	1962–1975	FEMC	Kampong Thom
UB027		1965–1966	Monastic	Kandal
UB028	FEMC d.942	2004	FEMC	Siem Reap
UB029		1995	Monastic	Kandal
UB030	FEMC d.943	1900–1925 (?)	FEMC	Unknown
UB031	FEMC d.944	1875–1925 (?)	FEMC	Unknown
UB033		1964	Monastic	Kandal
UB034		1962	Private	Phnom Penh
UB035	FEMC d.945	1925–1960 (?)	FEMC	Kampong Cham (?)
UB036		1960–1975 (?)	Private	Kandal
UB037	FEMC 097-B.06.06.01	1875–1925 (?)	FEMC	Kampong Cham
UB038		1995–2010 (?)	Monastic	Kampong Speu
UB039	EFEO-FEMC Photocopy 45	1979–2000 (?)	Monastic	Kampong Cham

UB041		1979–2000 (?)	Monastic	Phnom Penh
UB042	EFEO-FEMC Photocopy 64	1972–1973	FEMC	Kandal (?)
UB043		1988	Monastic	Siem Reap
UB044		1989	Monastic	Siem Reap
UB046		1979/1991	Private	Kandal/Siem Reap
UB047		1990–2005 (?)	Monastic	Tboung Khmum
UB048		1982 and 1983	Private	Kandal
UB049	FEMC d.946	1960–1975 (?)	FEMC	Kampong Cham (?)
UB051	FEMC 116-B.06.03.01	1900–1925 (?)	Monastic	Kampong Cham
UB052	FEMC 125-B.06.03.01	1900–1925 (?)	Monastic	Kampong Cham
UB053	FEMC 127-B.06.03.01	1900–1925 (?)	Monastic	Kampong Cham
UB055	FEMC 130-B.06.03.01	1875–1925 (?)	Monastic	Kampong Cham
UB057	FEMC d.948	1925–1960 (?)	FEMC	Kampong Cham
UB059	FEMC d.949	1875–1925 (?)	FEMC	Unknown
UB060		1994	Monastic	Phnom Penh
UB062	FEMC d.951	1999	FEMC	Kandal
UB065		2003	FEMC	Phnom Penh
UB066		2000–2010 (?)	FEMC	Phnom Penh
UB067	FEMC d.952	1875–1925 (?)	FEMC	Kampong Cham
UB068	FEMC d.953	1875–1925 (?)	FEMC	Kampong Cham
UB070	FEMC d.954	1875–1925 (?)	FEMC	Kampong Cham
	FEMC d.500	1875–1925 (?)	FEMC	Unknown

4. Print sources

Ang Choulean [Chouléan] អាំង ជូលាន. *Braḥ Liṅg ព្រះលិង្គ* [Spirits/the sacred liṅga]. Phnom Penh ភ្នំពេញ: Reyum រ៉េយំ, 2004.

———. "God of the Dead, God of the Living: Belief and Ritual Practices around Yama in Cambodia." *Renaissance Culturelle du Cambodge* 30 (2017–2018): 3–12.

———. *Les êtres surnaturels dans la religion populaire khmère* [Supernatural beings in Khmer popular religion]. Paris: Cedorek, 1986.

———. "Saṅkhep jaṃnīö lö braḥ yamarāj nau prades kambujā សង្ខេបជំនឿលើព្រះយមរាជនៅប្រទេសកម្ពុជា [Summary of beliefs concerning Lord Yama in Cambodia]." *Bulletin of Archaeology, Royal University of Fine Arts* 1 (December 2007): 25–38.

Ang Choulean អាំង ជូលាន, Preap Chanmara ព្រាប ចាន់ម៉ារ៉ា, and Ŝun Cān'ṭịp ស៊ុន ចាន់ឌីប. *Ṭaṃṇör jīvit manuss khmèr möl tām bidhī chlaṅ văy ដំណើរជីវិតមនុស្សខ្មែរ មើលតាមពិធីឆ្លងវ័យ* [The life passages of Cambodians as seen through life-cycle rites]. Phnom Penh ភ្នំពេញ: Yosothor យសោធរ, 2014.

Antelme, Michel. "Inventaire provisoire des caractères et divers signes des écritures khmères pré-modernes et modernes employés pour la notation du khmer, du siamois, des dialectes thaïs méridionaux, du sanskrit et du pāli [Provisional inventory of characters and various signs in premodern and modern Khmer scripts used for the notation of Khmer, Siamese, southern Thai dialects, Sanskrit, and Pali]." *Bulletin en ligne de l'AEFEK* 12 (2007): 1–81.

Appleton, Naomi, and Sarah Shaw. *The Ten Great Birth Stories of the Buddha: The Mahānipāta of the Jātakatthavaṇṇanā*. 2 vols. Chiang Mai and Bangkok: Silkworm Books and Chulalongkorn University Press, 2015.

Bernon, Olivier de. "About Khmer Monasteries: Organizations and Symbolism." In *The Buddhist Monastery: A Cross-Cultural Survey*, edited by Pierre Pichard and François Lagirarde, 209–18. Chiang Mai: Silkworm Books, 2003.

———. "'Des buddha aussi nombreux que les grains de sable': Note sur une métaphore figée dans la langue khmère [Buddhas as numerous as grains of sand: note on a fossilized metaphor in the Khmer language]." *Aséanie* 7 (June 2001): 13–17.

———. "Ieng Say: La métrique, cours traité pour la composition des poèmes [Ieng Say: Meter, a textbook for the composition of poems]." Mémoire D.R.E.A., Institut National des Langues et Civilisations Orientales, 1985.

———. "'Journeys to Jetavana': Poetic and Ideological Elaborations of the Remembrance of Jetavana in Southeast Asia." In *Buddhist Narrative in Asia and Beyond*, vol. 1, edited by Peter Skilling and Justin Thomas McDaniel, 177–93. Bangkok: Institute of Thai Studies, Chulalongkorn University, 2012.

———. "Le manuel des maîtres de *kammaṭṭhān*: Étude et présentation de rituels de méditation dans la tradition du bouddhisme khmer [The manual of the *kammaṭṭhān* masters: study and presentation of meditation rituals in the Khmer Buddhist tradition]." PhD diss., Institut National des Langues et Civilisations Orientales, 2000.

———. "Le rituel de la « grande probation annuelle » (mahāparivāsakamma) des religieux du Cambodge [The ritual of the 'great annual probation']." *Bulletin de l'École française d'Extrême-Orient* 87.2 (2000): 473–510.

———. "The Status of Pāli in Cambodia: From Canonical to Esoteric Language." In *Buddhist Legacies in Mainland Southeast Asia: Mentalities, Interpretations, and Practices*, edited by François Lagirarde and Paritta Chalermpow Koanantakool, 53–66. Paris and Bangkok: École française d'Extrême-Orient and Princess Maha Chakri Sirindhorn Anthroplogy Centre, 2006.

———. *Yantra et Mantra* [Yantra and mantra]. Phnom Penh: Centre Culturel Français de Phnom Penh, 1998.

Bernon, Olivier de, Kun Sopheap, and Leng Kok-An. *Inventaire provisoire des manuscrits du Cambodge, Première partie* [Provisional inventory of manuscripts in Cambodia, first part]. Paris: École française d'Extrême-Orient, 2004.

———. *Inventaire provisoire des manuscrits du Cambodge, Deuxième partie* [Provisional inventory of manuscripts in Cambodia, second part]. Paris: École française d'Extrême-Orient, 2018.

Bizot, François. *Le chemin de Laṅkā* [The path of Laṅkā]. Paris: École française d'Extrême-Orient, 1992.

———. "La consécration des statues et le culte des morts [The consecration of statues and the cult of the dead]." In *Recherches nouvelles sur le Cambodge*, edited by François Bizot, 101–40. Paris: École française d'Extrême-Orient, 1994.

———. *Le don de soi-même* [The gift of oneself]. Paris: École française d'Extrême-Orient, 1981.

———. *Le figuier à cinq branches: recherche sur le bouddhisme khmer* [The five-branched fig tree: research on Khmer Buddhism]. Paris: École française d'Extrême-Orient, 1976.

———. "La figuration des pieds du Bouddha au Cambodge [The portrayal of the Buddha's feet in Cambodia]." *Asiatische Studien - Études Asiatiques* 25 (1971): 407–39.

———. *Rāmaker: L'amour symbolique de Rām et Setā* [Rāmaker: the symbolic love of Rām and Setā]. Paris: École française d'Extrême-Orient, 1989.

Bizot, François, and Oskar von Hinüber. *La guirlande de joyaux* [The garland of jewels]. Paris: École française d'Extrême-Orient, 1994.

Braun, Erik. *The Birth of Insight: Meditation, Modern Buddhism, and the Burmese Monk Ledi Sayadaw*. Chicago: The University of Chicago Press, 2013.

Cāp Bin ចាប ពិន. *Nagar kāy នគរកាយ* [The city of the body]. Phnom Penh ភ្នំពេញ: Paṇṇāgār trairata(n) បណ្ណគារត្រៃរតន៍, 1952.

———. *Trairăta(n) pūjā niṅ trairăta(n) praṇām, buddhapravatti niṅ saṃvejanīyadharm ត្រៃរ័តន៍បូជា និង ត្រៃរ័តន៍ប្រណាម, ពុទ្ធប្រវត្តិ និង សំវេជនីយធម៌* [Worship of the Three Jewels, reverence to the Three Jewels, the life of the Buddha, and stirring teachings]. Phnom Penh ភ្នំពេញ, 1971.

Chhom, Kunthea. "Le rôle du sanskrit dans le développement de la langue khmère: Une étude épigraphique du VIe au XIVe siècle [The role of Sanskrit in the development of the Khmer language: an epigraphical study from the sixth to fourteenth centuries]." PhD diss., École Pratique des Hautes Études, 2016.

Cicuzza, Claudio. *A Mirror Reflecting the Entire World: The Pāli* Buddhapādamaṅgala *or "Auspicious Signs on the Buddha's Feet."* Bangkok and Lumbini: Fragile Palm Leaves Foundation and Lumbini International Research Institute, 2011.

Cœdès, George. *Inscriptions du Cambodge* [Inscriptions of Cambodia]. Vol. II. Hanoi: Imprimerie d'Extrême-Orient, 1942.

Cowell, E. B., ed. *The Jātaka or Stories of the Buddha's Former Births*. 6 vols. Cambridge: Cambridge University Press, 1895–1907.

Crosby, Kate. *Esoteric Theravada: The Story of the Forgotten Meditation Tradition of Southeast Asia*. Boulder: Shambhala, 2020.

———. "Tantric Theravāda: A Bibliographic Essay on the Writings of François Bizot and Others on the Yogāvacara Tradition." *Contemporary Buddhism* 1.2 (2000): 141–98.

Damrong Rajanubhab สมเด็จพระเจ้าบรมวงศ์เธอ พระองค์ดิศวรกุมาร กรมพระยาดำรงราชานุภาพ. *Mahādibaman(t) มหาทิพมนต์* [Mahādibbamanta]. Bangkok กรุงเทพ: bim(b) naï ṅān braḥ rājadān blöṅ śab āṃmāty do braḥyā aŕgani(dhi)niyam (samuy ābharaṇaśiri) ca ma, ca ja, ra ja ba. พิมพ์ในงานพระราชทานเพลิงศพ อำมาตย์โท พระยาอรรคนิธินิยม (สมุย อาภรณศิริ) จ ม, จ ช, ร จ พ, 2471 [1928].

Davis, Erik W. *Deathpower: Buddhism's Ritual Imagination in Cambodia*. New York: Columbia University Press, 2016.

———. "Weaving Life out of Death: The Craft of the Rag Robe in Cambodian Ritual Technology." In *Buddhist Funeral Cultures of Southeast Asia and China*, edited by Paul Williams and Patrice Ladwig, 59–78. Cambridge: Cambridge University Press, 2012.

Edwards, Penny. *Cambodge: The Cultivation of a Nation, 1860–1945*. Honolulu: University of Hawai'i Press, 2007.

———. "Making a Religion of the Nation and Its Language: The French Protectorate (1863–1954) and the Dhammakāy." In *History, Buddhism, and New Religious Movements in Cambodia*, edited by John Marston and Elizabeth Guthrie, 63–89. Honolulu: University of Hawai'i Press, 2004.

Ek Ñịm ឯក ញឹម. *Girimāmanadasūtr prè jā bāky kāby samrāp' sūtr oy manuss mān jamṅị គិរិមានន្ទសូត្រ ប្រែជាពាក្យកាព្យ សម្រាប់សូត្រឲ្យមនុស្សមានជម្ងឺ* [The Girimānanda Sutta translated into verse for recitation to the sick]. Edited by Cāp Bin ចាប ពិន. Phnom Penh ភ្នំពេញ: Institut bouddhique ពុទ្ធសាសនបណ្ឌិត្យ, 1969 [originally published 1933].

Ek Ñịm ឯក ញឹម, and Ras' Kèv រស់ កែវ. *Bhāṇavāra kiccavatt brịk lṅāc ភាណវារ កិច្ចវត្តព្រឹកល្ងាច* [Liturgical chants for morning and evening prayers]. Phnom Penh ភ្នំពេញ: Paṇṇāgār gim seṅ បណ្ណាគារ គិម សេង, 1965.

Gabaude, Louis. *Les cetiya de sable au laos et en thailande: Les textes* [Sand cetiyas in Laos and Thailand: the texts]. Paris: École française d'Extrême-Orient, 1979.

Gaṅ' V"ān'-nuon គង់ វ៉ាន់នួន. *Prajuṃ kauvatār abhidhamm niṅ dhammasaṅveg phseṅ2 ប្រជុំកៅវតារ អភិធម្ម និង ធម្មសង្វេគផ្សេងៗ* [Collection of Ākāravattā, Abhidhamma, and various *dhammasaṃvega* chants]. Battambang បាត់ដំបង: Paṇṇāgār pradīp khmèr បណ្ណាគារប្រទីបខ្មែរ, 1962.

Garling, Wendy. *The Woman Who Raised the Buddha: The Extraordinary Life of Mahaprajapati*. Boulder: Shambhala, 2021.

Gedney, William J. "Siamese Verse Forms in Historical Perspective." In *William J. Gedney's Thai and Indic Literary Studies*, edited by Thomas J. Hudak, 45–100. Ann Arbor: Center for South and Southeast Asian Studies, University of Michigan, 1997.

Giteau, Madeleine. *Le bornage rituel des temples bouddhiques au Cambodge* [The ritual boundary marking of Buddhist temples in Cambodia]. Paris: École française d'Extrême-Orient, 1969.

Godakumbura, C. E., ed. *Hatthavanagallavihāravaṃsa*. London: Pali Text Society, 1956.

Goodall, Dominic. "What Information Can Be Gleaned from Cambodian Inscriptions about Practices Relating to the Transmission of Sanskrit Literature?" In *Indic Manuscript Cultures through the Ages: Material, Textual, and Historical Investigations*, edited by Vincenzo Vergiani, Daniele Cuneo, and Camillo Alessio Formigatti, 131–160. Berlin: De Gruyter, 2017.

Gornall, Alastair. *Rewriting Buddhism: Pali Literature and Monastic Reform in Sri Lanka, 1157–1270*. London: University College London Press, 2020.

Grant, Catherine. "Social Shifts and Viable Musical Futures: The Case of Cambodian *Smot*." In *Ethnomusicology: A Contemporary Reader, Volume II*, edited by Jennifer C. Post, 97–110. New York: Routledge, 2018.

Guthrie, Elizabeth. "The Performance of the Māravijaya Episode during Buddhābhiṣeka." *Udaya: Journal of Khmer Studies* 4 (2003): 11–19.

———. "A Study of the History and Cult of the Buddhist Earth Deity in Mainland Southeast Asia." PhD diss., University of Canterbury, 2004.

Hallisey, Charles. "*Nibbānasutta*: An Allegedly Non-Canonical *Sutta* on *Nibbāna* as a Great City." *Journal of the Pali Text Society* 18 (1993): 97–130.

Hansen, Anne Ruth. "Buddhist Communities of Belonging in Early-Twentieth-Century Cambodia." In *Theravada Buddhist Encounters with Modernity*, edited by Juliane Schober and Steven Collins, 62–77. New York: Routledge, 2017.

———. "Khmer Identity and Theravāda Buddhism." In *History, Buddhism, and New Religious Movements in Cambodia*, edited by John Marston and Elizabeth Guthrie, 40–62. Honolulu: University of Hawai'i Press, 2004.

———. *How to Behave: Buddhism and Modernity in Colonial Cambodia, 1860–1930*. Honolulu: University of Hawai'i Press, 2007.

Harris, Ian. *Buddhism in a Dark Age: Cambodian Monks under Pol Pot*. Honolulu: University of Hawai'i Press, 2013.

———. *Cambodian Buddhism: History and Practice*. Honolulu: University of Hawai'i Press, 2005.

Holt, John Clifford. "Pchum Ben: Caring for the Dead Ritually in Cambodia." In *Theravada Traditions: Buddhist Ritual Cultures in Contemporary Southeast Asia and Sri Lanka*, 239–308. Honolulu: University of Hawai'i Press, 2017.

Huot Tāt ហួត តាត. *Kalyāṇamitt rapas' khñuṃ កល្យាណមិត្តរបស់ខ្ញុំ* [My spiritual friend]. Phnom Penh ភ្នំពេញ: Institut bouddhique ពុទ្ធសាសនបណ្ឌិត្យ, 1970.

Ind ឥន្ទ, Suttantaprījā សុត្តន្តប្រីជា. "Ārādhanā dhammakathik oy samtèṅ dhaŕm អារាធនាធម្មកថិកឲ្យសម្តែងធម៌ [Invitation to the preacher to preach the Dharma]." *Kambuja Suriya កម្ពុជសុរិយា* 1 (1926–1927): 34–37.

Institut bouddhique ពុទ្ធសាសនបណ្ឌិត្យ. *Bhāṇavār pālī ភាណវារបាលី* [Collected liturgical chants in Pali]. Phnom Penh ភ្នំពេញ: Institut bouddhique ពុទ្ធសាសនបណ្ឌិត្យ, 1936.

Jacob, Judith M. "Some Features of Khmer Versification." In *Cambodian*

Linguistics, Literature and History: Collected Articles, edited by David Smyth, 212–24. London: Routledge, 1993.

———. *The Traditional Literature of Cambodia: A Preliminary Guide*. Oxford: Oxford University Press, 1996.

Jaini, Padmanabh S. "The Apocryphal Jātakas of Southeast Asian Buddhism." In *Collected Papers on Buddhist Studies*, 375–393. Delhi: Motilal Banarsidass, 2001.

———. "(Introduction to and Translation of) *Ākāravattārasutta*: An 'Apocryphal' Sutta from Thailand." In *Collected Papers on Buddhist Studies*, 535–57. Delhi: Motilal Banarsidass, 2001.

———. "Mahādibbamanta: A *Paritta* Manuscript from Cambodia." In *Collected Papers on Buddhist Studies*, 503–26. Delhi: Motilal Banarsidass, 2001.

Jăy M"ai ជ័យ ម៉ៃ, Braḥ Vinăyadhar ព្រះវិន័យធរ. *Nānādhammasaṅveg នានាធម្មសង្វេគ* [Various *dhammasaṃvega* chants]. Phnom Penh ភ្នំពេញ: Paṇṇāgār gim seṅ បណ្ណាគារ គិម សេង, 1942.

———. *Nānādhammasaṅveg bistār នានាធម្មសង្វេគពិស្ដារ* [Various *dhammasaṃvega* chants, extended version]. Phnom Penh ភ្នំពេញ: Paṇṇāgār gim seṅ បណ្ណាគារ គិម សេង, 1949.

Jhịm Ŝum ឈឹម ស៊ុម. *Pad sarabhaññ បទសរភញ្ញ* [*Sarabhañña* chants]. Phnom Penh ភ្នំពេញ: Paṇṇāgār sumanasuvat(thi) បណ្ណាគារសុមនសុវត្ថិ, 1966.

Keo Narom កែវ ណារុំ. *Maratak tantrī khmèr / Cambodian Music មរតកតន្ត្រីខ្មែរ* [The heritage of Khmer music]. Phnom Penh ភ្នំពេញ: Reyum រ៉េយ៉ឹម, 2004.

Kèv Ûc កែវ អ៊ូច. *Parittasamodhān pālī បរិត្តសមោធានបាលី* [Collected Pali *paritta* chants]. Phnom Penh ភ្នំពេញ: Institut bouddhique ពុទ្ធសាសនបណ្ឌិត្យ, 1968.

Khing Hoc Dy ឃីង ហុក ឌី. *Suttantaprījā ind niṅ snā ṭai សុត្តន្តប្រីជាឥន្ទ និង ស្នាដៃ* [Suttantaprījā Ind and his works]. Phnom Penh ភ្នំពេញ: Paṇṇāgār aṅgar បណ្ណាគារអង្គរ, 2012.

Kobayashi, Satoru. "An Ethnographic Study on the Reconstruction of Buddhist Practice in Two Cambodian Temples: With the Special Reference to Buddhist *Samay* and *Boran*." *Southeast Asian Studies* 42.4 (March 2005): 489–518.

Kourilsky, Grégory. "La place des ascendants familiaux dans le bouddhisme des Lao [The place of familial ancestors in Lao Buddhism]." PhD diss., École Pratique des Hautes Études, 2015.

———. "Note sur la piété filiale en Asie du Sud-Est theravādin [Note on filial piety in Theravadin Southeast Asia]." *Aséanie* 20 (2007) : 27–54.

Kun Sopheap. "Les rituels accompagnant les prédications dans le bouddhisme traditionnel des Khmers [The rituals accompanying sermons in traditional Khmer Buddhism]." Translated by Olivier de Bernon. *Aséanie* 32 (December 2013) : 97–107.

Lagirarde, François. "Gavampati in Southeast Asia." In *Brill's Encyclopedia of Buddhism, Volume II: Lives*, edited by Jonathan A. Silk, 191–95. Leiden: Brill, 2019.

Langenberg, Amy. *Birth in Buddhism: The Suffering Fetus and Female Freedom*. New York: Routledge, 2017.

Lī Sumunī លី សុមុនី. *Kaṃnāby khmèr កំនាព្យខ្មែរ* [Khmer poetry] . Phnom Penh ភ្នំពេញ: Griḥsthān poḥ bumb niṅ cèk phsāy គ្រឹះស្ថានបោះពុម្ព និង ចែកផ្សាយ, 2009.

Lī Suvīr លី សុវីរ. *Bidhī dhvö puṇy buddhābhisek bī samăy purāṇ ពិធីធ្វើបុណ្យពុទ្ធាភិសេក ពីសម័យបុរាណ* [Procedures for performing Buddha image consecration rites from ancient times]. Phnom Penh ភ្នំពេញ, 2009.

———. *Bidhī dhvö puṇy khmoc satavatsa(r) dī 19 niṅ ṭöm satavatsa(r) dī 20 ពិធីធ្វើបុណ្យខ្មោច សតវត្សរ៍ទី ១៩ និង ដើមសតវត្សរ៍ទី ២០* [Procedures for performing funerals in the nineteenth and twentieth centuries]. Phnom Penh ភ្នំពេញ, 2002.

———. *Bidhī hau bralịṅ tām rapiep khmèr purāṇ ពិធីហៅព្រលឹង តាមរបៀបខ្មែរបុរាណ* [Procedures for the 'calling the spirits' rite in accordance with ancient Khmer practices]. Phnom Penh ភ្នំពេញ, 2010.

———. *Mar̊tak braḥ buddhasāsanā khmèr មត៌កព្រះពុទ្ធសាសនាខ្មែរ* [The heritage of Khmer Buddhism]. Phnom Penh ភ្នំពេញ, 2005.

Malalasekera, G.P. *Dictionary of Pāli Proper Names*. 2 vols. London: Pali Text Society, 1974.

Marston, John. "Reconstructing 'Ancient' Cambodian Buddhism." *Contemporary Buddhism* 9.1 (2008): 99–121.

———. "El Buda Jayanti en Camboya [The Buddha Jayanti in Cambodia]." *Estudios de Asia y África* 44.1 (January–April 2009): 9–30.

Miev Nand មៀវ នន្ទ. *Buddhapravatti bāky kāby ពុទ្ធប្រវត្តិពាក្យកាព្យ* [The life of the Buddha in verse]. Phnom Penh ភ្នំពេញ, 1951.

Mikaelian, Grégory. "Recherches sur l'histoire du fonctionnement politique des royautés post- angkorienne (c. 1600–c. 1720) [Research on the history of the political workings of post-Angkorian monarchies]." PhD diss., Université Paris IV–Sorbonne, 2006.

Ñāṇ Jhīn ញាណ ឈីន. *Visākhapūjā: gāthā bhāsit prè bāky kāby វិសាខបូជា*

៖ *គាថាភាសិត ប្រែពាក្យកាព្យ* [Visākhapūjā: Pali stanzas translated into Khmer verse]. Phnom Penh ភ្នំពេញ: Paṇṇāgār gim seṅ បណ្ណាគារ គិមសេង, 1952.

Ñāṇamoli, Bhikkhu. *The Path of Purification*. Seattle: BPS Pariyatti Editions, 1999.

Nū Kan នូ កន. *Bimbānibbān ពិម្ពានិព្វាន* [Yasodharā Bimbā's passing away into nirvana]. Phnom Penh ភ្នំពេញ: Paṇṇāgār gim seṅ បណ្ណាគារ គិមសេង, 1960.

Nuon Saṃ-ân នួន សំអ៊ាន. *Gihippatipatti gharāvāsadharm គិហិប្បតិបត្តិ ឃរាវាសធម៌* [Lay practices and Dharma texts for householders]. Phnom Penh ភ្នំពេញ: Sā īm, tūp lekh 66 jān' ḷau tīö phsār ūr ṛssī សា អុ៊ីម តូបលេខ 66 ជាន់ឡៅតឿ ផ្សារអូរឫស្សី, 2544 [2001].

———. *Gihippatipatti gharāvāsadharm គិហិប្បតិបត្តិ ឃរាវាសធម៌* [Lay practices and Dharma texts for householders]. Phnom Penh ភ្នំពេញ: Roṅ bumb bhnaṃ beñ រោងពុម្ពភ្នំពេញ, 2547 [2004].

Nyanaponika Thera and Hellmuth Hecker. *Great Disciples of the Buddha: Their Lives, Their Works, Their Legacy*. Boston: Wisdom, 2003.

Perreira, Todd LeRoy. "Whence Theravāda? The Modern Genealogy of an Ancient Term." In *How Theravāda Is Theravāda? Exploring Buddhist Identities*, edited by Peter Skilling, Jason A. Carbine, Claudio Cicuzza, and Santi Pakdeekham, 443–571. Chiang Mai: Silkworm Books, 2012.

Phibul Choompolpaisal. "Nimitta and Visual Methods in Siamese and Lao Meditation Traditions from the 17th Century to the Present Day." *Contemporary Buddhism*, 20.1–2 (2019): 152–83.

Pou [Lewitz], Saveros. *Un dictionnaire du khmer-moyen* [A dictionary of Middle Khmer]. Phnom Penh: Institut bouddhique, 2016.

———. "Inscriptions khmères K. 144 et K. 177 [Khmer inscriptions K. 144 and K. 177]." *Bulletin de l'École française d'Extrême-Orient* 70 (1981): 101–20.

———. "Les inscriptions modernes d'Angkor Vat [The modern inscriptions of Angkor Wat]." *Journal asiatique* 260 (1972): 107–29.

———. "La littérature didactique khmère: Les cpāp' [Khmer didiactic literature: the *cpāp*']." *Journal asiatique* 269 (1981): 454–66.

———. "Notes on Brahmanic Gods in Theravadin Cambodia." *Indologica Taurinensia* 14 (1988): 339–51.

Pou, Saveros, and Ang Choulean [Chouléan]. "Vocabulaire khmer relatif au surnaturel [Khmer vocabulary concerning the supernatural]." *Seksa Khmer* 10–13 (1987–1990): 59–129.

Preap Chanmara ព្រាប ចាន់ម៉ារ៉ា. "Braḥ baisraba(ṇ) ṛ deb srūv ព្រះពៃស្រពណ៍

ឬទេពស្រូវ [Vaiśravaṇa or the god of rice]." *KhmeRenaissance* [online] chapter 4, article 81, (2019–2020). https://www.yosothor.org/publications/khmer-renaissance/chapter-four/Preahpeisrop.html

———. "Phcāñ' mār ផ្ចាញ់មារ [The defeat of Māra]." *Magazine of the Ministry of Culture and Fine Arts ទស្សនាវដ្ដី ក្រសួងវប្បធម៌ និង វិចិត្រសិល្បៈ* 21 (November 2016): 2–26.

Pussadeva, Samtéc Braḥ Săṅgharāj สมเด็จพระสังฆราช (ปุสฺสเทว). *Svat man(t) chpăp hlvaṅ สวดมนต์ฉบับหลวง* [Pali chants, royal edition]. Bangkok กรุงเทพ: Mahāmakuṭ rājavidyālăy มหามุฏราชวิทยาลัย, 2496 [1953] (originally published 2423 [1880]).

Rama IV พระบาทสมเด็จพระจอมเกล้าเจ้าอยู่หัว. *Ṕraḥjum braḥ rājaniban(dh) bhāṣā pālī naï braḥ pād samtéc braḥ caam klau$_2$ cau$_2$ ayū$_1$ hvă ประชุมพระราชนิพนธ์ภาษาบาลี ใน พระบาทสมเด็จพระจอมเกล้าเจ้าอยู่หัว* [Collected Pali works of King Rama IV]. Bangkok กรุงเทพ: Mahātherasamāgam มหาเถรสมาคม, 2547 [2004].

Ras' Kèv រស់ កែវ. *Gihipratipatti bises bistār គិហិប្រតិបត្តិពិសេសពិស្ដារ* [Lay practices, special extended version]. Phnom Penh ភ្នំពេញ: Paṇṇāgār gim seṅ បណ្ណាគារ គិម សេង, 1966.

Ratnayaka, Shanta. "The Bodhisattva Ideal of Theravāda." *The Journal of the International Association of Buddhist Studies* 8.2 (1985): 85–110.

Revire, Nicolas. "Back to the Future: The Emergence of Past and Future Buddhas in Khmer Buddhism." In *Early Theravadin Cambodia: Perspectives from the History of Art and Archaeology*, edited by Ashley Thompson, 231–68. Singapore: National University of Singapore Press, 2022.

Reynolds, Frank E., and Mani B. Reynolds. *Three Worlds According to King Ruang: A Thai Buddhist Cosmology*. Berkeley: Center for South Asia Studies, University of California, 1982.

Rhys Davids, T. W., and J. Estlin Carpenter. *The Dīgha Nikāya, Vol. II*. London: Pali Text Society, 1903.

Roeské, M. "Métrique Khmère, Bat et Kalabat [Khmer meter, *pad* and *kalapad*]." *Anthropos* 8 (1913): 670–87 and 1026–43.

Samuels, Jeffrey. "The Bodhisattva Ideal in Theravāda Buddhist Theory and Practice: A Reevaluation of the Bodhisattva-Śrāvaka Opposition." *Philosophy East & West* 47.3 (July 1997): 399–415.

San Sarin. "Les textes liturgiques fondamentaux du bouddhisme cambodgien actuel [The basic liturgical texts of contemporary Cambodian Buddhism]." PhD diss., École Pratique des Hautes Études, 1975.

Sandhar Jā សន្ធរ ជា. *Lpök madrī ល្បើកមទ្រី* [The tale of Madrī]. Phnom Penh ភ្នំពេញ: Paṇṇāgār gim seṅ បណ្ណាគារ គិម សេង, 1960.

Santi Pakdeekham. "Court Buddhism in Thai-Khmer Relations During the Reign of King Rama IV (King Mongkut)." In *Buddhist Dynamics in Premodern and Early Modern Southeast Asia*, edited by D. Christian Lammerts, 417–28. Singapore: ISES–Yusof Ishak Institute, 2015.

Sèm Sūr សែម សូរ. *Prajuṃ dharm kāvatār niṅ sūtr braḥ dhămm ប្រជុំធម៌ការតារ និង សូត្រព្រះធម្ម* [Collected Ākāravattā texts and Abhidhamma chants]. Phnom Penh ភ្នំពេញ, 1972.

———. *Prajuṃ dharm pad niṅ dhammasaṅveg ប្រជុំធម៌បទ និង ធម្មសង្វេគ* [Collected Dharma songs and *dhammasaṃvega* texts]. Phnom Penh ភ្នំពេញ, [1970?].

Shulman, Eviatar. *Visions of the Buddha: Creative Dimensions of Early Buddhist Scripture.* New York: Oxford University Press, 2021.

Siyonn Sophearith ស៊ីយ៉ុន សុភារិទ្ធ. "Rak buddho រកពុទ្ធោ [The phrase '*rak buddho*']." *KhmeRenaissance* 2 (2006–2007): 148–49.

———. *Pidan (Bitān) in Khmer Culture ពិតាននៅក្នុងជំនឿនិងកិច្ចប្រតិបត្តិ* [Buddhist ceiling textiles in belief and practice]. Phnom Penh: Reyum, 2008.

———. "Smūt paṇtāṃ nāṅ mahāmāyā ស្មូតបណ្តាំនាងមហាមាយា [Chanting 'Māyā's Guidance for Gotamī']." *KhmeRenaissance* 7 (2011–2012): 137–38.

Skilling, Peter. "The Sambuddhe Verses and Later Theravādin Buddhology." In *Buddhism and Buddhist Literature of South-East Asia: Selected Papers*, edited by Claudio Cicuzza, 128–54. Bangkok: Fragile Palm Leaves Foundation, 2009.

———. "Some Literary References in 'La Grande Inscription d'Angkor' (IMA 38)." In *Buddhism and Buddhist Literature of South-East Asia: Selected Papers*, edited by Claudio Cicuzza, 69–79. Bangkok: Fragile Palm Leaves Foundation, 2009.

Som Suvaṇṇ សោម សុវណ្ណ. *Prajuṃ māghapūjā niṅ visākhapūjā ប្រជុំ មាឃបូជា និង វិសាខបូជា* [Collected chants for Māghapūjā and Visākhapūjā]. Phnom Penh ភ្នំពេញ: Paṇṇāgār khmèr niyam lekh 55 vithī p"äsdăr បណ្ណាគារខ្មែរនិយមលេខ ៥៥ វិថីប៉ាស្ទ័រ, 1966.

Thompson, Ashley. *Calling the Souls: A Cambodian Ritual Text / Le rappel des âmes: texte rituel khmer*. Phnom Penh: Reyum, 2005.

———. *Engendering the Buddhist State: Territory, Sovereignty and Sexual Difference in the Inventions of Angkor*. London: Routledge, 2016.

———. "The Future of Cambodia's Past: A Messianic Middle-Period Cambodian Royal Cult." In *History, Buddhism, and New Religious Movements in Cambodia*, edited by John Marston and Elizabeth Guthrie, 13–39. Honolulu: University of Hawai'i Press, 2004.

———. "Mémoires du Cambodge [Memories of Cambodia]." PhD diss., Université de Paris 8, 1999.

V"ėn Sun វ៉ឺន ស៊ុន, and Y"ān' Pūrin យ៉ាន់ បូរិន. *Rapāyakāra(ṇ) pūk sarup laddhaphal nai kār srāv jrāv pad smūtr kāṃṇāby របាយការណ៍បូកសរុបលទ្ធផលនៃការស្រាវជ្រាវបទស្មូត្រកំណាព្យ* [Report summarizing research into the melodies used for poetry recitation]. Edited by Thī Căndo ធី ច័ន្ទ and Iev Sukr-hān អៀវ សុក្រហាន. Phnom Penh ភ្នំពេញ: Samāgam rañjanabuddhibodhanamitt [CamboKids] សមាគមរញ្ជនពុទ្ធិពោធនមិត្ត, 2003.

Walker, Trent. "Bilingualism: Theravāda Bitexts across South and Southeast Asia." In *The Routledge Handbook of Theravada Buddhism*, edited by Ashley Thompson and Stephen Berkwitz, 271–284. London: Routledge, 2022.

———. "Carved Chants and Sermons on Stone: Epigraphic Evidence for Buddhist Literature in Middle Cambodia." *Udaya, Journal of Khmer Studies* 15 (2020 [appeared in 2021]): 57–93.

———. "A Chant Has Nine Lives: The Circulation of Theravada Liturgies in Thailand, Cambodia, and Vietnam." *Journal of Vietnamese Studies* 15.3 (Summer 2020): 36–78.

———. "Echoes of a Sanskrit Past: Liturgical Curricula and the Pali Uṇhissavijaya in Cambodia." In *Katā me rakkhā, katā me parittā: Protecting the Protective Texts and Manuscripts*, edited by Claudio Cicuzza, 49–116. Bangkok: Fragile Palm Leaves Foundation, 2018.

———. "Framing the Sacred: Cambodian Buddhist Painting." Exhibit catalog. Berkeley: Institute of East Asian Studies, University of California, Berkeley, 2013.

———. "How Sophea Lost Her Sight." *Peace Review* 23.4 (2011): 522–29.

———. "Indic-Vernacular Bitexts from Thailand: Bilingual Modes of Philology, Exegetics, Homiletics, and Poetry, 1450–1850," *Journal of the American Oriental Society* 140.3 (2020): 675–99.

———. "In Praise of Sister Queens." In *Out of the Shadows of Angkor: Cambodian Poetry, Prose, and Performance through the Ages*, edited by Sharon May, Christophe Macquet, Trent Walker, Phina So, and Rinith Taing, 4–5. *Mānoa: A Pacific Journal of International Writing* 33:2–

34:1, edited by Frank Stewart. Honolulu: University of Hawai'i Press, 2022.
———. "Quaking and Clarity: Saṃvega and Pasāda in Cambodian Dharma Songs." B.A. thesis, Stanford University, 2010.
———. "Saṃvega and Pasāda: Dharma Songs in Contemporary Cambodia," *Journal of the International Association of Buddhist Studies* 41 (2018): 271–325.
———. "Stirring and Stilling: A Liturgy of Cambodian Dharma Songs." Multimedia website. 2011. http://www.stirringandstilling.org. Paginated PDF version available at https://www.trentwalker.org/dharma-songs.
———. "This Heap Called a Body." *The Margins*, Transpacific Literary Project, Asian American Writers' Workshop (March: "A Notebook of Lullabies"). 2021. https://aaww.org/this-heap-called-a-body/
———. "Unfolding Buddhism: Communal Scripts, Localized Translations, and the Work of the Dying in Cambodian Chanted Leporellos." PhD diss., University of California, Berkeley, 2018. https://www.trentwalker.org/unfolding-buddhism. PDF version available at https://digitalassets.lib.berkeley.edu/etd/ucb/text/Walker_berkeley_0028E_17910.pdf

Index

Abhidhamma, 40, 61, 65, 191, 204, 240, 248, 268–69. See also *Paṭṭhāna*
"Absolving All Faults," 71–79, 204, 215, 219, 251
  sins in, attitude toward, 195, 253–55
  title of, 252–53
aggregates, five, 43, 200, 240, 267
Ākāravattā, 61, 204, 248
Allakappa, 52
alms, 30, 45, 67, 87, 90, 93, 95, 171, 288
Ānanda, 3, 43, 45–46, 161, 197, 243, 282
anger, 74, 133, 137, 184
Angkor Wat, xv, xix, 287, 289
animals, 75, 195, 253, 255, 258
arhatship, 192, 193. *See also* four stages of awakening (four fruits)
ascetic seers, 199
Ashoka, 141, 145, 276
Ashokan inscriptions, 211
"Asking for Mother's Forgiveness," 83–84, 190, 205, 216, 256–57
aspirations, 122–23, 261
  Buddha as model for, 149
  for buddhahood, 79, 255, 292
  in "Lotus Offering to Realize Awakening," 182–86, 192, 193, 289–92
  to meet Maitreya, 48, 55, 149, 164, 179, 186, 193
attachment, 14
  binding of, 119–20, 121, 137, 195, 271, 294n22
  as Māras, 194–95
Aṭṭhamīpūjā Gāthā, 245, 298n14
audio recordings, 213, 214, 258
austerities, 29, 236, 238, 241
authors, xv, xvii, 213–14, 228
Ayudhyā, 127, 129, 273
Ayutthaya, 285

Balahaka (horse king), 166
baṃnol meter, 216
Bejr Sukhā, 214, 258
Bhaddiya realm, 53
Bimbā, Princess, 23, 230. *See also* Yasodharā Bimbā
Bimbānibbāna, 230
birth, suffering of, 104, 264
bliss, 54, 106, 126, 147, 152, 277
Bodh Gaya, 203
Bodhi tree, 196, 199, 206–7, 244
  homage to, 163, 182, 283–84
  merit of, 36
  as symbol, 149
Bodhidatta, 143
bodhisattvas
  aspirations of, 192
  generosity of, 255
  as sprouts of buddhas, 54, 131, 247, 273
body
  abnormalities of, 76, 255
  binding of, 294n22
  braliṅ and, 107, 200, 265
  contemplating, 43, 106, 119–20, 125, 126, 127–28
  after death, 111–13, 119
  at death, 101–2, 109–11, 118–19
  debt to, 57
  doors/holes of, 112, 137, 140, 200, 294n38
  gift of, 263

body (*continued*)
  guṇ and heart syllables on, 67–69, 191, 250–51
  jewel hidden within (*maṇipaduma*), 131, 272
  like floating corpse, 103–4
  in meditation, 103
  Three Marks and, 97
Braḥ Dhammalikhit, 213, 287
Brahmā, 138, 140, 166, 184. *See also* Sahampati Brahmā
Brahmā realms, 35, 53, 123, 167, 173
brahmagīti meter, 215
  English structure and, 221
  poems in, 216, 239, 243, 249–50, 259, 263, 280, 288
  unrhymed poems, 242, 277, 279, 282–83
Brahmi script, 211
breath, 103, 109, 111, 126, 268
Buddha Gautama, 134, 192, 196, 275
  epithets for, 244
  footprints of, 144, 167–68, 285
  four pivots of, 48, 203–4, 244
  jewel of (*vaidurya*), 131, 272
  life span, 41
  passing of, 43–48, 242–44
  past lives of, 3, 14, 62, 197, 289 (*see also* Jātakas)
  praises and supplications, 61, 107–8, 153–54, 159, 181–82, 253–54, 279
  qualities of, 190
  as refuge, 155
  relics of, 199
  syllables representing, 65
  teaching career of, 41–42, 241
  See also feet, Buddha's; Siddhartha Gautama
Buddha images, 149
  consecrating, 171–79, 286, 288
  homage to, 163, 284
  purpose of, 154
Buddha within, 191, 192, 193
Buddhaghosa, 142–45, 240, 276. See also *Samantapāsādikā*; *Visuddhimagga*
buddhahood, 6, 79, 192, 255, 273, 292
Buddhapravatti bāky kāby (Miev Nand), 236
buddhas
  analogies for, 194
  of Fortunate Eon, 133–35, 136, 146–47, 275–76
  jewel of, 196
  merit of, 79
  names of, 191
  past and future, 192–93
"Buddha's Eightfold Array, The," 161–62, 197, 216, 282–83
"Buddha's Last Words, The," 43–44, 205, 216, 221, 242
"Buddha's Passing Away, The," 45–46, 205, 216, 243
Buddhavaṃsa, 239–40, 297n8
Buddhism
  and Buddhist poetry, relationship of, xv
  Cambodia's contributions to, xvi
  core values of, 211
  history of, 141–45, 276–77
  relationships in, 57

calendar, 57–58, 198–99, 203–4
Cambodia, xv–xvi, 285
  fashion trends, historic, 119–20, 270–71
  Kampong Speu province, 246
  mortuary practices, historic, 111–12, 263
  social upheavals in, 214
  Yasodharā Bimbā in, 230
Cambodian Buddhism, xviii, 189
  Buddha, view of in, 196
  buddhahood in, valorization of, 192
  complexity of, 200–201
  esoteric dimensions of, 57 (*see also* esoteric tradition)
  festival calendar of, 203–4
  guṇ in, 189–91, 293n3
  Pali texts in, 248, 249

Chaddanta, 7, 229
"Chaddanta's Lament," 5–6, 205, 216, 229
Channa, 238
channels, inner (*nāḍī*), 191
charnel grounds, 119, 263
Chiang Mai, 285
colonialism, 189, 214
compassion, 122, 196, 241, 279
consciousness, 126, 265
consecration rites, 149, 171–79, 203, 206–7, 288
cosmology, 198–99, 200, 206, 254
craving, 24, 104
cremation, 49–50, 205, 245, 263
"Cremation of the Buddha, The," 49–50, 204, 216, 244–45
Cūḷamaṇī stupa, 238

daily worship, 107, 149, 206
death, 97, 195–96
  dying process, 109–11, 118–19, 268–69
  inevitability of, 105, 114–15, 140, 264, 300n42
  and local deities, role of, 200
  suffering of, 24, 104, 264
deathbed rites
  corpse's mouth in, 269
  decline of, 207
  faults, reviewing in, 253
  recitations in, 203, 204–5, 270, 272
debts of gratitude, 57, 190–91, 193
  awareness of, 122
  dedication for, 265–66, 301n44
  lacking merit to pay, 133
dedication
  with iminā and pouring water, 105, 265–66, 301n44
  to parents, 84
  prayer for, 95, 260–61
"Dedication of Merit," 95, 198, 206, 215, 260–61
Deer Park, 241
"Defeat of Māra, The," 31–37, 199, 215, 236–38
  and "Leaving the Palace," relationship of, 235
  performance and recitation, 206–7, 238
Devanam Raja, 141
devotion, 149, 196
Dhajagga Sutta, 248
dhammakāya (spiritual Buddha body), 206–7
Dhammapada Aṭṭhakathā, 289
Dharma, 102
  as anchor, 103
  capacity for, 240
  death and, 137–38
  decorum of, 122, 271
  effort in, 64
  exhortation to study, 105–6, 114–15, 139
  homage to, 159
  jewel of, 156, 196–97, 280
  losing zeal for, 121–22
  qualities of, 40, 41, 240
  recalling, 138
  as rooted in body, 121
  syllable for, 65
"Dharma of Union, The," 171–79, 199, 206, 216, 286–88, 304n86
Dharma songs (*dharm pad*), xv, xvi
  composition, time of, 189, 200–201
  core themes of, 201
  emotions in, 3
  as living practice, 207
  performance of, 210–11
  purpose of, 218
  sources, 227
  survival of, 214
  titles, 227–28
  transmission, two modes of, xvi–xvii, 209, 210, 213
  as universal tradition, xvii
Dīgha Nikāya, 240, 263, 300n40
digital formats, 213
disciples, eightfold array, 161–62, 282–83
"Divine Messengers," 23–24, 216, 234, 238

Dukūlaka, 231
Duṭṭhagāminī Abhaya, 142, 145, 276

earth
debt to, 59, 62, 247
local religious beliefs about, 199–200
patience of, 57
Earth Goddess, 32–34, 59, 134, 199. *See also* Nāṅ Gaṅhīṅ Braḥ Dharaṇī
Ek Ñịm, 262
Eravana (elephant king), 166
esoteric tradition
in "Fortunate Eon," 276
Khmer alphabet in, 191
in "Lesson in Meditation," 272
nirvana in, 193, 194
sources for, 191–92
ethical conduct, 194

faith, 40
bright/radiant, 48, 106
cultivating, 126
during meditation, 129
merit and, 139
in offerings, 151, 177
pure, 147
in relics, 50, 54
vows and, 125
fathers
consonants of, 69, 250
debts to, 61, 67, 73
jewel from (*maniratna*), 130, 272
feet, Buddha's, 33, 149, 196
benefits of honoring, 169–70
symbols on, 165–67, 169, 182, 196, 285
"Filial Debts," 81–82, 190, 205, 216, 255–56
Five Māras, 40, 240
five obstacles, 120, 271
forgiveness, 57, 83–84, 252–53, 254–55, 256
"Fortunate Eon, The," 133–47, 197, 204, 215, 219, 274–75
arrangement of, 221–22
buddhas in, 133–35, 136, 193, 194
composition and recensions of, 276–77
on dying process, 195
Four Assemblies, 41, 240
four continents, 199
four elements, 118, 140, 191, 200, 269, 272
four foundations of awareness, 125–29, 272, 273
four jewels, 129–31, 272–73
four stages of awakening (four fruits), 146, 147, 268, 273, 278, 288
"Four Thieves, The" 103–4, 194, 204, 216, 219, 263–64, 267
Four Truths, 40, 99, 240
fourfold community, 196
"Funeral March," 99, 216, 261
funerary rituals, 57, 99, 203, 205, 206, 207
binding in, 271, 294n22
Pali recitations in, 263, 300n40
processions in, 261
stupas in, 248

Gandhara, 53, 172
Gavampati (aka Kaccāyana), 282, 283
gestation, 71–72, 83, 254, 257
ghosts and spirits, 200
after body's death, 111–13, 265, 269
debts to, 63
Girimānanda Sutta, 204
giving (Pali: *dāna*), 193–94
goddesses, 199, 200
gods, 198
intervention of, 16, 23–24, 232
as messengers, 23, 238
offerings by, 36
Group of Five, 41, 241
guṇ, 189–91, 247–48, 266, 293n3
internal and external, 272
meditation on, 269
of natural world, 57, 60, 62, 73, 198–99, 248, 253
of Three Jewels, 57, 60–61, 196–98
vowel symbols of, 249
See also debts of gratitude; virtue

Hatthavanagallavihāravaṃsa,
colophon, 289–92, 305n94
heart syllables, 57, 190–91
eightfold array and, 283
in four foundations of awareness, 125, 126, 129, 272
syllables used in, 249
hells, 59–60, 63, 106, 137
Himalaya Mountains, 174
Himavant forest, 127, 166, 199, 273
Hinduism, 198
"Homage Octet, The," 159–60, 204, 216, 280–81
"Homage to All Holy Sites," 163–64, 193, 206, 216, 283–84, 304n74
"Homage to the Three Jewels," 155–57, 206, 216, 279–80
humans, 265
inner virtues of, 272
rebirth as, 123, 136, 149
suffering of, 105
hungry ghosts, 88–89, 198, 200, 205–6, 258–59
"Hungry Ghosts' Lament," 87–91, 200, 206, 216, 257–59
"Hymn to the Buddha's Feet," 165–70, 196, 199, 204, 215, 259, 284–85

ignorance, 40, 103, 240
illness and disease, 97, 291
as karmic consequence, 75–76, 255
suffering of, 104, 264
impermanence, 21, 24, 99, 123, 133, 262–63, 275
"In Praise of the Earth," 59–64, 190, 199, 204, 215, 247–49
Ind, Suttantaprījā, 214, 239, 241–42, 297n12
Indra, 29, 138, 140, 142, 166, 185, 198, 236. *See also* Trāyastriṃśa Heaven
"Indra's Lute," 29–30, 204, 216, 219, 236
inscriptions, 211, 289, 296n8
intentional action, 195
intoxication, 75, 77, 253, 255, 292
"Invitation to Preach the Dharma," 39–42, 198, 204, 216, 219, 239–42, 297n10, 297n12

Jāli, 13–17, 232, 233
Jambudvīpa, 147, 172, 199
Jātakas
Chaddanta, 5–7, 229
Suvaṇṇasāma, 9–12, 231
Vessantara, 13–19, 232, 233, 248
Jăy M"ai, 214, 235, 236, 242, 243, 244
Jotikasetthi, 182, 289
Jūjaka, 14–16, 232, 233
Juon Ṇāt, 214, 278

Kailash, Mount, 166
kākagati meter
poems in, 215, 234, 236–37, 245, 247, 251, 260, 264, 266, 269, 271, 274, 284
rhyming and, 221–23
Kakusandha Buddha, 134, 192
Kampong Cham, 287
kaṃraṅ kèv ("garlands of gems"), 217, 232
Kanthaka, 238
Kapilavastu, 23, 52
karma
changing, 113–14
death and, 99, 110
for Dharma practice, 153
exhaustion of, 136, 139
merit and, 194
rebirth and, 155, 195
results of, 85, 89
Kassapa (disciple). *See* Mahākassapa
Kassapa Buddha, 134, 192
Ketumala, 144
Khmer alphabet, 191
consonants, 67–70, 191, 250–51
vowels, 65–66, 249–50, 272
Khmer Buddhism
body, view of in, 191
buddhas in, 192
ideological frameworks of, 189–90

languages of, 209–10
Nāṅ Gaṅhīṅ Braḥ Dharaṇī in, 238
nirvana in, 192
pāp (sin) in, 195
Khmer Empire, xv
Khmer language, xv, xvi, xvii, 3
manuscripts in, 211–12
and Pali, differences in, 209–10
script, 190, 211, 213
spoken, 190
symbols in, xviii–xix
Khmer Rouge, xvi, 214
killing, 77, 195, 253, 258, 291
kindness (*mettā*), 102, 122, 182, 231
Koet Ran, xvi, 218, 257
Koṇāgamana Buddha, 134, 192
Koṇḍañña, 161, 197, 282
Kṛṣṇā, 13–17, 19, 232, 233
Kruṅ Bālī (serpent king), 199–200
Kusinagara, 51, 52, 203, 246
Kuva kingdom, 53

Lanka, 53, 141, 142, 167, 172, 173. *See also* Sri Lanka
Laos, xv, 196, 238, 248, 273
laypeople, 82, 195, 197, 204, 205–6, 239, 243, 256, 283
"Leaving the Palace," 25, 215, 234–35
leporello manuscripts, 211–12, 213, 228, 275
"Lesson in Meditation, A," 125–32, 191, 194, 204, 215, 271–74
Lī Suvīr, 214, 261
life spans, 63, 195
lone buddha (*paccekabuddha*), 35, 238
Lord Death, 88, 89, 109, 136, 195. *See also* Lord Time; Yama
Lord Time, 105, 136, 140, 195. *See also* Lord Death
"Lotus Offering to Reach Nirvana," 151–52, 192, 207, 216, 277–78
"Lotus Offering to Realize Awakening," 181–86, 207, 216, 219, 285, 288
aspirations in, 182–86, 192, 193, 289–92
modern adaptation of, 277
"Lullaby of the Gods," 19, 217, 232–33
Lumbini, 203
lying, 77, 292

Madri, 13, 16, 232, 233
"Madri's Lament," 13–17, 205, 216, 231–32
magic diagrams (*yantra*), 190
Mahādibbamanta, 282
Mahākaccāyana, 161, 184, 197
Mahākassapa, 161, 184, 197, 282
Mahāmetrī (*Mahāmetti Sutta*), 63, 249
Mahāpajāpatī Gotamī, 21–22, 233
Mahāparinibbāna Sutta, 242
Mahayana, 192
Mahinda, 141, 143, 276
Maitreya Buddha, 135, 139, 176, 192–93
abode of, 198
aspiration to meet, 48, 55, 149, 164, 179, 186, 193
prediction about, 135, 146, 275
Malla monarchs, 49, 245
mantras, 190, 205, 264
manuscripts, xvi
bark-paper, xvi, xviii, 210 (*see also* leporello manuscripts)
palm-leaf, xvi, xviii, 196–97, 210, 211, 212, 213, 277
Māra, 46, 179, 194
abode of, 198
daughters of, 238
defeat of, 31–35, 134, 199, 206–7, 235, 237–38
See also Five Māras
marks (Pali: *lakkhaṇa*), 206–7
Māyā, 21–22, 27–28, 47, 233, 236, 248
"Maya's Guidance for Gotami," 21–22, 216, 233
"Maya's Lament," 27–28, 205, 216, 235–36
meditation, 63, 138, 248
on body parts, 251
exhortation for, 103, 264
forty-five subjects of, 120, 271

on foulness, 269
on goodwill, 288
success in, 121
Mekhala, 166
melodies (*smūtr*), xvi, 228, 258
affective dimensions of, 218
buddhapād prāṃ ṭhān, 266, 284
daṃnuoñ, 257
daṃnuoñ pret, 257
devatā paṃbe kūn, 232
dhaŕm yog, 286
Khmer lullabies, 233
lam-on, 277, 289
madrī, 230, 231
mahāmāyā, 229, 233, 262
number of, 217, 296n4
parābhavasūtr, 261
samrāy, 244, 280
sāṅ braḥ phnuos, 234, 243, 256
sarabhaññ, 278
sūtr rāy, 260, 279, 283
trailakkha(ṇ), 251, 262, 264, 266, 270, 274
vocal techniques and, 218
memorial rites, 203, 205–6, 207. *See also* funerary rituals
memorization, xvi, 69, 142, 183, 210–11, 290
mental cultivation, 194
mental factors, 125, 126, 129
merit, 63–64, 193–94
for ancestors, transferring, 90–91, 94, 206, 259–60
aspiration for, 185
Buddha's, 32, 34, 37, 42
of buddhas, relying on, 79
at death, 101–2
and debt, relationship of, 60
earth's, 59
exhaustion of, 136
field of, 156
fruit of, 106
in funerary rites, 263
of laypeople, three foundations, 82, 256
from offerings, 93
perfected, 147
rebirth and, 139–40, 193
sealing, 62
transferring, 206
See also dedication
Meru, Mount, 67, 174, 199
meter, 228
anuṭṭhubha, 245, 281
bāky 7, 216, 229–31, 233–34, 235, 243, 255–58, 262, 278
bāky 9 meter, 216–17, 236
extended, 219, 223
iambic, 222
indavajirā, 280
Khmer lullabies, 233
melodies and, 217
newer developments in, 216–17
paṭhyāvatt, 216, 244, 259, 261, 263
three primary, 215–16
See also brahmagīti meter; kākagati meter
middle way, 29, 153, 236
Miev Nand, 214, 236
Milinda, 141–42, 276
Milindapañha, 276
mind
and body, relationship between, 140
contemplating, 125, 128–29
cultivating, 136–37, 276
guarding, 102
rebirth and, 104, 265
winds and, 137
Mind, Prince and Princess, 126–27, 139, 273
modernization, 189, 201
Moggallāna, 161, 184, 197, 282
monasteries
eightfold array at, 283
misbehaving at, 78, 255
monasticism, 195
in Cambodia, 197, 214
faults in, 74–75, 254–55
robes in, 263
Mongkut (Rama IV), 245, 281
Moon, 60, 63, 73, 137, 198–99
Moon Sutta, 63, 249

mothers
consonants of, 70, 250
debts to, 61, 67, 71–73
forgiveness of, 83–84, 190, 256–57
jewel from (*manijoti*), 129–30, 272
See also Māyā
"Mourning the Buddha's Demise," 47–48, 204, 216, 219, 243–44

nāga realms, 172
nāgas, 129, 140, 238
Nāgasena, 142, 145, 276
Nammada river, 167
Namo Aṭṭhaka Gāthā (Mongkut), 281, 303n67
Nāṅ Gaṅhīṅ Braḥ Dharaṇī (earth goddess), 199, 238
National Museum of Cambodia, 277
natural world, 57, 60, 62, 73, 198–99, 248, 253
New Year (Khmer), 57–58
paying debts at, 62, 248–49
precepts during, 78
Nibbāna Sutta, 275
nirvana, 47–48
analogies for, 135–36, 194, 275–76
bliss of, 54
Buddha's, 3, 44, 46, 51, 242, 243, 244
as deathless country, 104
as journey, 193
peace of, 149
reaching, 64, 95, 147
not-self, 21, 123, 133, 270, 275

offerings
to Buddha, 35, 49, 151–52
in consecration rites, 175, 177–78, 288
faults in, 78
to hungry ghosts, 87, 90–91, 259
to monastics, 93–94, 206, 259–60
symbolic, 54, 165, 181, 186, 285, 289
on Visakha full moon, 48
water, 34
"Offerings for Monks and Ancestors," 93–94, 206, 216, 219, 259–60, 300n36
old age, 24, 99, 104, 117–18, 264
oral transmission, xvi, 210–11, 212
"Orphan's Lament," 85–86, 205, 216, 219, 257
Oudong, xv

Pali language, 242
body part meditation formula, 67, 251
chanting in, 296n7
Dharma tradition in, 196–97
iminā chants, 265–66, 301n44
"Invitation to Preach the Dharma" and, 239, 240, 241–42, 297n10, 297n12
in Khmer Buddhism, 209–10
"Relics of the Buddha" and, 246–47, 298n15
translations from Sinhala into, 142, 143, 276
Paññāsajātaka, 62, 248
Paranimmitavasavatti, 198
parents, 25, 235
debt to, 57, 60, 81–82, 190, 247, 255–56
faults of, 88, 90, 258–59
Pārikā, 231
"Parika's Lament," 9, 205, 216, 219, 230–31
parturition, 72, 254
Pataliputra, 173
patience, 49, 57, 114, 122, 183, 211
Paṭṭhāna, 131, 273
Pava realm, 52
Pchum Ben, 58, 205–6, 207
"Hungry Ghosts' Lament" during, 87–91, 258
offerings during, 259–60
precepts during, 78
performance tradition, 210–11
"Defeat of Māra, The," 206–7
"Hungry Ghosts' Lament," 258–59
length of texts used, 217
women in, 214
Phnom Penh, 144, 276, 278, 283, 287

pilgrimage sites, 163–64, 199, 283–84
Piliyakkha, 231
"Prayer for the People, A," 153–54, 206, 216, 278
preceptors, 60, 67, 95, 197
precepts, 95
  eight, 78, 79, 194
  five, 77, 79, 194, 255
  learning, 122
  upholding, 147, 288
predictions, 145–46, 193, 276–77
printing, 189, 210, 213
"Protective Chant on the Blessings of the Buddhas in All Directions," 282–83, 303n70
Prum Ut, xvi, 217
Puggalappaññatti, 240

Rāhu, 63, 249
Rāhula, 25, 161, 197, 235, 282
Rajagriha, 52
Ramagrama, 52
Rāmakerti (*Rāmāyaṇa*), 273
Ratanamālā, 204
rebirth, 79, 114, 139–40, 155, 193, 195
recitation and chanting, xvi–xvii
  benefits of, 61, 70
  monastic, 249
  performers of, 210–11, 296n7
  styles of, 278
  vowels, 65–66
relics, 49–50, 144, 196, 199, 206, 288
  Ashoka and, 141
  in consecration rites, inviting, 171–73
  division of, 51–55, 246–47
  homage to, 284
  in Phnom Penh, 278
  purpose of, 154
"Relics of the Buddha, The," 51–55, 215, 245–47, 288
renunciates (Khmer: *sramaṇ*), 238
repentance practices, 195, 254, 300n31
rhyme, 219–23
rituals
  modern development of, 207
  paṅsukūl, 263
  preparatory, 103, 264
  repaying debts in, 57–58
  types of, 203
  See also consecration rites; deathbed rites; funerary rituals
rūp (Pali: *rūpa*), 265

Saccabandha, Mount, 167, 285
Sahampati Brahmā, 39–41, 239–40, 241
sainthood, nine Dharmas (stages) of, 196, 294n26. *See also* arhatship
Samantapāsādikā (Buddhaghosa), 279–80, 302n66
samsara, 40, 104, 113, 194, 276
saṃvega (spiritual urgency), 97, 121, 218
Saṃyutta Nikāya, 249
Sandhar Jā, 214, 232
Sangha, 139, 156, 159, 197–98, 280
Sāriputta, 161, 184, 197, 282
Sarnath, 41
sensations, contemplating, 125, 128
Siddhartha Gautama, 3, 149
  birth of, 233
  departure of, 25, 235, 238
  ends asceticism, 29–30, 236
  four sights of, 23–24, 234
  journey to awakening, 237–38
  Māyā and, 28, 236
signs of progress (Pali: *nimitta*), 191, 197
  of contact, 126
  and counterpart images, 125, 127–29, 273
Sihanatha, 53
similes
  city, body as, 127, 130, 273
  crystal city, 135–36, 275–76
  four thieves, 103–4, 264
  roasting pot, 59–60
  treasure, protecting, 121
  tree, body as, 126–27, 273

sin (Khmer: *pāp*), 63, 169
attachment and, 194–95
cheating, 122
as dimension of life, 195, 253
against earth, 59
five of immediate retribution, 292
Śiva, 166, 183, 198
six realms, 198
"Song for the Hour of Death," 117–23, 195, 204, 215, 219, 263, 269
South Asia, 189, 250
Southeast Asia, xv
modernization in, 189
postpartum healing in, 254
Tantric Buddhism in, 191–92
spiritual teachers
debts to, 57, 60, 61, 74
need for, 137, 138
reverence for, 197–98
Sri Lanka, xv, 276, 278. *See also* Lanka
stanzas, 217, 221, 228
Stirring and Stilling, 213
stupas, 53–54
in Brahmā realm, 53
homage to, 163–64, 283–84
for paying debts, 62
purpose of, 248
Subhadra, 5, 7
"Subhadra's Lament," 7, 205, 216, 229–30
suffering, 21, 123, 133, 194, 275
ending, 153
freedom from, aspiration for, 292
letting go of, 113
of samsara, 40
at time of death, 117, 118
Sujātā, 206–7, 238
Sukhāvatī, 276
Sumanakuta, Mount, 167
Sumaṅgalavilāsinī (Buddhaghosa), 240, 243
Sumeru, Mount, 166
Sun, 60, 63, 73, 198–99
Sun Sutta, 63, 249
Sutras, 40, 65, 268
Suvaṇṇakesar, 54, 213, 245–46
Suvannamali, Mount, 167
Suvaṇṇapabbata, Mount, 167, 285
Suvannasama, 9, 231
"Suvannasama's Lament," 11–12, 205, 216, 219, 220, 231

tattoos, 190
Tavatiṃsa heaven, *See* Trāyastriṃśa Heaven
Temiya, 183, 289
Thai language, 239
Thailand, xv, 196, 238, 245, 248, 273, 282
Theravada Buddhism, 209
in Cambodia, xv
esoteric form, 190–91, 192, 273
"Thirty-Three Consonants, The," 67–70, 191, 204, 216, 219, 250–51
thirty-two vessels, 118, 270
"This Heap Called a Body," 109–15, 204, 215, 219, 266
death in, 267–69
mortuary practices in, 263
spirits in, 200, 269
translation approach, 219
"This Life Is Short," 101–2, 204, 216, 219, 262–63
Three Baskets (Pali: *tipiṭaka*), 190, 290
dominance of, 189
guarding, 139
in Khmer Buddhism, 197, 209, 253–54
memorization of, 142, 183
translation of, 143, 144, 276
Three Jewels, 196–98, 281
daily prayers to, 149
debt to, 57, 60–61, 196–98
homage to, 153–54, 155–57, 159–60, 171, 279–80, 281
meditation on, 138
venerating, 71, 106, 151
virtues of, 248
Three Marks, 39, 97, 240, 275
"Three Marks, beginning with 'Form is painful, form is impermanent,' The" 268–69, 301n46

Three Realms, 240
three treasures/attainments, 84, 147, 193, 257
Three Vedas, 183, 290
Three Worlds, 41, 42, 133, 151, 156, 176, 182
titles, 227–28
Trāyastriṃśa Heaven, 29, 53, 59, 172, 198, 236, 238, 248
"True Fate of Flesh, The," 105–8, 204, 215, 264–66
truthful aspirations (Khmer: *satyapraṇidhān*), 192
Tuṣita, 27, 79, 142, 198
tutelary deities and spirits, 78, 200, 255
twelve links of dependent origination, 240
"Twenty-Four Vowels, The," 65–66, 191, 204, 216, 219, 249–50, 272

ultimate truth, 125
universal monarch/wheel-turning king (*cakkavatti*), 138, 199, 276
Until Nirvana's Time
  sources, 212–13
  standardized poems in, 212
  structure of, xviii
  translations in, approaches to, 215, 218–23
Upāli, 161, 197, 282
Uposatha (elephant king), 166

Vaiśravaṇa (aka Kubera), 60, 62, 247–48
Vajrayana, 191–92
Vaṅkata, Mount, 14, 232
vegetarianism, 258
Vesak, 203–4, 207, 244, 245, 278
Vesali, 52
Vessantara, 14, 61, 182, 232, 233, 255
Vethadipaka, 52
Vietnam, xv
Vietnamese language, 209, 239
Vinaya, 40, 65, 240, 268
violence, xvi, 145, 149, 253, 254–55
vipassana meditation, Burmese-style, 189
virtue, 67, 169
  within body, 113, 269
  and debt, relationship of, 57, 60–61, 189–90
  of Dharma, 66
  of four jewels, 129–31, 271, 272
  of parents and relatives, 65, 67
  recalling, 139
  See also guṇ
Visākha, 45, 47, 48, 49, 203, 244, 245
Viṣṇu, 166, 185, 198
Visuddhimagga (Buddhaghosa), 191, 250, 269, 271, 273, 276
Viśvakarman, 183, 289
vows, 79, 82, 171
  of buddhas, 34, 79, 238
  dedicating, 95
  in esoteric practice, 125, 126, 272
  maintaining, 114
  pure, 106
  for rebirth in Maitreya's time, 48, 186

Wat Kien Khleang, 283
Wat Lanka, 144
Wat Saravan Techo, 283
Western music theory, 218
Western science, 189
White Lotus monastery, 54, 246
winds, 111, 137, 268–69
wisdom
  Buddha's, 174–75, 288
  cultivating, 126
world of desire (*kāmadhātu*), 198
written transmission, 211–12

Yama, 195–96, 259
Yama's henchmen, 109, 139, 140–41, 195, 267
Yan Borin, xvi, 217, 233
Yasodharā Bimbā, 230

Photo by Lan Le

About the Author

Trent Walker began his training in Cambodian Buddhist chant in 2005 under the guidance of Koet Ran, Prum Ut, Yan Borin, and Preah Maha Vimaladhamma Pin Sem. A specialist in Southeast Asian Buddhist music, literature, and manuscripts, he has published widely on Khmer, Lao, Pali, Thai, and Vietnamese Buddhist texts and recitation practices. After completing a PhD in Buddhist Studies at the University of California, Berkeley, he was the Khyentse Foundation Postdoctoral Fellow at Chulalongkorn University in Bangkok. He is the coeditor of a major anthology of Khmer literature, *Out of the Shadows of Angkor: Cambodian Poetry, Prose, and Performance through the Ages* (2022), and his literary translations of Southeast Asian songs, narrative poems, and stone inscriptions have appeared in *Words Without Borders*, *The Margins*, and other venues. His current research focuses on the intellectual history of translation in Laos and Thailand and the circulation of Buddhist literature in Cambodia. He serves as Director of Preservation and Lead Scholar for the Khmer Manuscript Heritage Project, an initiative of the Buddhist Digital Resource Center to digitize over 1.5 million pages of palm-leaf texts from Cambodian libraries and rural monasteries. A regular speaker at temples, retreat centers, and universities, he is currently a Postdoctoral Fellow at the Ho Center for Buddhist Studies and a Lecturer in Religious Studies at Stanford University. For more, see www.trentwalker.org.